INTER-SECTORAL
EDUCATIONAL
PLANNING

ORGANISATION FOR ECONOMIC
CO-OPERATION AND DEVELOPMENT

The Organisation for Economic Co-operation and Development (OECD) was set up under a Convention signed in Paris on 14th December, 1960, which provides that the OECD shall promote policies designed:
- — to achieve the highest sustainable economic growth and employment and a rising standard of living in Member countries, while maintaining financial stability, and thus to contribute to the development of the world economy;
- — to contribute to sound economic expansion in Member as well as non-member countries in the process of economic development;
- — to contribute to the expansion of world trade on a multi-lateral, non-discriminatory basis in accordance with international obligations.

The Members of OECD are Australia, Austria, Belgium, Canada, Denmark, Finland, France, the Federal Republic of Germany, Greece, Iceland, Ireland, Italy, Japan, Luxembourg, the Netherlands, New Zealand, Norway, Portugal, Spain, Sweden, Switzerland, Turkey, the United Kingdom and the United States.

* *
*

CONTENTS

EDUCATION AND INTER-SECTORAL PLANNING: AN OVERVIEW
by the Secretariat

INTRODUCTION

In the educational programmes of the OECD education is seen
increasingly in terms of its relationship to economic sectors, and
in terms of the whole range of other service sectors which are
directed toward the welfare of the various client populations for
education. Throughout the 60s and 70s the growth of OECD social
programmes, including education, has in fact been a reflection of
the recognition of the interrelationships between social and economic aspects of public policy, and of the interdependence of social
and economic institutions, of which education is an important part.

It is this recognition of the inter-sectoral nature of educational planning that lies at the origins of the present study
carried out under the programme of the Education Committee of OECD.
With the advice and criticism of OECD country representatives and
experts, an initial paper was prepared by the Secretariat, designed
to further this exploration. On the basis of this paper a number of
experts were invited to contribute the papers which are presented in
this volume.

In these papers an attempt has been made to explore:

1) the modern context for inter-sectoral relationships on a
   national level and involving education;
2) the structure and politics of inter-sectoral planning;
3) the major characteristics of the existing and projected
   organisation and programmes of inter-sectoral planning.

Most of the papers, though emphasizing different aspects of
this exploration from different points of view, tend to proceed
through the entire range of these issues; this holds true to a noteworthy extent even for those papers drawing mostly upon the experience
of a single country. This overview report attempts a synthesis of the
main arguments which emerge from the various experts' contributions
included in this volume.

The views expressed are those of the experts and do not necessarily represent those of OECD or of the countries concerned.

I.   THE MODERN CONTEXT FOR INTER-SECTORAL PLANNING

The meaning of inter-sectoral planning is essentially co-terminal with the original meaning of planning as a modern concept: that the main elements and sectors in the nation's economic and social life be developed and co-ordinated to achieve common societal goals at a specified future time.

This idea has found most acceptance in countries whose economic and social institutions being not yet modernised could be more readily directed toward common goals related to rapid modernisation. Planning has also been accepted more in those advanced countries having a long established tradition of centralisation through which an elite has usually controlled the major facets of national life. The logic of modern planning has tended towards the monolith: planning for any one segment of human activity is seen to be only as reliable as the control obtained of the factors which impinge upon this segment, and more comprehensive planning puts more of these factors under its control.

Most modern societies, however, have developed less formal systems of integration within which specialised activities have been grouped in order to fulfil specific public and social functions. When these activities have become sectors of national scope and organised under public authority, sectoral planning has appeared, usually of a relatively short-term nature and issuing from budgetary needs. Such sectors, as for example, education, may develop into complex and powerful entities. However, because of the nature of the interdependencies of modern life, they are increasingly subject to a network of inter-sectoral relationships. The most vital problems of modern life — social equality, environmental degradation, unemployment, urban development, life-long education - all cut across the established sectors. How to make policy planning take the realities of these sectoral interdependencies into account is a characteristic issue of modern public policy.

The contributions to this book largely agree in characterising the history behind the current situation in most OECD countries. Cohen has outlined three major periods for the public service sectors, dating from the 19th century to fairly recent times. First, there was the period of modest level and narrow areas of public intervention into the total field of human activity, for instance orphanages or soup kitchens or veterans' homes, etc. There was little concern for overlap or co-ordination. Second, when in the late 19th century government began to accept more responsibility for social welfare, there was a struggle to achieve minimal standards in each identified area such as education and public health; just to establish what would be the relevant social service and expand it was the pre-occupation. Third, the professions have gone through a hundred-year period of defining their special competencies with respect to these service fields, pushing up the standards in various sectors, delineating them to suit professional specialities.

The situation of the social service sectors has changed in very important ways. First, the professions, now well-established, are becoming somewhat less defensively insistent on specialisation. Second, the extent of public responsibility for social policy has grown immensely. Minimum standards have moved upward and the scope of public service has expanded laterally. The standards of minimum decency have risen, and the spheres of social relations thought to be appropriate for a public welfare policy have expanded beyond "education", "health", etc., to new areas such as community development, social security, labour relations and environment, to name a few. Affecting all of these have been changing criteria and rising standards for fairness and equity. Finally, this expansion of the social responsibilities of the state has meant a deeper and more complex involvement with private sectors of society.

Thus, need for developing effective forms of co-ordination or integration has become apparent. As Eide puts it:

"When government activities were confined to a small number of isolated programmes in scattered areas, while most societal activities were of no concern to governments, it was still conceivable to look upon individual government programmes as 'autonomous'. However, modern government in all countries implies a much more general concern for societal developments, and in this situation the notion of 'programme autonomy' becomes illusory."

II. THE STRUCTURE AND POLITICS OF INTER-SECTORAL PLANNING

The general agreement on the need for co-ordination among public sectors has nowhere been followed by effective answers to this need. The "answers" come and go with history. For example, in many countries a response to gaps and boundary collisions between sectors and their services was to consolidate existing agencies in some manner, making administrative units larger and more comprehensive. This approach may now be yielding to another focus of attention on the problems of bureaucratic gigantism and inefficiency, and the idea that the clients of such services should be given more power to determine what is to be co-ordinated on their behalf and toward what ends (Cohen).

Thus history and politics are inseparable from "technical" facts and they together form the working data necessary to comprehend the issues of inter-sectoral planning. In the search for a general framework and principles which would facilitate interpretation of these data, it is convenient to begin with the single sector - for clarity, and as the first step toward comprehending the complex relationships among sectors.

The logic of this approach is matched by reality in this case: most efforts at inter-sectoral planning will involve action by people within established sectors such as education. The following discussion will define the sector by reviewing its economic, social and organisational aspects. Some of the main problems of making relationships among sectors which emerge from this description lead to a statement of the main technical problem for the development of inter-sectoral planning and operations (p. 13). Experience in a representative group of countries provides a basis for examining the politics connected with this problem, particularly when it involves education.

A) MAIN CONCEPTS AND PROBLEMS OF THE SECTOR

The Economic Definition. Making use of economic concepts Peston defines the sector as:

"a set of activities. Each activity involves the use of

resources, or inputs, and generates a flow of benefits, or outputs."

Pursuit of the implications of this definition in the case of education takes Peston far into major problems of inter-sectoral analysis. The procedure he proposes begins with a careful description of the resources used within the sector. He sees, however, that the resources applied to education cannot easily be measured against achievements even when these are narrowly interpreted, because educational outcomes are incidents in a process that are beyond simple categorisation and measurement. Peston's effort to deal with this problem leads him to the idea of an elaborate listing of a "vector of items" which would include a great variety of academic achievements and personal, social developments seen as consequences of education. Then, as these items are classified and studied they would be recognised as containing elements from other sectors such as health, family life, or community services.

Peston outlines how activities in education and other sectors could be systematically observed to discover, for example, whether their combinations are additive or sub-additive, bring economies or diseconomies. However, he finds that education is a sector whose "...activities themselves are not simple input-output relationships in which given one, the other follows with certainty". This uncertainty makes it apparent that recognising economic parameters is only the first necessary step toward a description of the dynamic realities of education as a sector of human activity.

The Education Sector as Social Organism. Peston notes the sector's "creative" functioning:

"...we postulate the existence of sectors at two levels. Each sector comprises a set of activities, actual and potential, the set itself changing as a result of its own operations. While in the sense a sector is there to do a job set from the outside, in large part it determines its own job and the way in which it is judged. Thus, while what is called consumer sovereignty is relevant, it is not correct to interpret the sector as analogous to the firms and industries of neo-classical economies, competing to satisfy a given demand. Quite the contrary, their role must be seen as a creative one, to generate and make the case for new demands."

Thus, while the sector may be observed to share its objectives and even its resources and outcomes with other sectors, it often distinguishes itself by transforming activities in terms of its own traditions, perceptions, concepts of service and modes of operation which prevail in the services it offers. The sector is a social organisation which reinterprets problems, generates or discovers new

9

ones which it diagnoses largely according to its particular competence. It states the case for new demands which it is prepared to satisfy. Thus, the social functioning of the sector develops along certain pathways which often narrowly confine its creative ability. <u>The problem for inter-sectoral policy planning is to find the means to affect these lines of social relationships in the sector, making them more open to outside influences and genuine creativity</u>.

<u>The Sector in Organisational Terms</u>. Eide's definition of a sector as a convenient grouping of specific policy instruments, measures and activities calls attention to its manifest administrative and organisational nature. Thus, the sector for education is seen in terms of educational institutions, broadly defined. Identified in this way, as an organised set of policy instruments, education must be described so that the relationships of its organisations to those of other sectors are apparent. A number of the accompanying papers attempt such analytical descriptions, and it is possible to portray them in the following way.

First, the educational sector may be characterised by <u>inter-level</u> <u>inter-agency and inter-sectoral "fragmentation"</u> (Etzioni's term). The first two of these are internal to the educational organisation itself. It is fragmented into various types and levels, from the local level to the national level, and from the single educational institution to regional and national administrative bodies as well as corresponding professional agencies. Secondly, further divisions of education are found in various other government agencies - which often perform quite formal educational functions (the military, for example) as do various private educational organisations and agencies. Then, these various divisions of the educational sector are each related in various ways to non-educational entities: first, to other governmental social service sectors; second, to other governmental sectors such as agriculture, environment, commerce, sectors dealing with economic policy, etc.; and finally, to other sectors outside the government in the private sphere.

While the emphasis in the following papers is on the relationships between other government social sectors and education, it is not exclusively so, and it is recognised that the topic cannot be realistically handled unless the major elements of this whole system of sectors are included.

Viewed in this abstract way, there could be a huge number of possible inter-relationships among sectors but, in fact, such inter-relationships involving education have taken on a number of recognisable patterns, in some cases well-developed institutionally and in others in more experimental form.

<u>Types of co-ordination/integration</u>. Thus, types of co-ordination/integration may be treated as possible strategies which have already

made their appearance. A number of administrative strategies aim to establish new, more integrative patterns of authority and hierarchic structure. For example, there have been attempts at administrative consolidation or integration of social service sectors within a single new agency. Within such agencies the original sectors often show great capacity to retain their original identity. A second strategy has been to create a new agency operating in a newly defined inter-sectoral field, such as environment or urban development. A third type of co-ordinating organisation is an umbrella planning body. This may operate through advice and persuasion to foster voluntary co-ordination among existing agencies and sectors; or such an agency may have some prescriptive powers to require such co-ordination. Finally, the example may be considered in which an agency, or sector like education, is in a position to impose an effective co-ordination over other sectors through the co-optation of other services. This may happen, or be facilitated, at central levels of decision-making but more often operates at local levels - in "the field".

This latter example illustrates the relationship between centrally organised strategies and those which as a whole attempt to bring about co-ordination at the point of the delivery of services. Such strategies may be very little concerned with actual reorganisation above the local level.

One such strategy involves co-ordination at the point of delivery by local multi-agency institutions, but not necessitating the consolidation of the agencies themselves. Another strategy involves the notion of the co-ordination of services by the clients of these services, through a) increasing the local political power of the clients in the governance of local agencies, or through b) effectively increasing their power as consumers.

Autonomy and Authority in the Definition of the Sector. Since striking, or even moderate, success cannot be cited as a reliable outcome of any of the above types of co-ordination/integration or any combination of them, they provide important evidence for defining the task ahead in this field. What we have gained so far from the above discussion is a recognition of a sector's typical lack of autonomy from other sectors: in terms of input and outcomes (economic analysis) and in terms of social and organisational relationships. Recognition of the main features of a sector's lack of economic, social and organisational autonomy is fundamental for the self-definition of a sector, and such self-definition is crucial to the engagement of the sector in inter-sectoral planning and action.

Why does this recognition usually fail to develop, or when it does, is subject to manipulations and distortions? A first clue is to be found in observing that the co-ordination/integration schemes summarised above may not modify the essentials of the hierarchial

bureaucratic organisation of existing social service sectors, and
may therefore be limited by the politics, motivations and incentives
characteristic in such organisational structures. This means that
another step toward understanding the meaning of co-ordination/inte-
gration schemes which aim to bring together the units of different
sectors, is to recognise the main content of the authority relationships which these schemes involve. Eide calls attention to three
general forms of co-ordination/integration which develop within the
framework of hierarchic and bureaucratic organisation and which can
be viewed in this way:

a) co-ordination of subordinate units by a superior organisational unit which is equipped to take prescriptive or in-
formational measures; subordinate units ultimately must accept
the superiors' goals and values, and these may derive from
professional groups strategically placed to play the co-
ordinating role - educators, medical people, economists, or
planning analysts, for example.

b) collaboration between two or more units at the same hierarchic
level, none of which is subordinate to the others; prescriptiv
measures are excluded, with bargaining the characteristic mean
of inter-action; each unit accepts the other's objectives and
modes of operation only insofar as each assesses the benefits
and costs of the collaboration positively in terms of its own
value structure.

c) integration of units from different sectors, eventually mergin
their values and goals, including the development of a common
structure of weights attached to these goals and merging their
missions and resources.

Experience cited in the accompanying papers is that in hierarchic
organisations co-ordination by superior units tends to be the dominant
form, but this is not a testament to its success. The original units
demonstrate a great capacity for satisfying the formal requirements
of the superior body while giving very little to effective co-
ordination. If such co-ordination efforts attempt to provide technical solutions for political problems, as is often the case, then these
problems and the divisions between sectors may be aggravated.

Nevertheless, collaboration and integration are seldom stable,
and, in fact, tend to be transformed into co-ordination by a superior
body. This is because incentives are notably lacking for horizontal
collaboration between organisations whose structure of sanctions and
rewards moves in a vertical direction.

Finally, mergers of organisations can bring unwanted results.
A tightly logical merger of separate units may destroy other valuable
and well-established inter-sectoral relationships which do not fit

into the scheme. Then, also, weaker segments in a merger may not be able to defend themselves against "institutional" or "cultural imperialism". Who yields most in the merging of value structures when units are integrated and how to build up the bargaining power of weaker parties, are major questions for inter-sectoral policy planning.

Thus, an outstanding problem for inter-sectoral policy planning is how to modify hierarchic structures to a point at which they can sustain the development of at least a collaborative style of inter-unit relationships. This is readily recognised as both a technical and political problem which has particular historical dimensions in each country. Political and historical experience in a number of OECD countries, which is the basis for the following section, can provide a necessary context for thinking about the problems and characteristics of this kind of planning for education.

B) THE POLITICS OF INTER-SECTORAL PLANNING

1. Some OECD Countries' Experience

Experience in OECD countries - exemplified in a series of papers which form the final section of this book - shows that the introduction or development of inter-sectoral planning of public services such as education involves changes, gains and losses, in power and influence - politics in the broad sense of that term.

Magnussen in his assessment of the Norwegian Perspective Plan for Education, 1971-1975, comes to the conclusion that this plan emphasizes decentralisation as a reflection of changing functions and positions among major social groups in Norwegian society:

"A more basic factor is the structural change which is taking place in the Norwegian labour market, away from the traditional authoritarian organisation of production on the factory floor, towards a wider participation of workers in the decision-making units of firms and enterprises. Pilot experiments have been undertaken for some years already with self-controlled groups, and these experiments are yielding encouraging results. A law providing the legal basis for participatory democracy in industry has been passed by the Parliament. Educational planning without any consideration for these clear signs of change in the power-structure of Norwegian society could hardly be politically relevant.
The philosophy of this plan is that the educational system can be regarded as a preparatory testing ground for participatory democracy in all important fields of public life. Instead of concentrating on education as a product influencing the

development of other sectors as well as over-arching goals through a centrally determined process, this perspective analysis argues that any contribution of education to over-arching social problems is best handled by training people to undertake a variety of tasks in a largely self-controlled way."

Professor Piven describes a different situation for education in the United States. The educational agencies in that country are not in a position to anticipate public trends or policy. In a large and complex polity such as the United States, it is more difficult for education authorities to identify major economic or social directions for which they could plan. The 50 state school author-ities and about 20,000 local school authorities operate separate systems which must respond to a great variety of local situations. However, the overriding fact, says Piven, is that in the United States the leverage of public policy is small compared to powerful forces in the private sectors of society, and education, like other public agencies, has insufficient foreknowledge concerning the main forces affecting its own operations, its budget and relevant legis-lation; and therefore, it cannot genuinely engage in planning.

Piven comes close to a statement of the idea that planning requires certain minimum conditions for it to function as a tool of public policy:

"In sum, American school systems cannot plan, largely because they have no ability to predict, much less control the economic, political and social changes which necessarily affect educa-tional institutions in critical ways. The schools can only adapt to these changes. But they do not merely adapt, for in the process of responding to external crisis, the educational system, like other public and quasi-public services, has grown to become a complex and formidable bureaucracy, representing in its own right large concentrations of money, and controlled by the powerful vested interests that have stakes in this bureaucratic agglomeration. That process has not been planned, but it has been facilitated by activities called 'planning'."

Thus, Piven observes, planning functions less as a guide to public agency decisions and more often may be recognised as a public rela-tions exercise or as agency efforts to entrench, expand or defend their domain.

The contrasting material presented by Magnussen and Piven illustrates how the politics of institutionalised social services at all times contains two elements: one is the politics responsive to social needs outside the service, and the other is the politics internal to the institutional functioning of the service. Of course, these two elements are always closely related, but the overall

14

politics of the organisation has a distinctly different quality
depending upon which of these two kinds of "politics" is predominant.
It is the latter, inward-turning politics of the educational establishment upon which Piven has focused attention in her assessment of
educational planning in the United States.

In contrast to the situation of education in the United States,
the unitary governmental structure of France seems to give its
authorities control over many of the main operational elements needed
for the planning of education. However, in his paper Malan shows that
this structure actually operates as a social organism of remarkable
equilibrium that is capable of resisting most of those changes called
for in such planning.

Malan's comprehensive survey of French experience in inter-
sectoral planning related to education serves to illustrate how careful investigation might be expected to provide insights in this field.
Malan outlines the strenuous and often ingenious efforts of French
authorities to establish planning in an essentially centralised
system. French planning is rich in concepts. Among its major
features is the distinction established between centralised advisory
planning represented by the work of the Commissariat du Plan and
administrative planning, which exists in each government sector.
Collective functions are determined which are meant to harmonize
actions of different ministries and agencies, while the finalised
programmes of the Commissariat's Five-Year Plans give guidelines
which are meant to influence their annual budgeting decisions.

The French central planning system provides for elaborate
arrangements for participation under the Commissariat du Plan, but
Malan describes a lack of co-ordination on priorities between
national, regional and local government. This, for example, shows
up in the demand for social services equipment expressed as an inter-
sectoral need at the local level but interpreted as a precise demand
for the type of equipment supplied by each national service under its
own national standards.

Furthermore, Malan documents that the politics affecting planning
in France are tied to the public agencies' established bureaucratic
relationships with their clientele. He quotes Crozier who says French
centralised administrations "are not capable of changing the equilibrium (or symbiosis) which exists between the local services and the
social environment; this equilibrium has crystallised independently
of them and against them". Malan concludes that decentralisation
is discussed but actually not desired by most groups and lobbies
within the educational sector. Co-ordination with other sectors
might mean greater dependence on them whereas responsibility to one
ministry offers "a form of protection".

While public services have long been decentralised in the
United Kingdom, national initiatives in recent years to reorganise
and unify these services on a local level are based on an awareness
of a broad national consensus that the wide-ranging public services
involved in the welfare state cannot be adequately provided by means
of a local administration pattern dating from pre-welfare days. In
order to look more closely into developments in the United Kingdom
arising from these initiatives, Melo examines a promising example,
the corporate system of the city of Coventry, and traces the organisation under this system of inter-sectoral co-ordination for one
aspect of education - early childhood ("under-fives"). A major feature of this system is the organisation of "Programme Area Teams"
(PATs) on the basis of "prime objectives" set for specific population
groups, and consisting of the relevant departments or agencies.
This new structure is meant to cut across the "...traditional local
authority departments, with their professionalisation of particular
disciplines...", while leaving the operations of these traditional
departments intact. The Programme Area Team for education developed
local plans to expand educational services to the "under-fives", but
when implementation was blocked by national developments and policies,
discouragement and resistances to this system became manifest. A
system of communication and negotiation between the national authorities and the local PATs had not been established to permit adjustment of local commitments based on a longer time span within the
framework of changes in national policy. Decentralisation to be
politically operational must be supported by such a framework.

In New Zealand, co-ordination among established public and
private agencies, without necessarily requiring a radical restructuring of these agencies, also seems to be a major objective of inter-
sectoral planning for new public services. Based on developments
dating back to the early 1950s, New Zealand's planning organisation
includes national sector councils whose reports are ultimately
considered inter-sectorally by the Cabinet Committee on Policy and
Priorities. Numerous ad hoc inter-agency committees, formed with
wide public participation to cover particular fields or issues, are
another important part of this system. The education sector has its
Advisory Council on Educational Planning, and since 1955 at least
30 public committees have closely affected government policy in what
is now called a consultative planning system. Just how this system
has been working in recent years is illustrated in some detail in
the New Zealand paper by describing organisational activities for
pre-school education. If, in New Zealand, planning plays a significant part in the political process through which inter-sectoral
issues and interests are constructively brought together and resolved,
it may be a noteworthy demonstration.

2.   A broad political objective

The political value underlying this brief account of inter-sectoral educational planning in a number of countries is that the services involved would be made more available and responsive to the clients, and this implies an increase in their influence and power - in other words, increased decentralisation. Progress towards this end is not easy to evaluate. Piven offers a simple test of the effectiveness of decentralisation:

"Finally, activities which are called decentralisation can be evaluated not merely by observing the shifts in intra-agency chains-of-command, or the formal procedures for 'citizen participation' or feedback, but by evaluating the actual political leverage on the agency, particularly leverage in matters regarding the allocation of tangible resources, including the hiring and firing of personnel, which accrues to citizen groups, especially those citizen groups which have not previously been regarded as significant constituents of the agency. While such a 'test' of decentralisation may seem crude, in the turgid realms of bureaucratic policy, the simplest tests of power may be the most reliable."

This formulation suggests a way to assess developments in the political aspects of education, but it does not cover the pedagogical operation of the schools associated with such developments, and this further step is essential for educational planning. Magnussen offers a concise summation of the field which goes farther in this direction by examining the relationships between the main outcomes of education and the two main aspects of inter-sectoral planning for education:

1. consistency in the total system; and
2. decision-making along a scale of centralisation/
   decentralisation.

He argues that the main outcome of education is not so much a product, such as certified graduates but, rather, this outcome is a process - the creation and maintenance of the experience undergone by the people involved throughout the whole extended time of this education. It is now recognised that the wide variety of preferences and needs of pupils and students requires great flexibility in this educational process. A planning process which would facilitate flexible educational provision certainly could not stress centralised decisions nor great consistency of objectives between the central levels of the agencies concerned and local and individual preferences. Furthermore this attention to the process of education adds further weight to the potential role of the individual in educational planning, since those undergoing education are in the best position to contribute to the

corrective evaluations which should be an essential feature of
planning.

Thus, in sum, the co-ordinated planning of agencies related to
education would aim for effective decentralisation and only a very
moderate consistency between central objectives and those of local
institutions and individuals concerned and engaged in education.
This broad political objective for inter-sectoral educational planning arises out of the need to confront what seems to be the dominant
force behind most planning - that of agency aggression and self-
defence. What would be the main features of a planning system based
on this broad political objective? For example, what centrally-
based commitments, initiatives, planning and information are essential to make an inter-sectoral system and decentralisation workable?
Such planning should promote the development of greater specificity
of political objectives for inter-sectoral educational development
which reflect the particular trends and needs of each country. The
general features of this kind of inter-sectoral planning will be the
subject of the final section of this paper.

III. THE SEARCH FOR OPERATIONAL INTER-SECTORAL PLANNING

A) ORGANISATION, INCENTIVES AND THE PEDAGOGY
OF INTER-SECTORAL PLANNING

The paradox of inter-sectoral policy planning is that although
it involves and requires great organisational reform, it is not
primarily an organisational problem. In fact, development of an
inter-sectoral system would involve organisational reform in great
depth requiring a profound change of behaviours, away from separation and competition and toward collaboration among groups and individuals. Furthermore, they would have to engage in the modification
of the structure of incentives and rewards to support this collaboration. The overwhelming conclusion of the evidence presented is that
no organisational scheme is a reliable generator of inter-sectoral
collaboration. At best, certain organisational arrangements provide
a necessary container for collaboration.

Behind most proposed organisational changes is a preoccupation
with the unsolved problem of operational incentives for collaboration.
Cohen and others refer to the weakness of bureaucratic incentives,
the inoperative character of economic incentives in social service
sectors, and the divisiveness of political incentives reflecting
the competition among the groups involved. Eide, Dror and Peston
in various ways suggest changes in the organisational form of the
bureaucracy. Eide goes farthest in seeking to change the structure
of incentives by proposing a "redefinition of tasks" which would
eliminate the old boundaries of specialisation between units. But
where is the incentive to be found to make such changes? It is
obvious that this ultimately involves the appearance of a political
will which would express itself in the form of the gradual organisation of a "matrix" of horizontal relationships across sectors.

The content of this political will is essential not only to
provide the energy behind inter-sectoral reform but to establish
its specific nature. Gans, Westley and Magnussen particularly
demonstrate that in the case of education, a fundamental task of
policy planning is to facilitate attempts to define the nature of
education and the kinds of values expected from it. This would
provide fundamental support to the formulation of the needed political will which would underlie genuine collaboration with other

19

sectors. Thus, the main tasks of educational inter-sectoral planning turn out to be political and broadly pedagogical - to contribute to the development and the public acceptance of knowledge about
education which would inform the political will behind its planning.

B) INTER-SECTORAL PLANNING AND PROCEDURE: MAIN CHARACTERISTICS

The purpose of the foregoing discussion of the structure and
politics of inter-sectoral planning has been to provide a basis
for examining some of its main characteristics involving education.
It should be borne in mind that the development of inter-sectoral
planning in each country or jurisdiction would have its own history,
organisational orientation and task emphasis. Nevertheless, the
following treatment of main characteristics of inter-sectoral planning and procedure will be somewhat a-historical in order to keep
the discussion at a cross-country level of generalisation.

1. The role of central initiative

Dror, making use of a systems analysis approach, assesses the
typical situation of education in relation to other sectors to the
effect that any notable increase in integration will almost invariably represent an improvement. From this viewpoint, more integration can be treated as positive and desirable in itself, and
Dror looks for central government initiatives and measures which
can be expected to affect an entire inter-sectoral system.

Dror is aware that centrally organised inter-sectoral approaches
are only effective insofar as cross-sectoral operations are carried
down to the local levels of the social services involved, which
research now shows they seldom are. To meet this problem he proposes strategies initiated by central authorities which would
develop a new system of communication in its broadest sense, particularly among professional personnel. These strategies would include, for example:
   a) Similar elements being introduced into the various sectoral
      units, such as: data, goals, basic assumptions, decision
      doctrines, professional personnel, images and preferences
      concerning the future.
   b) Distance between sectoral components being reduced - facili-
      ties put under one roof, common clubs, professional associa-
      tions, career rotation, joint in-service training, etc.
   c) Common data banks, feedback of information and evaluations
      shared among sector components.
   d) New "overall system-direction units" being established.
The new system direction units would be the most essential
element in this strategy. These could be called inter-sectoral

planning agencies, but Dror in using the word "direction" seems to
mean something more since in fact they would be related to general
changes in organisational structure and personnel. Dror does not go
far in describing such planning agencies but does point to their
proposed variety and proliferation:

> "...complexity of issues, multiplicity of useful approaches
> and variety of relevant interests and values require a redundancy
> of such units which take different forms, such as: inter-
> sectoral planning units in central government; integrated
> service units on the field level; comprehensive social policy
> research units at universities; and policy research units of
> the Think Tank type in special relationships with various
> public agencies."

To suggest the deliberate introduction of a new redundancy into
modern bureaucracies as a means of promoting efficiency may seem
like a surprising contribution from the field of systems analysis.
Nevertheless, this may be the practical recommendation from study
of the disordered state of relationships among the social sectors,
including education. Writers from other points of view seem also to
reach this same position. A main feature of centrally initiated
inter-sectoral planning is that since it is seldom accompanied by
the power to abolish old structures, it merely adds new elements to
the existing structures. <u>This may thus suggest that centrally
organised inter-sectoral approaches, of themselves, tend toward the
creation of organisational redundancy</u>. Such developments, which of
course may take various forms, may nevertheless make useful contributions to further development.

Nevertheless, the point to be emphasized here is that no scheme
for inter-sectoral development seems to be operational without the
support of central initiatives. This central initiative may involve
efforts to integrate policies at the higher administrative levels
without necessarily attempting to effect an integration of the vertical organisation of the services themselves. Participatory modes
at local levels of social services would, in this case, be viewed
as subordinate means to the centralised strategy of integration.
On the other hand, if an inter-sectoral system is seen to be inseparable from the development of a participatory system, stressing
participation at the most local point of delivery of service, such
a development would require a framework of central policy no less
difficult or technical in its content. The emphasis on a central as
against a decentralised strategy may upon investigation be shown to
be related to the point in history during which the development of
an inter-sectoral system takes place.

2. Decentralisation

The majority view of the accompanying papers is that some form and a substantial amount of decentralisation must occur in the development of inter-sectoral policy planning. Obviously, the subject for systematic observation of country experience and research would be the relative balance between centralised and decentralised organisational elements. There is also the technical and political question of how much deviation from overall consistency is provided for by the specific rules governing the decentralisation. Eide reiterates a number of conditions which must govern the decentralisation of decision-making power in order for it to operate according to equity values and considerations:

a) Decentralisation must not put local units in a position in which they are without central protection from external pressures emanating from larger national forces.

b) The remnants of central decision-making power should not be allowed to expand and undermine formal decentralised decisions.

c) A reasonable balance of resources and bargaining power should exist between independent units at the same level.

d) A sufficient participation in decision-making for all those involved in the activities of subordinate units should be ensured so as to prevent a loss of freedom for the individual under the local hierarchy compared to what existed under the national one.

e) Decentralised decisions should be significant and of consequence to those invited to participate and questions for decision regarded as essentially controversial.

(A note on regional planning. It should be particularly noted that at the regional level horizontal collaboration is seldom effective because, as Eide suggests, "...as long as each of such organisations and institutions has its place within a separate national hierarchy, the willingness to enter into such local collaboration and to accept the outcome of decisions by local authorities has very narrow limits". This observation leads to the proposition that local co-ordination can only be achieved by cutting the separate vertical lines of control and support and inserting instead one single line from the local co-ordinating body.)

3. The inter-sectoral "grids of information"

Another point of consensus among contributors to this subject is that the development of inter-sectoral planning would be directly dependent on the establishment of networks of communication and of information within and between sectors. Of course, styles and the type of information and modes of delivery would vary to suit the character of the inter-sectoral system being developed. Eide stresses that such grids of information should be "purely non-directive", their products "non-prescriptive", and particularly divorced from the weight of higher authority. Dror and Kogan more readily accept information as an instrument for a more rational exercise of authority. Etzioni and Peston postulate entire organisations whose main task would be the development and dissemination of information, but with a different emphasis on its relationship to the authority. It is worth noting briefly the main lines of these proposals.

Peston suggests the creation of the "inter-sectoral sector", a new agency that would "discover" or "generate" problems which are beyond or outside the conceptual tools and instrumentalities of existing operating sectors. Primarily exploratory, innovative and evaluative, the activity of the inter-sectoral sector would stop short of putting its information in the hands of the existing operational agencies. This idea generally fits into the category of super-planning agencies which have largely advisory and persuasive powers. (See Section II A above.) If this is so, then experience in such widely different jurisdictions as France, Ontario, Canada, New York City and the United States Federal Government, shows that such super-planning agencies do not seem to function as expected. Since the operating agencies remain largely unchanged, the inter-sectoral sector finds it necessary to develop some kinds of prescriptive powers to get its proposals acted upon or, if unsuccessful in this, it tends to sponsor or create new inter-sectoral operational units. This is the general history of such super-planning agencies, unless they tend toward atrophy for want of influence.

Etzioni proposes the organisation of policy research centres, which would be "think tanks" organised within the operating agencies concerned. To help ease the problems of co-ordination such centres would have to bridge the inter-level, inter-agency and inter-sectoral fragmentation of the educational sector, by means of a largely pedagogical role, stimulating and affecting the thinking of people engaged in the work of the sector. The relatively small permanent staff of such centres, which would include people with particular competence in communications skills, would be always greatly augmented by people on loan from key positions in the operating agencies who would regularly rotate and constitute a growing informal "club" associated with the work and thinking of the policy research centre. The research done, which could stress specific cross-sectoral plans, would be worked out, explained and carried into the various operating agencies but would have no prescriptive authority. Thus, while this scheme, elaborated by Etzioni, meets Eide's non-directive stipulation, it is aimed at key operational personnel and therefore shares some of Dror's concern to establish the authority of superior information.

A system of information which is non-directive and non-prescriptive and which is also sufficiently pointed and likely to stimulate innovation and collaboration, is of course an ideal construction. Etzioni's proposed "think tanks" would be an integral part of their operating agencies but would be guaranteed an academic-style independence. He carefully delineates these internal research centres from existing types of policy research organisations, showing his proposal to be an untried model which could be open for experimentation, the kind of experimentation through which new organisational norms for information might be realised.

4. Inquiry for inter-sectoral policy planning: its nature and purpose

The hallmark of inter-sectoral planning study, as it emerges from the papers in this volume, may be said to be a recognition of sectoral interdependence. Such recognition is much more likely to come to people if it develops close to them than if it is "dropped" on them from afar. This argues for such studies to be assumed less by inter-sectoral planning agencies than by investigational units and activities established within each sector. However, it is not the discovery of interdependence which should be the main point of such study in education. Rather, the aim should be a deeper immersion in the nature of the problems of education itself, which would lead normally to a recognition of interdependence with other sectors. Inter-sectoral study and plans would be designed to bring to bear the functions of various sectors on problems which have been illuminated by new knowledge.

Planning study for inter-sectoral policies might be said to be aimed at the creative function of the sector, identified by Peston, a function which normally is seriously flawed. Peston projects the discovery of new major problems requiring innovative solutions which he thinks might belong to no sector or to an "inter-sector". But apart from the solution of creating a new agency or sector for each such problem, such problems must be worked out within existing sectors, a perspective which implies that they themselves must develop or resuscitate their creative functions.

Thus, the papers point to what may seem to be the paradoxical conclusion that the road to inter-sectoral policy approaches will best be found through a deeper comprehension of problems within individual sectors. For example, it has been noted before that inter-sectoral approaches in most circumstances must be implemented within each sector and at the field level, and these sectors usually thwart innovation that does not fit their establishments. The alternative of establishing new "inter-sectoral sectors" is viewed with caution in an age fighting to limit the development of bureaucracy.

Furthermore, if the motivation and incentives either for collaboration among sectors or for the creation of new "inter-sectors", depend upon the redefinition of tasks, such a redefinition requires new knowledge and comprehension among the people engaged in the existing sectors.

Insight into a new order of problems and tasks is unlikely to be accomplished by simply bringing together the sector specialists and their specialties and "adding them up". Like interdisciplinarity, this kind of study is not brought about by administrative tactics, structures or procedures; it is rather that people themselves must evolve into "interdisciplinarians", people with a tendency to recognise problems beyond the confines of their own disciplines and with sufficient appreciation of other disciplines to be able to understand them without at the same time attempting to dictate to them.

5. The major pattern of inter-sectoral study

It is only possible here to sketch what appears to be a pattern of planning studies which would be effectively supportive of inter-sectoral planning in education.

    a) The economics of inter-sectoral planning. The general character of this kind of study is indicated in the earlier section on the economic definition of the sector. Such study would deal with the sectoral interdependencies of goals, instruments and results in terms of resource flows and costs in as practical and concrete a manner as possible, and would recognise also the limits of this approach. Peston outlines further what would be involved in developing an inter-sectoral budget process and calls attention to the need to investigate the actual value of sectoral resources and comparative sectoral costs and the adverse relative price movements which affect such sectors as education.

    b) Institutional analysis of sectors. Kogan sketches and illustrates a method for making a comparison of major institutional characteristics of the social services recognised to be serving overlapping clientele. He shows how a number of categories subjected to parallel examination for each of the services could form a basic grid of data from which possible relationships, conflicts and congruences among these services could be recognised. Based upon observations of British institutions, Kogan makes an illustrative comparison of the following characteristics for education, social welfare, service housing and social security.
      - basic values
      - objectives or intended outputs and activities or intended inputs

- the client population
- training and recruitment patterns
- statuses of professional groups
- patterns of delegation between constituent administrative bodies, agencies, units or institutions
- size of institutions
- effect of building stocks and other facilities on development of the service.

Kogan and other authors, particularly Cohen, make it clear that other items for study could be added to this list, for example, the concepts of service, traditions and traditional practice which govern the professions dominant in each service; the knowledge base, operational procedures, and techniques and technologies available to each service, and the geographical scope (such as catchment area) of institutions particular to each service. Kogan's proposal represents a practical approach for gathering and organising data of prime importance for inter-sectoral study, since it would be more readily available from the usual bureaucratic and institutional sources.

c) <u>Study of the policy systems of sectors</u>. Study of sectoral policy systems would require a level of investigation taken beyond bureaucratic and institutional characteristics to research into the social system and the political culture of the sector. The objective of such study would be to describe the main formal and informal relationships among the main groups involved, including client groups and the community beyond the sector, which would reveal its policy system. Policy systems of different sectors could then be compared and their points of interrelationship better recognised. Planning of the most sophisticated kind would also include taking account of the planners' own position and role within the social system. (Reference, Cohen. Also extensively treated in <u>Participatory Planning in Education</u>, OECD 1974.)

d) <u>Socio-technical analysis</u>. Study of this kind requires that the facts of the policy system outlined above would be further specified in terms of educational practice. That all productive organisations have both a technical system by which the work of the organisation is done and a social system which is interrelated with the technical system, is an accepted general fact. Yet most innovative development flounders on the common failure to grasp the practical outcomes of this relationship. In schools, for example, the great amount of unwanted results which come from applying promising new equipment, new techniques and new organisational forms, emphasizes the need here to take carefully into account the relevant socio-technical relationships. (References: Westley and Hayward)

e) <u>Monitoring the development of main problems, reported practices and scientific findings</u>. Inter-sectoral study would involve keeping abreast of the major policy issues and intellectual problems of the sector and attempting to interpret experience in all fields which seem promising for the improvement of the social service offered by the sector. Special attention could be given to certain problems which appear as strategically important or to areas in which certain scientific developments seem ripe for exploitation. This kind of study would aim to promote and communicate developments in the state of the art relevant to services in the sector, looking for what would be major improvements in technical systems.

f) <u>Inter-sectoral plans</u>. Study and analysis of relationships with other sectors along the above lines could be the basis for attempts to develop sectoral plans which have strong inter-sectoral components. Such plans and broader ones attempting a more general inter-linking of sectors on a national scale could be major heuristic exercises, especially if their underlying assumptions are clearly explained. Also such plans are instruments of inter-group bargaining in the politics of inter-sectoralism, and therefore should not be monopolised by any one group. Inter-sectoral plans of more limited scope and featuring specific practical proposals, might also be effective in opening up problem areas for new study and action.

6. <u>The role of the planning agency</u>

"The distinction between 'planning', 'policy-making' and important decision-making is unclear and, I think, quite unessential for the purposes of this paper..." says Dror, and this is precisely the point of division on the question of the role of the planner and planning agency. The opposite view insists that there <u>be</u> a sharp division between the planning agency and decision-making. Planning can be restricted to primarily an informative function, but connected to decision-making it has prescriptive power. From all that has been said before, it can be seen that the general issue is whether the inter-sectoral planning agency is to be a new power centre in the organisation or an instrument for the broader distribution of power. Opinion in these papers seems to lean towards the planning agency to be organised primarily as an informative source which could contribute to the broad redistribution of competences

among people and to a dimunition of splitting and compartmentalisa-
tion in human activities.

C) HISTORY AND PERSPECTIVE FOR THE FUTURE

The level of commitment to a long-term perspective determines
the quality of any planning effort. How historical and future perspectives provide a necessary vitality to inter-sectoral strategies
for education is doubly illustrated in papers by Westley and Gans,
notable for the clarity of their policy content. Westley summarises
a long-term perspective for the future development of modern western
society and education is placed within it. This perspective is
that the major task of the future is to develop a reintegration of
work, education and leisure, which in the industrial age of the
past 150 years have been artificially compartmentalised as a result
of their institutionalisation. Therefore the institutions of work,
education and leisure would be directed toward an inter-penetration
in which children would be early introduced to socially significant
work, work would be vitally concerned with the development of the
workers, and the supposed major period of leisure, old age, would
be largely redistributed as self-recreative periods throughout a
life career. When its task is to work out the implications of this
kind of explicit perspective, inter-sectoral planning is in a
position to make practical contributions to the larger political
debates of our times.

Gans' paper illustrates another approach to the development of
perspective for inter-sectoral planning. He focuses his study for
a future planning model by choosing well-defined social goals to be
achieved by a designated population group in one country, in this
case, the United States:

"...(1) the economic integration of the poor, particularly
the urban poor, i.e. underemployed and unemployed and unemployable - and their children - into the 'mainstream' economy; and
(2) the dynamic use of education by this population."

Gans demonstrates the historical dimension of relationships
between sectors which must be considered if these goals are to be
achieved. In the United States the children of the lowest social
groups are not given the kind of schooling which allows them to be
dynamically related to labour market sectors; that is, they ordinarily do not move up the economic ladder. However, if as youths,
at say age 16 onwards, they are given reliable work and good and
increasing incomes, the next generation of these people shows itself
able to make use of the schools as they are to promote their upward
movement in the world of work. Into this model goes an assessment
of the way schools function for certain populations, and how the

labour market operates for them. In his argument Gans develops views
on prospects for reform of the schools as compared to prospects
for the reform of the labour market. Ultimately this examination
illuminates how the reforms of the school sector and of the labour
market sector must support each other if progress is to be made towards the stated social goal, the rescue of the very poor from their
inter-generational cycle of poverty in the United States.

D) CLIENT POWER, ANTI-BUREAUCRATIC GIMMICKRY AND NEW BASES FOR UNDERSTANDING IN EDUCATION

Any examination of the possibilities for inter-sectoral planning affecting education should bear in mind that the ultimate aim
is the education of the clients. Of course, genuine integration
between education and other services could result in conceptualising
goals somewhat differently. For example, "the healthful development
of the individual" could be substituted for "the education of..."
The feeling persists, nevertheless, that such decisions may
be too important to be left in the hands of the decision-makers, and
participation has moved from the status of an "in" slogan to that
of a long-term problem of social organisation. Participatory schemes
can be accepted as useful instruments for the integration of services, but they may also share in the criticism usually reserved for
various types of bureaucratic manoeuvre. Are teachers or doctors
or social workers, or any combination of the three, for example, in
an integrated service, likely to perform in a satisfactory manner
if they have to be forced to pay attention to their clients' needs
and aspirations by means of the organisation of client power? Are
such social services likely to be effective through the processes
of advocacy and confrontation? These questions bring us back to the
problem of the nature of the service which is desired in the first
place. While the voice of the client should indeed be clearly heard
and highly influential as the social services embrace a larger part
of their lives, such participation should supply the motivating
force to organise the knowledge concerning the nature, the meaning
and the techniques of these services, and to make it available both
to the service professions and to an increasingly informed public.
Essential to the notion of inter-sectoral planning is the provision
of a framework for collaboration and participation. This idea can
be illustrated by looking at the notion that clients, such as pupils
or students and their families, can best be their own co-ordinators
by giving them a free choice in a public service market. Having
some amount of anti-bureaucratic appeal, experiments along these
lines have been instituted in the United States and are the subject
of a fair amount of comment and serious evaluation. In these cases

29

the key question would be the extent to which this particular model of sellers providing buyers with social services promotes the mutual comprehension and empathy between the services and the clients which should be characteristic in the process of education.

In its ordinary operation education might very well be the most "natural" inter-sectoral sector among the public services. It might be said that people are in fact "inter-sectoral" and education is the institution beyond the family with the longest concern for their development. Not only does the popular demand for more effective education for more people oblige educational agencies to recognise the broad forces affecting their operations, schools have become the most obvious "dumping ground" for unloading some of society's serious problems. Thus, it is not surprising that perhaps the most effective examples of inter-sectoral policy approaches involve the co-option by education of other services. These examples sometimes reflect an increasing comprehension of the need for other instrumentalities in order to reach even traditional educational goals, to say nothing of the larger values shared with other sectors. On the basis of this experience inter-sectoral planning for education could mean that the educational establishment may in turn be better prepared itself to be co-opted by other sectors - prepared to give a large part of its energies as a resource drawn into educational activities developing throughout society.

Part I

APPROACHES TO INTER-SECTORAL

EDUCATIONAL PLANNING

AN ECONOMIC APPROACH
by Maurice Peston

I. THE NEW ECONOMICS OF INTER-SECTORAL PLANNING

It is difficult to think of any area of research that involves
a broader range of new problems than the economics of inter-sectoral
planning. Moreover, as these problems are examined more closely,
they prove to be neither elementary nor open to quick resolution.
Inter-sectoral study of costs and expenditures gives rise to difficulties that are usually ignored when a single sector is being inves-
tigated, but on the benefit and output side these difficulties are
increased by several orders of magnitude.

Equally, this study to a very great extent must break entirely
new ground, which means that its initial contribution must be chiefly
theoretical and methodological. This also means that it could be
regarded as the first stage of a long investigation, the major part
of which would comprise testing new procedures in practice. How far
existing planning bodies can take cognisance of the inter-sectoral
idea is a matter for conjecture. It seems more likely that new bodies
need to be brought into existence and new kinds of personnel trained
for them. Developments of this kind would seem likely at all levels
of government and administration from local authorities, through
national bodies up to international agencies. Furthermore, as we
argue below, changes in the operations of the sectors themselves,
education, health, housing, law and order, etc. will be necessary,
which may call into question the nature of various professions. In
sum, intersectoralism can involve significant changes and upheavals
in the status quo and must be founded as much as possible on experimental evidence and solid analysis.

The key issue of intersectoralism - a term adopted in this paper
as convenient shorthand expression - from the economic viewpoint, is
not measurement, but rather it is the very characterisation of the
flow of outputs from the system under consideration. Of course, for
such systems as education, it is customary to avoid all this by talking about "improvements in the person" or "amelioration of society",
but such expressions are of no help. The planner's objective must be
to specify in observable form the outputs of an overall system comprising education, health, law and order and other sub-systems.

Since we are still some way even from being at all confident that we understand and can specify the main outputs of the individual sub-systems, a good deal of caution, informed by some sense of pessimism, must be exercised when it comes to something so much larger.

The chief purpose of this paper is to throw a critical light on the nature of the inter-sectoral problem examined at a convenient level of generality. The main theme is the argument that any attempt to produce a complete solution is doomed; and while an overall view is of interest theoretically, practice demands something more limited. We shall argue that what can be of most help at the moment is posing quite small problems in an inter-sectoral way and attempting to solve them while taking account of sectoral interrelationships. In other words, emphasis should be on "social phenomena", which are usually not seen or dealt with in a rounded form because they are pushed into one or another sector. Examples would be: truancy, which is typically referred to "education"; violence, which is referred to "law and order"; absenteeism, which is referred to "employment"; neurotic illness, which is referred to "health"; urban blight which is referred to "housing", etc. The well-worn bromides about how all these problems are due to "society" (society itself comprising all these problems), are true but of little help. It may take a long time for new forms of organisation to appear and, for many years to come, existing sectors will remain. The responsibility for particular problems will be seen as falling chiefly within one sector or another. What can be suggested is that to approach them intersectorally may help to show how their worst aspects can be mitigated, and a little progress made in social policy making.

Interest in this area of research arises from experience in individual sectors where concentration on a narrow range of activities and their consequences has led to sub-optimal decision making. Its point of departure must be criticism of and dissatisfaction with the status quo. As a preliminary caveat, however, it is worth emphasizing, right from the outset, that it would be wrong to regard the existing planning situation as entirely disastrous. The desirability of new thinking does not necessarily arise from the need to meet an existing crisis. Suggestions for improvement are easily misinterpreted as criticism of an existing state of affairs, but that is not the view of this paper. In particular, there can be no doubt that public sector planning has advanced considerably in recent years, notably from 1960 to the present day.

II. A GENERAL ECONOMIC FORMULATION

The purpose of this section is to provide a general economic formulation of the inter-sectoral problem. Our concept of the sector is that it comprises a set of activities. Each activity involves the use of resources, or inputs, and generates a flow of benefits, or outputs. The fact that the activities are similar or complementary is what causes them to be placed in the same sector, the sector itself being defined to include not merely the activities it currently uses but also all those (possibly infinite in number) that it might use. This similarity of activities might refer either to the benefits or to the resources. It might be thought natural to concentrate on the former, and to assume essentially that the sector is to be defined in terms of its objectives or achievements. But in practice the reverse is frequently true, sectors being differentiated according to the types of resource they use. In education, for example, the tendency would be to characterise the sector in terms of its use of teachers and schools. In health similarly the emphasis would be placed on hospitals and doctors. It is taken for granted that this will ensure that what these resources produce is sufficiently similar also to warrant their being in the same sector.

Even if we invent a notional history and assume that originally sectors emerged or were started to deal with classes of objectives called education, health, law and order etc., it is apparent that they rapidly transform themselves into concentrations of resource use. This is because the objectives themselves are usually so abstract that it is next to impossible to isolate a sector in those terms alone. It is much easier to concentrate on inputs which refer to particular physical locations and specific brands of professional expertise. It is a chicken-or-egg question to ask which came first, the sector (i.e. the objective) or the professionalism, but there can be no doubt which gained the ascendancy. Indeed, one force that sustains the professional is that he comes to be regarded as a repository for expert knowledge or judgement of objectives.

The economist will also want to define sectors not simply in terms of a class of objectives which they aim at, but also as possessors of criteria by which achievements are to be judged. He would be tempted to concentrate entirely on criteria of evaluation, and assume that the activities used by and open to each sector would then follow as a matter of course. As a matter of practice this does not happen, but it also does not make a lot of theoretical sense. The reason is that the sectors are not to be thought of as static entities solving problems thought up somewhere else in society according to principles which are also given to them outside. Rather they themselves are intended to be problem seekers and innovators with respect to ends as well as means.

We return to the question of criteria of evaluation below, for it lies at the heart of intersectoralism. First, however, we must look at the demarcations between sectors, and the question of co-ordination. If the set of activities comprising a sector is well defined, no problem of demarcation arises. But in practice the edges of each sector are not clear-cut, and they are constantly being blurred by the discovery of new activities. To a large extent demarcation disputes are avoided by the professionals of the sectors themselves; thus, the teachers do not interfere with the general practitioners who in turn rarely attempt to take over from the lawyers.

Apart from matters of demarcation, and long before inter-sectoralism itself is properly recognised, it is seen that some sectoral activities need to be co-ordinated with others. Thus, the division into what might be called primary or operating sectors gives rise to the existence of secondary or co-ordinating sectors. Now, in the present context, these sectors too would be defined according to a set of activities in which they engage. In this case, however, the outputs which they generate must be regarded as inputs to the other sectors or intermediate to the system as a whole. The trouble is, of course, that the co-ordinators or planners, too, become professional-ised, and begin to regard what they do as a pure output or something valuable in its own right. Within the primary sectors one comes across the pathological cases of success in education and health being seen in terms of the job satisfaction of teachers and doctors. Now, at the secondary level, there appears the more extreme pathol-ogy of successful planning or co-ordination as such with scant regard to the activities of the primary sectors at all. At the extreme one finds planning departments of central governments claim-ing for themselves all kinds of successes while accusing all the operating departments of failure.

To summarise so far, we postulate the existence of sectors at two levels. Each sector comprises a set of activities, actual and potential, the set itself changing as a result of its own operations. While in a sense a sector is there to do a job set from the outside, in large part it determines its own job and the way in which it is judged. Thus, while what is called consumer sovereignty is relevant, it is not correct to interpret the sectors as analogous to the firms and industries of neo-classical economics, competing to satisfy a given demand. Quite the contrary, their role must be seen as a creative one, to generate and make the case for new demands.

This creative role is obviously partly to do with the invention and introduction of new activities, but it also involves exploration within the existing activities set. While we can define the exist-ence of that set in the abstract, it is worth emphasizing that much of its content will not be known to individual decision makers.

35

Moreover, the activities themselves are not simple input-output relationships in which given one, the other follows with certainty. Quite the contrary, the decision-making procedure is fraught with uncertainty and unforeseen effects. Much of this is the inevitable uncertainty due to social processes and our lack of knowledge of how they work. In part, however, it is the result of the sectoral partition itself, and within any one sector is attributable to what is going on and being decided elsewhere.

There is one other characteristic of the sectors that actually exists, at least in the United Kingdom. It is that as systems responding to both inside and outside forces they are extremely sluggish. They do respond to outside forces but at a rate measured in quinquennia or decades rather than months and quarters. It might be argued that this is inevitable given that we are dealing essentially with government operations, and also desirable in the context of the low information states within which decisions are taken. What is relevant to the present discussion, however, is that taking account of the overlap between sectors must also occur as a long-term or trend response to deviations from a desired state of affairs, rather than as an immediate capacity for adjustment. To put the point differently, it might well be desirable to make these systems much more quick acting, but this is separate from intersectoralism and might well not be fostered by it.

III. TOWARD ESTABLISHMENT OF AN "INTER-SECTORAL SECTOR"

If we accept this formulation of the sectoral situation we are led to the problem of intersectoralism in a variety of ways. Firstly, it will not always be the case that the effects of particular activities are additive. The result of combining several activities will not be the sum of their effects taken separately. They may be complementary so that the value of them taken together exceeds the sum of their values taken separately, or they may interfere with one another so that the value of them taken together is less than the sum of their values taken separately. Now, if all these activities are placed within the same sector, it is at least possible that the relevant interrelationships will be recognised and taken into account. If they are within separate sectors, this is less likely to happen, particularly if it is assumed that effects are not there for all to see but have to be discovered.

Having argued that the effects of groups of activities might be superadditive or subadditive, it is easy to go on and argue, secondly, that this will be true of their costs as well. There may be economies or diseconomies in the joint use of resources. Different inputs may

complement each other, or the successful use of one may interfere
with another. Where there are fixed quantities of particular resources (albeit temporarily) there is an obvious problem of choice
of use, but this remains true of an expanding system. It is also
worth bearing in mind that a decision to expand certain related activities simultaneously may be more efficient than expanding them separately at different times. But on another occasion the crucial question may be to decide which activity is to go ahead first and which
are to remain in the queue.

Thus, although in an elementary analysis we may take it for
granted that we may treat each activity as separate, merely adding
their costs and benefits when necessary, we rapidly become obliged
to see how much more complicated are their interconnections, if for
no other reason than because otherwise the division into sectors
would appear to be arbitrary. But, having gone that far, we are
then forced to check whether there are gaps between the activities
so that the interconnections do not occur across sectors but only
within them. What is now apparent is that these gaps are not as
large as might be thought, and that resource use and benefits in one
sector as conventionally defined are closely related to resource use
and benefits elsewhere. While this may be blurred by the professional
work of the sectors (teachers teach, doctors cure, policemen maintain
law and order), ultimately it is impossible to hide the social reality
which is there. Curiously enough, this is not solely because social
scientists study these fields and find the conventional divisions
unsatisfactory. It is also because the professionals themselves (or
some of them) have begun to see how they are constrained by choices
taken in other, often distant, areas.

The third point, and perhaps the most significant of all,
derives from the role of the sector as the creator of problems and
the inventor of criteria of evaluation. To a considerable extent the
problems that emerge and the method of dealing with them are not sui
generis, and are dependent on the sectoral structure that exists.
The case for intersectoralism is then no longer solely the negative
one, i.e. that the existing system is unable to provide satisfactory
solutions to problems. It is also the positive one that the present
system is unable to generate the appropriate problems in the first
place. (If one prefers to take the point of view that in some sense
the problems are always there, then the relevant proposition becomes
that the system cannot discern the appropriate problems.)

All of this can be illustrated by example. An obvious one would
be what is encompassed under the general heading of truancy. In the
narrowest educational terms this is merely a matter of non-attendance
at school. In the narrowest police terms it is a matter of law
breaking. To the social worker it may not even be a problem at all,

but a symptom or even partial solution to another problem, namely breakdown of the family unit. To the economist it may be an early warning of future difficulties concerning labour force participation and employment. Lastly, the psychologist may see irregular school attendance as just one aspect of the mental illness of the individual and possibly not as a social problem at all.

Now, as a matter of simple fact, all of these sectors are operating on the same individuals, and may be thought of as dealing with different facets of the same situation. It is by no means obvious, however, that each treatment reinforces all the others, and it could well be that much effort is wasted simply because it is not fully integrated into a complete strategy. More serious in this example is the likelihood that quite different criteria of evaluation are being employed by the different sectors. The education sector's concern may be simply with school attendance and good behaviour in the classroom. The truancy problem interpreted in terms of the physical (as opposed to mental) presence of the child in the school is then solved. The solution for the law and order sector may simply be to get the child anywhere that is off the streets and out of public places. For the social worker the reduction of truancy may be to exacerbate the home situation, while the economist may be indifferent to it if the child eventually makes a successful entry to the labour force. All of this may still leave the health sector with an uncured patient.

What one now argues is that there should come into existence a sector or a part of a sector which is able to examine the truancy problem as a whole. It would endeavour to discover whether it is one problem or a whole class of problems, and, if the latter, construct a method of diagnosing particular cases. In terms of treatment it would again provide a uniform approach with individual variations corresponding to individual differences. Above all it would see that the solution actually applied to the problem.

It is impossible to emphasize too strongly how important this last comment is. As things stand at the moment, the sector in which a problem appears is obliged to deal with it, even though it may not have been shown that the solution is actually in the hands of the people who are deemed to be responsible. This occurs to a great extent in the education sector and truancy provides almost a classic case. It is by no means obvious that truancy is an educational problem at all in the sense that it is capable of being solved by the methods which teachers and school administrators have at their disposal. Similarly, if the problem is then placed in the hands of truancy officers and the police, they may find means of solving it in their own terms which appear to be effective and inexpensive. But the result may be to place enormous costs on the other sectors so that in no overall sense is the solution efficient.

Truancy exhibits all the bad characteristics that intersector-alism is designed to overcome. It involves duplication of effort, a confusion of costs and benefits, treatment of the symptoms rather than the disease, and a separation of responsibility for action from capacity for action. In discussing it the setting up of a sector to cover truancy as a whole was referred to. This was an idea intended to cover two related developments. One is that the different sectors should approach each problem in what might be called an inter-sectoral spirit. The other is the need for a sector devoted to intersectoralism.

The rationale for this is that truancy is not an isolated, unusual phenomenon, but one example of a whole range of inter-sectoral phenomena. It is fascinating because it involves virtually all sectors together with an explicit overlap of the individual and the social. It is not, however, unique. (Of course, it is somewhat special in that the problem arises in one form because of the legal requirement of school attendance. It would be a mistake, quite typical of the sectoral approach, to assume that the problem would be solved if the legal requirements were abolished. Rather it would exist in a different form. This is not to say that the school leaving age in the U.K. should have been raised to sixteen or that it would not be worthwhile reconsidering the relationship between home, school and workplace, but the reason for that would not be to define the problem of truancy out of existence.)

The natural generalisation of the truancy problem is absentee-ism in general from work and from the home. Indeed, an inter-sectoral approach might discover a great deal in common between absenteeism in all its forms. Instead of the present situation in which failure to attend school is a matter of education, absentee-ism from work is a matter of economics, and disappearance from home a matter of social psychology, they would all be placed in the general framework of abstention from normal activity.

This leads me to the central conclusions of this part of the paper. They are, firstly, that formal procedures need to be developed for separate sectors so that the kind of difficulties and potential waste that we have mentioned are reduced, possibly to the vanishing point. Secondly, that a systematic attempt should be made to cate-gorise and then investigate a number of inter-sectoral problems. This would be along the lines of our discussion of truancy, but, of course, on a much larger scale and in greater depth. The objective of the first approach would be to develop the philosophy of inter-sectoralism while the task of the second would be to prepare the ground for the setting up of an "inter-sectoral sector".

IV. PROCEDURES TO DEAL WITH INTER-SECTORAL PROBLEMS

Given the existence of a class of problems, actual and potential, that may be placed under the general question of intersectoralism, the development of a procedure or set of procedures to deal with them is needed. As things stand at the moment, the approach is one of co-ordinating the activities of existing individual sectors, each sector calling on the relevant expertise of the others when it sees this to be necessary. The operation of the sectors themselves is to a considerable extent conventional and habitual in that they get along without an explicit specification for output for their activities and tend to take their own effectiveness and efficiency for granted.

It follows that an appropriate procedure must start from a rather elementary level. If, for example, the education sector is not at all clear what it is doing in its own terms, it might appear to be quite beyond its capacity to re-examine its operations in intersectoral terms. To put the point differently, an attempt to bring inter-sectoral ideas to bear must act as a stimulus toward the rational examination of all sectoral activities.

This suggests, therefore, that the first step must be a complete description of resource use within each sector in as fine detail as is possible. This means, in particular, not so much an account of expenditure, but rather an account of the resources available at a given time and the rate at which they are being used up. The economic point here is to give due weight to capital and to the dynamic consequences of current decisions.

Secondly, the resources must be related as closely as possible to what they are designed to achieve in individual sectoral terms. The aim here is to develop a picture of the set of activities discussed above.

Thirdly, the individual sectors will see their operations not only in the basic form of these teachers, and those books, and that heat and light go into something called a school, and those doctors and those drugs, and that heat and light go into something called a hospital, but also in the form of objectives defined more broadly as education, health, etc. It is at this stage, of course, that most research has broken down, and we are usually left without an explicit specification in terms which correspond to the raison d'être of any sector.

There have, however, been a growing number of attempts to account for particular sectoral activities not so much in the broad terms of something called education, but more as a vector of items describing a variety of academic achievements, personal developments, and social characteristics. While most people would agree that there is more

to "education" than such a listing, it is recognised as giving some
guidance towards a rational appraisal of the resources being used.
At least one benefit of as complete a listing as possible is that it
prevents decisions being taken according to performance along the one
dimension that is fashionable at that time. It is now agreed that
such a listing provides a discipline in that (a) it leads to an
attempt to establish the facts pertaining to any category in the
vector, (b) it acts as a stimulus to search for other dimensions of
performance and extension of the vector, (c) it focuses on the problem
of transforming the vector into the ultimate objective, i.e. education
itself.

For our purpose, however, it has one other advantage, namely
that it should lead towards the isolation of particular aspects of
the inter-sectoral problem. An attempt to classify the consequences
of education activities will immediately give rise to a list containing elements belonging more properly to health, law and order etc.
This will also be true for the other sectors. Naturally, this would
not have to be left to chance, and instructions could be given to
search for such overlaps. But, even if no conscious attention were
paid initially to coincidence of interest with other sectors, it
would be bound to emerge within the procedure indicated.

This leads on, of course, to the education and training of administrators and others within individual sectors. If, in fact,
attempts are made to rationalise decision-making processes so that
they focus much more on their outputs or results, a concomitant would
be the necessity of reorientating the individuals concerned towards
an inter-sectoral approach. One would, indeed, go further and argue
that the ultimately desirable state of affairs is one in which the
practitioners themselves have a much stronger inter-sectoral element
in their education and training. Curiously enough, this is recognised
in many quarters although it is often not expressed in what might be
called inter-sectoral language. The need for teachers, doctors and
policemen to gain a broader understanding of the social and psychological effects of what they do is taken for granted in most statements on curriculum reform, even though much less than what is desirable is yet incorporated into current practice. The trouble is that
this broadening is often in conflict with what are taken to be the
needs of professionalism, and each profession is anxious to protect
its preserve from the encroachment of others.

The teachers are subject to the greatest pressures of all, for
they can see how everything they do is closely involved with all
other social activities, but sometimes have great difficulty in isolating their own particular contribution. Indeed, one unfortunate
consequence of the existing structure is that education becomes the

residual legatee of all social problems which fall between the inter-
stices of the other sectors. Thus, teachers and educational administrators are forced into intersectoralism whether they like it or not.

While the ultimate solution might be to create a new profession
of social engineer who specialises as a teacher, doctor, psychologist,
policeman or social worker, and who with appropriate retraining can
transfer from one sector to another, it is utopian to believe that
anything like that will develop in the near future. The most that
can be hoped for, therefore, is that curriculum change in the direction of intersectoralism will gather strength, and that practitioners
and administrators can be guided towards seeing their work in an
inter-sectoral framework.

This leads to a last practical proposal for procedural reform.
The philosophy that we have outlined is based on the view not that
intersectoralism is simply to be interpreted as an overlap between
sectors, but rather that there exist problems of a type that must
transcend any individual sectoral arrangements. Moreover, to approach
these problems as having educational, health, legal, etc. aspects whic
need co-ordinating is to miss their significance as phenomena in their
own right. To revert to our example of truancy, the issue here is not
merely to get a number of experts to take account of each other's
expertise, and it is not just to ensure that all forms of expertise
are brought to bear. Rather what is necessary is that someone is
responsible for truancy as such. A similar comment would be made
about other intrinsically inter-sectoral phenomena. Within the
present system they are neglected altogether or at best dealt with
on an ad hoc basis. What is now needed is a sector devoted to them,
capable of isolating these phenomena, analysing them, and feeding
back the results of their discoveries to the individual operating
sectors. It would be a sector devoted to social problems as such,
including their evaluation and costing, and its primary role would
be investigatory and innovatory, operations continuing to be left to
the sectors that exist already.

V. THE RELATIVE PRICE EFFECT AND EDUCATIONAL EXPENDITURE

The purpose of this section is to approach the problem of inter-
sectoralism from another standpoint altogether.

It is widely recognised that one of the most significant developments in the planning of the public sector in the past decade or so
has been concerned with the projection and control of government
expenditure. The published figures are classified according to the
sectors we are discussing here, and in somewhat finer detail, but
not, of course, down to the level of individual projects. It could

almost be argued that the area of present debate is that defined by the structure of sectors as set out in the Public Expenditure White Paper published in the United Kingdom.

Although governments have an interest in the actual money expenditure that they incur, of more importance are the figures for expenditure at constant prices. There may be technical difficulties involved with predicting the rate of inflation, and even if there were not, governments would find the publication of such figures politically embarassing. The result is that the figures for planned expenditure are all expressed in base period prices.

Projections of expenditure at constant prices enable the government to anticipate and plan the volume of resources going into individual sectors and into the public sector as a whole. There may also be an interest in the cost of some or all of public sector activity especially in relation to the likely growth of gross domestic product. It might be thought that a measure of the volume of resources going into the public sector would also be a measure of the cost of those resources at constant prices. In fact, in general this is not the case because of the existence of the so-called "relative price effect". In essence this amounts to the proposition that over time public sector activities become expensive relative to economic activity in general. This is partly the result of what might be thought to be rather peculiar national accounting conventions, but it is also due to a difference in factor intensity in the public sector compared with the economy as a whole.

The purpose of this section is to explain in more detail how the relative price effect arises. We then go on to argue that it is in principle a serious complication for inter-sectoral planning, but that above all it reinforces the need to solve the problems of specification, measurement and evaluation of the outputs of the public sector. (We shall concentrate on the United Kingdom case, but much the same sort of problem must arise in other countries.)

Public expenditure at constant prices may be divided into public current expenditure and public capital formation at constant prices. To a considerable extent these series are obtained by deflating expenditure in actual prices by indices of prices or costs. A whole variety of price indices are used pertaining to the goods and services bought, and in cases where the expenditure is for the employment of people, an index of pay will be used. This is true on both the capital and current sides, and to obtain a constant price series for the former there is in general no difference between the methods employed for the public sector and the private sector. It is true, however, that for some items of current expenditure a different method is used to obtain figures at constant prices. Instead of deflating actual expenditure by a price index, a volume indicator is

used. Thus, dispensing cost at constant prices by the National
Health Service is measured by the number of prescriptions dispensed.

IMPLIED PRICE INDICES (1963 = 100)

	I		II		III		IV		V	
1961	94.7		93		94.7		94.7		87.1	
1962	97.9	3.4	96	3.2	97.1	2.5	96.1	1.5	96.1	10.3
1963	100.0	2.2	100	4.2	100.0	3.0	100.0	4.1	100.0	4.1
1964	102.6	2.6	105	5.0	105.4	5.4	104.7	4.7	102.8	2.8
1965	106.8	4.1	112	6.7	111.7	6.0	112.5	7.5	110.8	7.8
1966	110.4	3.4	118	5.4	119.1	6.6	118.2	5.1	117.4	6.0
1967	114.4	3.6	124	5.1	123.2	3.4	124.7	5.5	124.5	6.1
1968	117.7	2.9	131	5.7	131.7	6.9	131.1	5.1	130.3	4.7
1969	121.8	3.5	140	6.9	139.9	6.2	139.4	6.3	139.0	6.7
1970	131.1	7.6	153	9.3	158.5	13.3	153.3	10.0	149.3	7.4
1971	145.1	10.7	169	10.5	175.5	10.7	172.2	12.3	161.0	7.8

I. Gross Domestic Product Deflator

II. Public Authorities' Current Goods and Services Deflator

III. Public Authorities' Current Expenditure on Goods & Services:
Military Defence

IV. Public Authorities' Current Expenditure on Goods & Services:
NHS

V. Public Authorities' Current Expenditure on Goods & Services:
Education

In each case the first column gives the level of the index number
and the second its annual change.

Given these statistics at expenditure at constant prices, we
can derive the implied price indices for such broad aggregates as
public authorities' current expenditure, public authorities' fixed
capital formation, and total public expenditure. In the United
Kingdom constant price estimates are also published for such broad
sectors as 'military defence', 'national health service', 'education', and 'other' so that the implied price indices for these may
also be calculated.

Now, an examination of these indices (given in the preceding
table) shows that they rise more rapidly than prices in general (i.e.
consumer prices, prices of capital goods, and the gross domestic
product deflator). It is this which is meant by the relative price
effect. It implies that if the volume of resources going into education, for example, is planned to increase at the same rate as

44

national income, the cost of those resources will increase faster
than that. The result will be that expenditure on education will
rise as a share of national income even though the volume of resources going into that sector does not.

How does the relative price effect come about? The answer at
the simplest level is that public expenditure tends to involve the
purchase of goods and services, the prices of which rise relative to
those of goods and services in general. If we examine why particular goods and services become relatively more expensive through time,
the answer lies partly in the change of productivity in one line of
production compared with another, partly in what happens to wage rates
compared with the return to capital, and partly in the behaviour of
demand.

Typically, in the sort of economic systems we are talking about,
capital is accumulated faster than the growth of the labour force,
and there is a tendency for the real wage to rise relative to the
return on capital. It is also the case that technical progress pro-
ceeds more rapidly in the capital-intensive sectors. If, thirdly,
demand shifts so that the labour-intensive sectors expand relative
to the capital-intensive, this will reinforce the rise in the real
wage compared to the return on capital.

It follows that goods and services produced in labour-intensive
sectors, and in sectors in which technical progress is below average,
will rise in price compared with goods and services in general. If
public authorities concentrate their expenditure on these goods and
services, for the same money they will be acquiring a smaller volume
of resources. Alternatively, a given volume of resources will require
increasing money expenditure. That is the way the relative price
effect arises, from a difference between its pattern of expenditure
and that of the economy at large. In the extreme case the public
sector (or a large fraction of it) is itself extremely labour-
intensive so that the relevant price index for it would be the wage
rate which in a growing economy must rise in real terms. Another
way of putting this would be that the money wage rises relative to
the general level of prices, which, of course, is an example of the
relative price effect.

The discussion so far has proceeded on the assumption that what
happens to relative prices is independent of government expenditure
which merely reflects what is happening in the economy at large. In
fact, government activity itself may be a significant cause of the
relative price effect. In the first place, government demands for
the past decade or so have been rising compared with demand in
general in the economy. This has involved a direct recruitment of
people into the public service or has been devoted to other labour-
intensive activities. Secondly, the output of the public sector

itself as conventionally measured shows a zero or below average rise in productivity. Again, insofar as the government purchases its own output, there will be a relative price effect.

If there can be a relative price effect between the public sector and the economy at large, there can also be a relative price effect between the individual sectors comprising the public sector. This is seen in the table in which the price index for expenditure on education rose over the decade more slowly than that for health. It is here that the problem of intersectoralism emerges in a stark form because it is necessary to enquire what are the consequences for policy when the activities of one sector seem to become expensive compared with the activities of another.

VI.   AN INTER-SECTORAL FORMULATION FOR THE BUDGET

At the micro-level of the individual project intersectoralism amounts to the view that there are problems the full solution of which cannot be reached by individual sectors acting on their own, and there are problems the very existence of which will fail to be recognised by the existing sectoral structure. We have argued that the attempt to do this leads inevitably to a more careful examination of the output or outputs generated by the solution to the problem and also to a different specification of the cost. If carried out correctly, it would be expected that the relative price effect will be taken into account.

It is unlikely, however, that in the near future the control of public expenditure will be based on the appraisal of projects in such detail. It is much more likely that something resembling the existing situation will persist for some time. It then follows that some attention must be paid to the broader estimation of the outputs of the individual sectors, their comparative costs, and the extent of their inter-sectoral overlap.

In the United Kingdom the real output of the public sector is measured broadly speaking by the number of people employed by it. This means that in essence productivity in health, education, etc. is assumed to remain constant. What we have therefore, is a system in which the real volume of resources going on is rising, their relative cost is rising even more, and productivity is unchanging. The danger is then that the economic value of the public sector as a whole is underestimated, and the significance of different parts of it confused.

This has led most economists who have studied the subject to emphasize the need to determine much more precisely the outputs of individual sectors, and also to distinguish the annual expenditure on each sector from the value of the resources it uses.

On the latter, the key point is to obtain an estimate of the stock of capital used by each sector and the value of capital services flowing into it. In particular, it is important not to interpret the figures for capital expenditure as one for capital inputs. This is complicated by the fact that a part of public authorities' current expenditure should really be treated as capital expenditure.

On the former point, the question of output, the obvious pitfall is to talk about the inefficiency of the public sector when, correctly measured, its flow of outputs may be rising more rapidly than the value of the resources it uses up. Within the present context, however, there is another danger. It arises from concentration on the relative price effect, and leads to conclusions such as (a) if the public sector is becoming more expensive relative to the private sector, we should, other things being equal, switch demand from the former to the latter, and (b) if health is becoming more expensive relative to education, we should again switch resources from the former to the latter. Both types of argument are fallacious in that they confuse expenditure with cost, but no correct estimate of cost can be obtained without paying attention to the output interrelationships between the sectors.

Thus, while the relative price effect shows that the prices of goods and services being purchased in the health sector is rising relative to the corresponding prices in the education sector, this is quite compatible with "the price of a unit of health" not rising relative to "the price of a unit of education". Moreover, a unit of health and a unit of education may not be strictly separable in that each may contain elements belonging to the other sector, and there may be elements belonging jointly to the sectors that end up being assigned to neither.

This suggests that the allocation of the government budget must partly have an inter-sectoral foundation, and the distribution of funds to any one sector may have consequences for others. In particular, it cannot be taken for granted that the sectors left to operate on their own will achieve entirely satisfactory results. Moreover, an attempt to assess the performance of the sectors separately could easily lead, as it almost certainly has in the past, to a misallocation of public funds.

VII.   CONCLUSION: THE ECONOMIC PLANNING OF SOCIAL POLICY MUST BE INTER-SECTORAL

The concluding section of this paper can be brief. The purpose has been to clarify the nature of intersectoralism, and to show where it is relevant to policy. The existing structure of sectors, while it is clearly relevant to any future organisation for public policy making, has obvious limitations. Its rationale lies much more in the professionalism to which it gives rise and which fosters it than in the social problems which are emerging at the present. In particular, it fails to see these problems in the broad, or to predict and prepare for the nature of the problems likely to arise in the future.

It seems reasonable to argue, therefore, that the next developments in social policy will be on inter-sectoral lines. Certainly this seems to be the case as far as both the administration and the economic planning of social policy is concerned. This means, therefore, that attempts must be made as rapidly as possible to incorporate this type of thinking into new curricula for educating and training all the many types and levels of people who will be engaged in this kind of work. This is not simply a matter of reform in the level of first degree and post-graduate study. It is much more an item to be emphasized in all the multifarious courses that make up permanent education in the social fields.

Lastly, while this and other papers are based on experience of work on a variety of social problems, they are bound to be largely theoretical. What must also be given priority, therefore, is a serious research effort to examine in more detail actual problems in which the inter-sectoral element is dominant. It is on the basis of such studies that precise plans for intersectoralism can be drawn up, yielding practical solutions to real problems.

<u>CONCEPTS TOWARD DECENTRALISED COLLABORATION</u>
by Kjell Eide

I. THE SECTOR CONCEPT

Like so many other organisational terms, the use of the term
"sector" has its origin in military organisation. A battlefront was
divided into sectors, and each sector was the responsibility of one
local command. When seen from headquarters, the analogy between a
battlefront divided into sectors and the geometric sector concept
is evident, as shown in Figure 1.

Figure 1

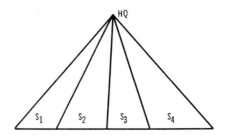

Even in a military context, however, the analogy with a two-
dimensional geometric concept is far from perfect. Behind the geo-
metrical surface lies division of responsibilities between the
various military branches - infantry, cavalry, artillery, air-force,
etc. - constituting an underlying grid of command, which together
with the sectoral divisions forms a kind of organisational matrix.
It is interesting to note that in a military context, the sectoral
divisions are temporary, while the underlying grid of military branches is a permanent feature. When the latter begins to become too
rigid, the central military command may try to break up this rigidity
with the help of specialist services running across the border-lines
between the various branches. MacNamara's(1) use of systems analysts

---

1) Reference here is to Mr. MacNamara's tenure as U.S. Secretary of
   Defence.

and programme budgeting specialists was in part an attempt to break
down such rigidities. An independent set of premises provided by
such specialists offered the central command a means to judge the
firmly established premises of each of the individual military
branches. One can understand the desperate need felt by a central
command faced with such firmly entrenched sub-systems. Yet, whether
the decisions reached on the basis of the new, alternative premises
were any better, and where such decisions were in fact located are
debatable issues.

When used in the more general context of public administration,
the tactically oriented sector concept becomes even more problematic.
It is often used interchangeably with the loose concept of a "field
of policy". We talk about educational policy, research policy,
cultural policy, health policy, social policy, economic policy, and
even innovation policy, regional policy, information policy, etc.
The way we use those terms makes it clear that we are dealing with
overlapping phenomena, as illustrated in Figure 2.

Figure 2

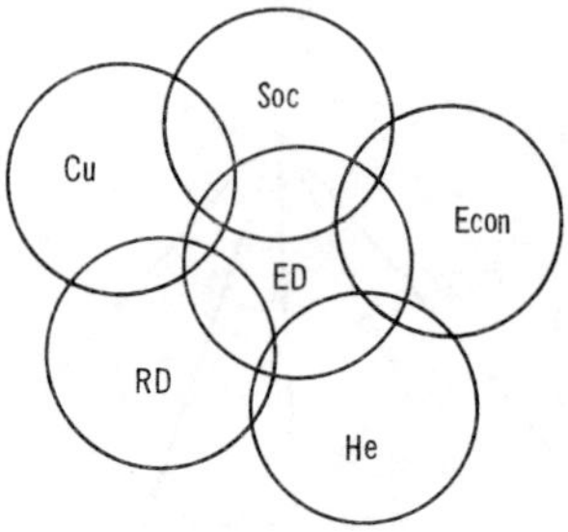

To a considerable extent, one and the same policy measure may
belong to several fields of policy. Thus agricultural education is
part of educational policy, but also an important instrument in
agricultural policy, and it may be viewed as part of economic policy,
social policy, regional policy, innovation policy, etc. Correspondingly, remedial primary education is certainly a part of educational
policy, but also essential in the context of social policy and health
policy.

The reasons for this overlapping are not difficult to see. We
may define a field of policy, or a sector, in terms of specific
policy instruments. Educational policy may, for instance, be seen
as the use of educational institutions for a variety of policy objectives, most of which would also appear as objectives for policies
in other fields. But we may also define a field of policy, e.g.
education, in terms of a specific set of objectives to be served.

In that case, we regularly discover that such objectives are also
influenced by policy instruments applied in policy sectors not at
all associated with education. Most sectors or fields of policy
have thus little autonomy - their activities cannot be judged without reference to their interrelationships with other sectors.

When government activities were confined to a small number of
isolated programmes in scattered areas, while most societal activities were of no concern to governments, it was still conceivable to
look upon individual government programmes as "autonomous". However,
modern government in all countries implies a much more general concern for societal developments, and in this situation the notion of
"programme autonomy" becomes illusory.

In most governments we try to handle this complexity of
"policy sectors" with the help of a bureaucratic administrative
structure. By vertical lines of command, we connect superior and
inferior units, each with its specific and distinctive responsibilities. We apply, in other words, the two-dimensional sectoral concept, quite analogous to its military use, including the division
of individual sectors into subsectors, etc., as illustrated in
Figure 3.

Figure 3

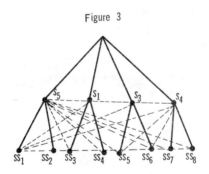

A key principle in bureaucratic organisation is the clear-cut
division of responsibility among units at the same level. This
means that any policy measure "belongs" to one, and only one, bureaucratic sector. Consequently, within such an organisation we act as
if the overlapping between sectors illustrated in Figure 2 does not
exist. The real interrelationships between bureaucratic sectors,
as illustrated by the dotted lines in Figure 3, are, in principle,
only a concern for superior co-ordinating units.

The bureaucratic structures actually found in governmental
administration can only be explained as the result of a historical
process. At some stage, it appeared convenient to organise activities of a certain kind in an administrative sector (e.g. a ministry)
or sub-sector (e.g. a department). However, once established, such

structures may outlive the specific reasons for their establishment. Thus, traditional sector divisions may gradually lose meaning both in terms of political priorities and instrumental convenience. Yet, no re-organisation can more than partly remedy the lack of sectoral autonomy of such bureaucratic units. There is no way in which the cake can be cut so that full sector autonomy is achieved. The most one can hope for is that, in a given situation, certain bureaucratic structures may cut less essential interrelationships than others.

It should be noted, incidentally, that administrative regroupings may have considerable costs. Alternative structures should thus represent significant gains in order to be worthwhile. However, quite frequently, actual attempts on restructuring government administration appear as a kind of desperate search for solutions which cannot be found within any bureaucratic structure.

The actual structuring found in government administration does not follow any clear-cut principles. Generally, interdependent activities tend to be grouped together. A school, for instance, may serve many purposes, but it appears practical to keep such activities within one organisational unit. By and large, government structures are oriented towards convenient grouping of policy measures rather than interrelated clusters of policy objectives. This distinction, however, is somewhat dubious, as there is hardly any way to distinguish clearly between ends and means in this context. However, the fact that different units serve overlapping objectives tends to make the co-ordinating function of superior units somewhat easier, and even provides some common grounds for horizontal contacts between units at the same level.

The obvious shortcomings of organisational structures of this kind have led to various attempts to find better criteria for their structuring. One such attempt is often labelled "functional organisation"(1). Its starting point is the fact that the world of professional people is also divided into what may be called sectors of competence. Such sectors are related to traditional divisions into scientific disciplines and professions. "Strong" professions may also be related to fields of policy, such as health, economy or education, while others, such as law and science, run across policy sectors and bureaucratic sectors.

"Functional" organisation tends to group individuals with similar professional competence in specific units, such as technical, legal, medical or economic branches, but also in expert units for such functions as "budgeting", "personnel management", "planning", "evaluation", "analysis", etc. The assumption appears to be that organisational structuring along such lines will increase the professional strength of decisions taken.

_____
1) It should be noted that the term "functional" in this context has a rather particular meaning; not excluding the possibility that it may be rather disfunctional.

Within an hierarchical bureaucratic organisation, what regularly happens in this case is that such "functional" units are forced by the system itself to act as if they were operational. They tend to draw operational conclusions, apparently based on their professional competence, but in fact derived from value structures built into their professions. The consequence is internal struggle within the organisation about what kind of decision should be taken on what kind of "professional competence". The outcome is usually that essential functions are taken away from operational units to become the monopoly of "functional" units, sharing the market of "professional" decisions between themselves.

Some of the latter may operate on the basis of value structures of their own, derived from broad professions such as medicine or teaching, while others may seek political alliances, establishing themselves as control mechanisms between operational units and the political leadership. The latter applies more typically to units for planning, budgeting, evaluation, analysis, etc. Some units may even seek alliances outside their own administrative structures. Units for planning, budgeting, efficiency control and even certain technical branches within an operational ministry may, for instance, view themselves as extended arms of the Ministry of Finance.

Bureaucratic structures with strong elements of "functional" organisation may be viewed as abortive matrix structures. Within an hierarchical bureaucratic structure the simultaneous functioning of both an operational grid and a "functional" grid will tend towards either the complete domination of one grid by the other, or a sharing of power between elements of the two grids, following the principles of division of responsibilities. As mentioned above, the top leadership of an organisation will often feel the need for premises for judgement alternative to those of operational units. However, such premises will hardly be provided by the kind of structure described here. It appears even less capable of handling intersectoral problems than a structure based mainly on operational units.

Another approach to the restructuring of bureaucratic organisations is to use individual objectives of the organisation as the basis for the division of responsibility. This is often referred to as "management by objectives" or "programme budgeting". The idea that such an organisational structure should facilitate the judgement of "efficiency" of individual programmes implies that the ideal unit should have responsibility for one objective only, and this responsibility should not be shared with any other unit.

In principle, such an organisational structure should facilitate the co-ordinated use of instruments aiming at a particular objective. The problem is, of course, that most activities have effects on a variety of policy objectives, but an organisational structure of this kind provides direct incentives for individual units to neglect such consequences of their activities. Furthermore, the possibilities for superior co-ordinating bodies of taking care of such neglect are hampered by the fact that individual units do not share goals and tend to become purely competitive on behalf of their particular objective. Incentives for horizontal collaboration are, of course, non-existent within such a structure.

A common feature of the alternative approaches to organisational structuring outlined above, is their technocratic bias. Implicit in the "functional" structuring is the assumption that "professional" solutions can be found to most political problems. In a somewhat more indirect way, "management by objectives" has similar implications, but restricted particularly to economic expertise. Experts on "budgeting", "efficiency", "programme analysis", etc., are singled out as judges of administrative performance and obtain strong political powers in their capacity as "experts".

It is interesting to note in this context that when organisational goals are listed, there is an increasing tendency to add "efficient utilisation of resources" as a separate goal. This is quite illogical, as commitment to the other objectives clearly implies exactly such a use of resources. The efficiency goal must thus either be redundant, or make the statement on goals over-determined. The way such an additional objective functions, however, is to provide "experts" on efficiency with a means by which they can apply their own ideas on objectives, as built into their measures of efficiency. The apparent over-determination is solved by substituting such interpretations of the organisation's objectives for interpretations held by operational units.

The two approaches described above are often advocated as providing better means of political steering and control. In all likelihood, the technocratic biases built into those approaches will, in fact, mean <u>reduced</u> political control, both because of the substitution of "professional" competence for political competence, and because of the difficulty of controlling professional mystification of political issues(1).

The basic problems of intersectoral interrelationships in public administration are thus not solved by redefining the criteria for organisational structuring. Whether we use "professional"

---

1) In principle, programme budgeting refers to budgetary decisions, and not necessarily to organisational structures. The distinction is, however, not too easy to draw. When in the case of the Swedish universities, budget decisions are made jointly for all the universities for each major field of research and training, each university has very little control of its own affairs. From a policy point of view one can almost properly describe the structure as a countrywide faculty structure, rather than a structure of universities.

sectors or "goal-oriented" sectors, the problems of intersectoral co-ordination remain, and are even likely to grow worse when the latter approaches are tried. Partial approaches to problem solving do not become less partial when biased towards professional value structures or specific objectives. Superior co-ordinating bodies may become even more overburdened than before, and may find the task of co-ordinating even more difficult.

A serious attack on the problem of intersectoral planning leaves only two roads open: either a functioning matrix organisation can be established by abandoning or modifying essentially the bureaucratic structures of the organisation, including its hierarchical nature and the notion of separate and distinctive responsibilities of individual units; or, if a bureaucratic structure has to be maintained, an operationally oriented organisation structure may be supplemented by <u>purely non-directive</u> grids of information based, for instance, on "functional" or "goal-oriented" criteria. Later on I shall comment briefly on such possibilities.

II. CO-ORDINATION, COLLABORATION AND INTEGRATION

For the moment I shall stick to a hierarchical bureaucratic organisation as the frame of reference. It may be interesting to see what meanings we can attach to such concepts as co-ordination, collaboration and integration within such a framework.

I would suggest that the term <u>co-ordination</u> should be taken to mean activities of an organisational unit aiming at improved co-operation of two or more subordinate units. In this sense, co-ordination represents the traditional answer in hierarchical organisations to the need for intersectoral planning. Co-ordination is often achieved by exertion of prescriptive authority, though financial or informative policy measures may also be applied for this purpose.

By <u>collaboration</u> I shall mean interaction for some common benefit between two or more units within a hierarchical structure, none of which is subordinate to any of the others. Defined this way, collaboration excludes the use of prescriptive measures by any of the partners, the usual means being financial (including exchange of services) or informative. Typically, such an interaction will be characterised by bargaining. Each party wants some benefit from the collaboration in terms of its own goal structure, while the costs involved should be reasonable in relation to such expected benefits.

As mentioned previously, the lack of incentives for collaboration may be even more marked if the organisation is structured according to "functional" criteria, and probably only negative if difference in objectives is the structuring principle.

55

By _integration_ I shall mean a situation in which two or more units come to share not only a common set of goals, but also a common goal structure, in terms of relative weights attached to such goals. Bringing a number of units together under the umbrella of a superior unit is not a sufficient condition for integration. It requires a redefinition of the mission of each unit involved, so as to make them coincide.

However, what is often called "integration" in hierarchical organisations is just the establishment of a co-ordinating body on the top of the units to be integrated. In practice, this means the insertion of an additional level in the decision-making hierarchy. It relieves superior co-ordinating bodies from some of their work load, though in itself it does not necessarily lead to integration of subordinate units in the sense indicated above. As in the case of "collaboration", "integration" in hierarchical systems tends to be transformed into co-ordination by a superior body.

Examples of this form of integration are easy to find: we "integrate" preprimary and primary education by putting the two activities within one institution with a common leadership; we do the same with general and vocational education at the secondary level, with specialised post-secondary institutions within the framework of community colleges, and with academic "schools" of medicine, engineering, etc. within universities. What happens is sometimes that the "integrated" activities go on as before, according to their own value structures, their practical interplay, however, somewhat facilitated by the nearness of a co-ordinating body. Sometimes, however, a more genuine integration is achieved through the gradual merger of the value structures governing the various activities. Such a merger may be the result of changes in the incentive system, possibly combined with an increased awareness of problems as seen by those responsible for related activities and of the nature of the interrelatedness.

In the latter case, an interesting question is who yields most in the merging of value structures governing the behaviour of the integrated unit. Administrative mergers of the kind described here will normally lead to a predominance of values held by the institutionally and professionally most well established party. In the cases mentioned, integration of preprimary and primary education will tend to favour values and standards established in primary education even in preprimary activities. At the secondary level, integrated institutions may become dominated by standards set by theoretical schools with an academic orientation, and when shorter post-secondary education is integrated in the universities, they will mainly have to adapt to standards set by the latter.

Our belief in integration as a value in itself may thus often fail to bring intended results; we may find ourselves in a less desirable situation than before the integration.

Such concepts as institutional imperialism and cultural exploitation come easily to the mind in such contexts, and some lessons from conflict theory in a wider context should be borne in mind. One of them is that if an integration process is not to lead to the exploitation of one of the parties involved, one has to build up the bargaining power of the weakest party to a reasonable balance with the others.

But even if such a balance exists, administrative integration raises a number of problems. Most units have extensive interrelationships with a variety of other units. Normally, a unit has arrived at what it conceives as a reasonable balance between concerns legitimately due to various other units. Merging such a unit with one other may mean that their common concerns are taken particularly well care of, but possibly at the expense of interrelationship with other units.

If we use for illustration the recent merger of the two parts of the OECD Secretariat dealing with education on the one hand and manpower and social affairs on the other, the problem comes out very clearly. If it means a genuine integration, the implication is that educational affairs will be run with much more emphasis on its particular relationship to manpower affairs and such social matters as taken up by the OECD. The question is, of course, which other equally appropriate educational concerns will suffer from this. If before the merger the organisation's educational activities had found a reasonable balance between a number of valid concerns, such a merger is likely to lead to less relevant educational activities. Similar considerations could be put forward in relation to activities on manpower and social affairs.

A possibility is, of course, that the establishment of a common head of the two parts of the Secretariat may mean nothing else than that the activities go on as before, with somewhat better chances of sorting out the interrelationships which have existed all along. This appears to correspond fairly well to the previous situation, which formally joined activities in the fields of education and science policy. The question remains, however, whether the leadership of such a joint unit can accept a variety of value structures operating within its field of responsibility, or whether it feels the need for some sort of consistency in relation to a common value structure. It might be felt that if the latter is not achieved, the merger has been a failure.

The conclusion I would draw from this is that problems of intersectoral co-operation rarely find real solutions through administrative regroupings within a hierarchical bureaucratic system. Collaboration sounds good and integration even better, but in such an organisational structure they are not very likely to occur in any genuine sense, and if they do the consequences may not be the ones hoped for.

Some additional comments should be made on <u>co-ordination at a regional or local level</u>, a fashionable subject today. What happens when such co-ordination is attempted frequently corresponds to the case when horizontal collaboration is asked for between subordinate units. If local activities have strong vertical lines of authority to regional or central bodies, attempts on horizontal co-operation or collaboration at the local level will rarely succeed.

Integrated actions by schools, libraries, cultural organisations, adult education organisations, etc., are in principle regarded as very desirable. Yet, as long as each of such organisations and institutions have their place within a separate national hierarchy, the willingness to enter into such local collaboration and to accept the outcome of decisions by local authorities has very narrow limits. Local co-ordination can only be achieved by cutting separate vertical lines of control and support, and inserting instead one single vertical line from the local co-ordinating body.

III. DECENTRALISATION

There is nothing new in pointing out that traditional bureaucratic organisations offer little scope for intersectoral collaboration, and that planning units within such a system tend to become units monopolising a function called "planning", which in fact mainly consists of control and political screening of activities in the rest of the organisation. The justification for pointing this out once more is the increasing tendency within traditional bureaucracies to pay lip service to "intersectoralism", and to undertake various forms of organisational acrobatics offering only fictitious solutions to the basic problems of such organisations.

More real solutions can only be found through modifications in the basic structures of hierarchical bureaucratic systems. A keyword in this context is "decentralisation", though even this term is frequently used to describe changes of a purely symbolic nature, with no real impact on organisational structures.

Some basic conditions must be fulfilled before we can talk about decentralisation in any real sense. Firstly, the idea must be dropped that an effective organisation is one with the highest possible degree of consistency and predictability of behaviour in all its parts. It must be accepted that a variety of value structures will exist inside the organisation and influence behaviour in ways which are not fully compatible with any centrally-conceived goal structure.

In return, an organisation of this kind may be much more adaptable to dynamic external and internal circumstances; it satisfies at least some minimum conditions for organisational learning to take place. Furthermore, the potential of individuals within the organisation is utilised much more fully as individual judgement, energy and creativity is released.

In a previous paper for the OECD(1) I have outlined in more detail the conditions under which decentralisation of decision making power may lead to such consequences. In this context, I shall only summarise the main points:

Centralised decision making shelters subordinate units from pressures external to the system. Decentralisation of decision making power to subordinate units must not put them in a position in which they can do nothing but yield to such external pressures.

In education, such pressures may, for instance, be exerted by teachers' unions. A strong centralised union is able to dictate its terms to local educational authorities if central educational authorities yield their power. It is also conceivable that the priesthood of pedagogical expertise may occupy the power vacuum left by central authorities when power is formally decentralised.

A second condition for genuine decentralisation of decision making power is that decisions taken by subordinate units are not threatened by "spill-over effects" from what remains of central decision making power. The right to appeal may be used in a way which completely undermines formally decentralised decisions. When both local minorities and majorities know the outcome of an appeal, the local decision is more or less given. The same applies in cases where unwanted local decisions are punished by decisions in other fields where central power remains.

Subordinate units are mutually interdependent, but this interdependence may well be strongly asymmetric. The formal autonomy of one unit may be quite fictitious, as it is fully dependent upon decisions taken by another unit formally at the same level, and with no means of influencing those decisions. An example here would be the dependence of certain parts of the school system upon entry conditions set by the most attractive parts of the educational system at the next higher level. Correspondingly, low prestige institutions may have no other possibility than adapting to standards set by high prestige institutions, even if the latter have quite different ideas about missions to be performed.

1) Participation and Participatory Planning in Education, OECD, 1973.

Thus a third condition for genuine decentralisation is a reasonable balance in terms of resources and bargaining power between interdependent units at the same level.

A subordinate unit has its own <u>internal authority</u> structure which may imply very different positions for individuals involved. Little power for federal authorities in school matters may mean more strict control by local authorities of individual schools. Great formal independence for individual schools may mean very strict control of individual teachers or pupils, etc. As a general rule, institutions and individuals tend to prefer external control to be located far away, or high up in the hierarchy, possibly because slack in the control system increases with distance.

As a fourth condition for genuine decentralisation of decision making, we may thus put down full participation by all those involved in the activities of a subordinate unit in its decisions.

The right to take part in decisions is not always used. A feeling of lack of competence may be the reason, but more frequently it simply means that the decisions in question are of little interest to the individuals involved, or possibly that questions for decision are regarded as uncontroversial.

As a fifth condition, we must insist that decentralised decisions should be of consequence for those invited to decide, and that the issues are potentially controversial.

This last point may need an additional comment. In education, teaching is often so structured that the issues involved in each subject are relatively non-controversial. This is partly because they do not touch problems of essential importance to the non-educational world, or because answers are seen as a matter of professional expertise within the limited field in question.

One may suspect that the delicate <u>balance of power</u> between educational institutions and the external world is based upon a professional subject structure which prevents professional experts from dealing with essential political problems, while on the other hand questions which can be raised inside the subject are left to the internal hierarchy of authority within the profession. This might explain why interdisciplinary approaches within educational institutions are met with such suspicion from the outside world, and even stronger reprisals from the institutions themselves. They threaten both the established power balance, and the internal authority structure of the institutions.

A way of meeting the claim for decentralisation, without really disturbing the basic features of hierarchical organisations, is thus to offer considerable independence to units which are so specialised, small and powerless that they cannot take any decisions of consequence. The maintenance of a wide variety of small,

specialised educational institutions is a typical example, ensuring
that all decisions of any consequence relating to them must be taken
at the central level. Only when the specialisation is broken at a
local or institutional level is there a real chance that decentralisation of decision making can become meaningful for the individuals
involved.

Decentralising decision making power is no panacea for the release of hidden human potentials in bureaucratic organisations, and
even less for intersectoral contacts. The kind of decentralisation
that could lead to such effects must at least be defined in multi-
dimensional terms, involving a complex mixture of horizontal and
vertical organisational relationships.

In all likelihood, some such form of decentralisation is a
necessary condition for intersectoral collaboration, but it is far
from sufficient to secure such relationships. If horizontal interaction between administrative units is seen by the units as a zero
sum game, in which gains can only be achieved at the expense of
similar losses for other parties, the scope of such collaboration
is nil. The typical outcome of such interactions will be a kind of
sharing of the power market with peaceful, but non-co-operative co-
existence as the best possible outcome. We shall have to look for
additional conditions for genuine intersectoral collaboration.

Such conditions are clearly related to the existence of possibilities for net gains for all parties involved through interaction.
Stated in other terms, there must be a certain overlapping in the
value structures governing actions of the parties concerned. As
stated before, this is very often the case if the objectives of various administrative units are associated with the actual consequences
of their activities.

The second major modification of traditional bureaucratic organisations needed for intersectoral collaboration is thus the explicit recognition of overlapping objectives and responsibilities
for units at the same level. The idea of separate and exclusive
responsibilities for each unit must be abandoned, and even more so
ideas of exclusive goal orientation implied in theories on "management by objectives" or "programme budgeting". Such a recognition
must first of all lead to a change in the incentive system, which
today is largely adapted to the traditional forms of division of
responsibility. Awareness of actual interrelationships with other
units and concern for the totality of consequences of one's own actions can be used actively as criteria for such incentives as resource
allocation, promotion, recognition, etc., instead of negatively, as
is mostly the case today. It also means, however, that incentive systems must be less individualised and less oriented towards the encouragement of competition between units. Such conclusions are firmly
established, e.g. through the experiments with semi-autonomous groups
in industry.

The abolishment of distinctive border lines of responsibility does not necessarily mean horizontal integration in the sense the term is used here. The definition of partially overlapping value structures does not in itself lead to a merger of such value structures. Individual units will tend to maintain their own profiles, based on their particular competence and loyalties. The development of a multilateral system of collaboration, reflecting the variety of concerns of individual units, is more likely than a tendency towards the merging of units.

IV. PLANNING AGENCIES AND OTHER SPECIALISED UNITS

In our discussion of intersectoral collaboration it has been assumed implicitly that such collaboration also includes planning and other more special functions. A third major condition for intersectoral collaboration is, in fact, that the trend towards specialisation and division of labour along "functional" lines is profoundly reversed in bureaucratic organisations. The task structure must be revised, not only to permit job rotation, but to bring back under the real responsibility of operating units a majority of specialised functions essential to their operations.

Today, one may find operational units deprived of control of their budgets by specialised budget units, of their personnel policy by specialised personnel units, of documentation and reproduction of documents by other special units, building and technical matters by technical units, etc. Their formal responsibility for activities in a certain field is matched only with a certain control over legal measures, even those subject to the approval of legal specialists. The idea that such operational units can operate with any genuine responsibility towards their formal mission is completely unrealistic, and even more so the idea that they can enter into any form of genuine intersectoral collaboration. Widespread practical experiments with organisational restructuring in industry, services and also schools fully confirm that task restructuring breaking down the organisational border lines between specialist functions is a necessary condition for intersectoral collaboration.

This does not necessarily mean that there is no room for specialist units based on specific functions, for instance, planning units. Their role, however, must be defined quite differently from the traditional pattern of bureaucratic organisations. Their prime task must be to assist in the development of their specialist function all through the organisation, in operational units at all levels. Instead of monopolising their particular function and the set of specific decisions associated with it, their task must be to help others in the performance of such functions.

A pre-condition for this is that specialist units, such as planning agencies, renounce all means of exerting prescriptive authority within the organisation. They must act solely on the basis of informative authority, and accept the value structures of operational units as the premises for their advisory functions. In practice, it means that their vertical lines of communication with co-ordinating bodies at superior levels must be virtually cut. Appeals to superior co-ordinating bodies when specialist advice is not accepted by operational units inevitably turns the horizontal interaction into a bargaining process with all its usual aspects, information absorption, passive sabotage and fight for power. We are back in the traditional interaction patterns of hierarchical bureaucratic systems.

It should be mentioned in passing that the establishment of separate planning agencies outside an organisation is quite incompatible with the structural changes advocated above. Such separate planning agencies regularly develop into competing politic centres, leaning on to other parts of the political superstructure ("planning ministries", special bodies reporting directly to the Prime Minister, etc.), or to other external power groups, such as industry or professions. Planning agencies may even develop their own "constituencies", through "participatory planning" establishing direct links with various power groups in society, contact networks developing "goals for education", or at the extreme a Gallup poll approach to policy making.

Such separate agencies may achieve sufficient political strength to force their policies upon the organisation formally responsible for policies in the field concerned, for instance, a ministry of education. The interaction between the latter organisation and the agency will inevitably develop into forms for bargaining, as in the case of internal planning agencies using superior co-ordinating bodies as a means for exerting prescriptive authority.

The functioning of specialised units within a revised task structure may act as an informative matrix structure within the organisation. It may also function constructively, contrary to matrix structures provided with prescriptive authority. Such informative functions are essential for the dynamic development of an organisation and its ability to deal with changing external pressures. It would serve as a built-in critical function within the organisation, complementary to the power oriented critique directed towards the organisation from external sources. Only the proper combination of the two forms of critical functions may ensure a government administration capable of handling turbulent environments, and at the same time promoting what the majority would associate with "quality of life".

CENTRAL PLANNING BASED
ON A SYSTEMS MODEL
by Yehezkel Dror

INTRODUCTION

In both theoretic paradigms and applied orientations, this
paper attempts to apply my previous broader work on policymaking
to the particular issues of educational and intersectoral planning,
especially at the central level. It is assumed that the readers are
familiar with the basic ideas of policy studies, both in their behavioural and in their prescriptive forms. Particularly relevant
for the present paper are: a) an aggregative view of policy-making,
resulting from dynamic interaction between a multiplicity of diverse
variables; b) an integrated approach to abstract study of systems
and their applied improvement; and c) an instrumental attitude to
the subject matter detached, as far as possible, from subjective
preferences for particular versions of "good life" and similar value
judgments.

The main ideas and propositions of this paper are summed up in
the form of concise recommendations for further OECD inquiry. These
recommendations deal respectively with a) relevant theoretic knowledge, b) design for country field studies and c) operational recommendations for improving the integration of education in inter-
sectoral planning. Within the four main sections which form the
structure of this paper, these recommendations (signalled by the
letters "a", "b", and "c") are distributed throughout this paper
under the titles:

a) Theoretic research recommendations
b) Field study recommendations
c) Improvement recommendations.

Of course, summing-up of my discourse in the form of recommendations carries with it the dangers of overstatement and of reliance
on additional, more elaborate analysis which remains unexplained.
Nevertheless, I hope that the formulation of such recommendations,
even if oversharp, may be useful for the specific purposes of this
paper.

I. VALUE SENSITIVITY ANALYSIS

In an area as subject to ideology as education, it is especially important to distinguish between advocacy and instrumental contributions: particular ideas, ideals or solutions on the one hand and, on the other, contributions which help legitimate value-judges such as elected politicians, a local community, a peer-group of professionals, etc., to maximize their changing values. This requires explicit value-analysis and explanation of assumptions, as far as humanly possible. For instance, when discussing allocation of more authority to local levels, a clear distinction should be made between the value-basis of such a recommendation on the one hand, and an instrumental claim, supported by evidence, that such devolution of authority actually aids inter-sectoral planning (which - in turn - must be justified too).

The need for analysis of value sensitivity and for an approach which is instrumental and based on agreed ideologies, leads to the following recommendations:

a) <u>Theoretic research recommendations</u>:

a)1. Improved methodologies for value-sensitivity analysis should be developed, with particular reference to education and related areas.

a)2. Researchers should exercise strict self-discipline and distinguish as clearly as possible between their own values and their professional knowledge-based contributions. Explicit value-sensitivity analysis should be a part of every study dealing with so value-dependent a subject as education in particular and social policy in general.

b) <u>Field study recommendations</u>:

b)1. Value-mapping of the main actors in respect to education and intersectoral planning should constitute an important part of the field study - both for explaining reality and identifying leverage points for change.

c) <u>Improvement recommendations</u>:

c)1. Awareness of one's own values and improvement of value-sensitivity of main actors may be useful for better intersectoral planning, if combined with awareness of values of others and tolerance for other values.

c)2. Intersectoral planning professionals (a concept to be discussed later, see section IV.4) must make value-sensitivity analysis an integral part of their work, together with readiness to accept value-judgment of legitimate value-judges (which may vary for different locations). This is necessary in order to increase probability of utilisation of such professionals in actual policymaking as well as, to inject a value of my own, for ethical reasons.

II. BASIC MODEL

The basic model proposed for treating the subject of education and intersectoral planning, on which this paper is based, is a systems model. According to this model, policymaking is viewed as a systems process where policies are the result of interaction among various components which can be classified in different ways, depending on our interests and needs.

Applying such a systems view, in its simplest form, to the subject of education and intersectoral planning, the following implications, among others, emerge:

1. Policies are the result of interaction among components. Therefore, policies should be viewed as an aggregate product the characteristics of which can be changed through various alterations in the components and their interaction modes.

2. Educational policies are made by a subset of the policymaking system. Therefore, one way to identify interrelations between educational policies and other policies is to examine overlaps, interdependencies, interfaces and other relations between the educational policymaking sub-system and other sub-systems of the policymaking system. In particular, the following types of interrelations can be identified:

i) The same components may make policy for education and for other sectors (e.g., central budgeting units, overall policy analysis units, and overall civil service units).

ii) Educational policymaking components and other components compete for scarce resources (e.g., money, manpower, prestige, attention, location on political agenda).

iii) Educational policymaking components and other policymaking components share some target populations (e.g., children). When they share the same target population, the policy effects of the educational and other policymaking components may reinforce one another, be mutually insensitive or may contradict one another - depending on the goals of the policies and the behavioural interactions of different policies applied to the same or interacting target populations.

iv) Educational policymaking components and other policymaking
   components have goals which may be consistent or inconsistent, logically and behaviourally. The degrees and forms
   of consistency and inconsistency may vary marginally for
   different mixes of goals (i.e. no fixed linear relation can
   be assumed).

v) Policy instruments used by educational policymaking components and other policymaking components may be actually
   shared, specific, or actually specific but potentially
   shared.

3. The model should be viewed within the time dimension, with
all the interrelations taking place within the temporal stream.
Therefore, insofar as value-relevant interactions exist, the problem
is not one of co-ordination alone (i.e., controlled interaction of
different sectors during the same time), but also and even more so,
one of synchronisation, (i.e., controlled interaction of different
sectors over a long time-span).

4. Because of both inherent and imputed (because of limited
knowledge) uncertainty, the policymaking system must be viewed as
stochastic, with statistically arbitrary elements. Furthermore
the system environment is, to use Trist's term, turbulent - thus
further increasing uncertainty.

5. In principle, changes in system outputs, e.g., better
integrated (i.e., both co-ordinated and synchronised) policies can
be achieved by two approaches to system management: detailed system
management and system dynamics management. The first requires
detailed understanding of the system; the second requires general
understanding of the system dynamics and operates through changing
the systems dynamics (e.g., through different incentives) and changing some system components (e.g., introducing new units and professionals). Because of the complexity of the policymaking system,
its stochastic, arbitrary nature and its rate of change (which may
include ultra-change), the second mode of systems management is
the more appropriate. Furthermore, every systems change strategy
has to be adjusted to uncertainty, using uncertainty-patterning and
uncertainty-absorbing methods, such as experimentation and sequen-
tial decision-making.

6. The problem of critical mass applies. In other words, as
opposed to an incremental change orientation, the question must be
faced whether too small an amount of directed change may not be
absorbed by the system without any impact on system outputs.
Therefore, in order to achieve better integration of education with
intersectoral planning, a set of changes in the relevant systems
may be required. At the same time different combinations of

changes may lead to equifinal results - providing approximately
similarly useful combinational alternatives.

I will return later to some additional implications of the
system model adopted by me for handling the subject (especially in
respect of the necessary meta-system). But, at this stage, enough
has been said to illustrate the usefulness of a broad system model
for handling the issues of education and intersectoral planning.
Let me now transform these suggestions into a number of
recommendations:

a) Theoretical research recommendations:

a)3. Work should be devoted to developing systems models of
educational policymaking within intersectoral policymaking. The
basic models should be conceptual, with more advanced languages
being used whenever possible. I do not expect metric quantification.
But well-worked-out non-metric models should permit clear identification of the interrelations between educational policymaking and
policymaking in other sectors. (For instance, in the form of cross-
sectoral input-output matrices).

a)4. A system model such as proposed above should be advanced
iteratively, on the basis of information gained through further
theoretic work, field research and experimentation with innovations.

a)5. The model should be action-oriented, with special
emphasis on identification of system direction instruments. Therefore prescriptive systems analysis will provide more inputs into
the models than pure or general systems theory.

b) Field study recommendations:

b)2. The field-study should be carefully designed on the basis
of clearcut theoretic concepts, derived from systems models such as
proposed above. Priority should be given to facets more useful for
system-guidance; but all the country-studies should be carefully
programmed on the basis of shared basic models - to permit compara-
bility and significant theoretic as well as applied findings.

c) Improvement recommendations:

c)3. Improvement recommendations should be derived from the
above-mentioned systems view. In particular, attention must be
given to the features of complexity, uncertainty and critical-change-
mass.

c)4. Improvement unavoidably operates through changes in
system-components. Therefore the dangers of system-bias which
contradicts sub-system-improvements must be faced. Constant awareness of the overall system features and careful monitoring of changes
are essential.

c)5. This leads to a very important institutional recommendation: Improvement of policymaking involves changes in the policymaking system. For this purpose, it is necessary to have meta-policymaking units, that is, units in charge of policymaking in respect to the policymaking system. Applied to education and intersectoral planning, this leads to the recommendation to establish some unit in charge of constant study, monitoring, evaluation and improvement-proposal initiation in regard to intersectoral planning and education. Without a suitable unit dealing with the subject on a continuous basis, few reliable improvements can be achieved. Such a unit must be appropriately staffed, including professionals in the relevant subjects (education, social policies, etc.) and in policymaking improvement.

A semantic comment is in order: The distinction between "planning", "policymaking" and "important decision-making" is unclear and, I think, quite unessential for the purposes of this paper (and for many aspects of OECD work in this area). Therefore I will not discuss different strict or tacit definitions of these terms, but use them more or less as synonyms.

To complete the system view shortly sketched above the political and bureaucratic characteristics of the relevant system and its components should be emphasized. Power mapping, political feasibility analysis, interest divergence and similar concepts are tools from the domains of political science; organisation theory and even conflict studies are, therefore, relevant for the study and should be extensively used. Indeed, power models and inter-organisational models may be useful for all dimensions of the study in addition to the economic, inter-professional, formal-structural, cultural and cybernetic models used in most of the papers prepared for the project.

III. SOME SPECIFIC INTERACTIONS

Some of the interactions between educational and intersectoral planning are well explored in the various other papers prepared for the OECD project. Others, that require additional study, are indicated above. Therefore, at this stage of the project I will limit my treatment of interactions to a short exploration of some items susceptible to identification at the present state of knowledge. The items to be dealt with in this part of my paper are: 1) preferable degrees of integration; 2) macro-micro relations; 3) integration in the time dimension; and 4) policy instrument interdependencies.

1.   Preferable Degrees of Integration

There is no axiomatic reason to believe that the more integration between educational and intersectoral planning the better. Distinct advantages of non-integration under various circumstances may include: reduction of risks of unitary and mistaken policies; ability to satisfy a larger variety of demands and values; better fit with special characteristics of particular clienteles; more scope for innovation and for spontaneous semi-market experimentation; more elasticity in facing uncertainty and fit with semi-market models of policymaking (e.g. Lindblom's). To these particular possible advantages of non-integration one must add the avoidance of the burdens on intellectual, political and administrative capacities involved in integration and the reduction of the risks of mistakes caused by bad integration.

On a theoretic level, it is possible to try and handle the issues of preferable degrees of integration and to evolve a mega-policy (i.e., "master-policy" or "policy-strategy") which specifies desired degrees of integration and preferable patterns of non-integration, such as through a "mixed-strategy" (in the theory of games sense) approach. In respect to the detailed study of particular issues and cases such an approach may even be operationalised with detailed policy-implications. But, in general, at the present state of knowledge, specification of a general mega-policy on desirable degrees of integration of educational with intersectoral planning is over-ambitious. This leads to the following recommendations:

a) Theoretic research recommendations:

a)5.   Theoretic attention should be devoted to the preferable degrees of integration of educational planning with intersectoral planning, with special attention to the formulation of operational criteria which can be applied to concrete conditions.

b) Field study recommendations

b)3. In the field study, the problems of actual and preferable degrees of integration of educational planning with intersectoral planning should be studied within the contexts of specific issues.

When we pass on to the prescriptive dimension, all available material indicates that 1) more integration is actually needed and 2) because of anti-integration factors actually operating, there is little danger that attempts to improve integration will result in over-integration. Therefore:

c) Improvement recommendations:

c)6. The existence of a hypothetical optimal degree of integration should, in most circumstances, not be taken as a reason to
reduce maximum efforts actually to increase integration. Or, in
positive formulation: Maximum efforts should be made to improve
integration of educational planning with intersectoral planning,
even though counterproductive results are hypothetically possible.
At the same time, awareness of such a possibility should result in
some consideration of possible negative results of concrete integration steps.

2.   Macro-Micro Relations

The problem of macro-micro relations in respect to education
and intersectoral planning is rather complex. These relations
include both the dimension of macro-policies and their relations
with micro-actions and the dimension of macro-levels of policymaking
and their relations to micro-levels of action. Differences in the
discrete location of various forms of authority and resources-control
and in the uses of macro-policy-instruments versus micro-action-tools
between education, health, community planning, social work and other
related sectors (as pointed out, for instance, in the paper of
Maurice Kogan) further complicate the issue. An additional complication stems from ideological and professional preferences for macro-
versus micro-levels respectively. Thus economists have often a
macro-policy-tools preference, while social workers have often a
strong attachment to the micro-level of action. On the structural
dimension, pro-local-autonomy ideologies tend to emphasize the
micro-level.

An easy verbal escape from the problem is to recommend better
integration both on the macro and at the micro levels, in all their
dimensions. But this is an unjustified avoidance of an issue which
is of critical importance, both theoretic and applied. Because of
the need already pointed out to achieve more integration in the face
of strong anti-integration barriers, a multiple approach attempting
to achieve more integration by simultaneous action on both macro-
and micro-levels can, in principle, be justified. But any rational
approach to the matter requires more than that. At least, the following facets of macro-micro relations must receive specific
attention:

- Changes on the macro-level and on the micro-level are closely
related. Therefore, they must be handled simultaneously. For instance, to encourage better integration on the local level and make
it feasible, incentive structures must be changed and decision-
authority must be granted, together with guidelines and monitoring.

- Some of the relevant literature seems to assume that changes are easier to introduce on the micro-level. This assumption has no basis. In particular, it is dangerous to generalise the results of single small-scale experiments done under artificial conditions.
- General trends (at least in many of the OECD countries) to improve central policymaking may provide convenient entry-points for improving also the integration of educational and intersectoral planning, a possibility that should be carefully explored (in due relation with relevant OECD projects).
- The rather obvious observations that social policies find their final effects in respect to individuals (born and unborn) should not lead to the conclusion that the micro-level has an inherent advantage because of its apparent proximity to the individual. Abstract macro-policies may have as powerful and even more powerful effects on individuals, even though the connection moves through different mechanisms.
- Studies in recent years (e.g., by Aaron Wildavsky) emphasize the difficulties of building bridges between central decisions intended to be implemented through local units and actual implementation in the field. Problems of implementation must, therefore, receive attention within any attempt to improve integration of education and intersectoral planning through local-action-oriented macro-decisions (including decisions granting local units more power and authority).

Summing up these points in the form of recommendations, the following emerge:

a) Theoretic research recommendations:

a)6. Macro-micro relations should constitute a main subject for research.

b) Field study recommendations:

b)4. In the OECD country studies, the macro-micro relations should be carefully studied, an attempt being made to identify the main mechanisms through which they interact.

b)5. Implementation problems deserve special attention in the field studies.

c) Improvement recommendations:

c)7. Improvement recommendations should deal with both the macro and the micro-levels, as an integrated set.

c)8.   All recommendations directed at local implementation
should be feasibility-tested with respect to actual probability of
being implemented.

c)9.   Improvements in respect to education and intersectoral
planning should be tied in, insofar as practical, with ongoing reforms in central policymaking.

c)10. Ideological preferences and professional prejudices
should not be permitted implicitly (as contrasted with explicit
value preferences or legitimate value judges) to influence
recommendations.

c)11. Assumptions about ease of achieving changes on the
local level should be subjected to critical re-examination.

3.   Integration in the Time Dimension

The importance of the time dimension in handling integration
of education and intersectoral planning has already been emphasized.
Here, I want to carry this point one step further, by emphasizing a
number of related issues:

- Differences in the time perspective and time preferences of
  the policies of different sectors constitute a main barrier
  to their synchronisation. Thus, physical planning often has
  a very long time perspective, while large parts of health
  policy - despite talk to the contrary - seem to have a short
  time perspective.
- Differences in the images of the future on which policies of
  different sectors are based, constitute another main barrier
  to their integration. Thus educational planning may be
  based on one image of the future, while welfare planning (if
  any) may be based on quite different images of the future.
- The lead time needed for introducing changes may be quite
  different for various sectors. Thus the rigidity of
  buildings and of highly but narrowly-trained professionals
  constitutes a main factor reducing short-range elasticity.
- For the same reasons and the time-bound effects of present
  "sunk costs" (including political and organisational ones)
  in general it is often easier to achieve integration in
  the future, if one starts to plan for it now, than in the
  present.

To understand better the importance of the time dimension, it
should be combined with the systems view. Doing so, the following
widespread trends emerge. Different sectors are influenced by different images of the future and by different goals for the future;
these influences are especially pronounced during "planning", which -
by all definitions - is distinguished by concern with the future.

What often happens is that sector one plans for futures A and B (assuming planning in the sector is sophisticated enough to admit uncertainty), while sector two plans for futures C and D. But when we check the possible co-existence of A or B and C or D in any one social system (through cross-impact analysis simulation or any other appropriate technique), then fundamental contradictions between the assumptions, images and goals of the different sectors emerge. This danger of cross-purpose results in the future of single-sector planning may well constitute a main reason for requiring more integrated intersectoral planning, especially because of the "counter-intuitive" (to borrow Forrester's apt phrase) features of many necessary implications. This counter-productive effect of single-sectoral planning also indicates some of the means that can be utilised in order to reduce these dangers, viz., to improve intersectoral planning.

Leaving for later consideration* some applied recommendations in improving time-treatment in better integrated educational and intersectoral planning, our discussion can be summed up in the following recommendations:

a) Theoretic research recommendations:

a)7. Prediction methods, alternative futures, uncertainty-patterning methodologies and uncertainty-absorbing approaches in respect to educational and intersectoral planning should be intensely studied.

b) Field study recommendations:

b)6. The time perspectives, time preferences, future images and goals-for-the future of the main actors should be studied within the country studies.

b)7. The concept of "time-rigid resources" should be utilised in the field studies.

b)8. The extent and forms of future inconsistencies between education and other sectors resulting from single-sectoral planning oriented towards different future images and future goals should serve as one of the foci of the country studies.

c) Improvement recommendations:

c)12. Better integration of educational and intersectoral planning should itself be planned so as to handle different variables according to their time-rigidity and with different lead times.

c)13. Achievement of better integration in the future should be accepted as a main goal, rather than exclusive concern with better integration in respect to pressing current issues. In other

---
*) IV-3 ("Process") below.

74

words: building up a policymaking system promising better integration of educational intersectoral planning should constitute a
main goal, at the cost of somewhat less attention to integration in
respect to current concrete policy issues.

For recommendations in respect to concrete methods and techniques to be used in respect to the future dimension, see recommendations c.21 and c.22.

4.   Policy Instrument Interdependencies

As mentioned in section II above, policy instruments are one
of the interfaces between education and other sectors, and this
point should be emphasized. Planning and all other policymaking
activities are (or should be) oriented towards influencing reality.
Therefore one of their main expressions is in sets of policy instruments applied in various combinations and different settings to
target populations. In a more advanced treatment, further distinctions are in order, such as between primary and secondary policy
instruments, elastic and rigid ones, short-range and long-range
ones, etc.; but for the limited purposes of this paper, it is
sufficient to clarify the term and mention its utility.

The main point to notice is the interdependence between policy
instruments used by education and intersectoral planning. This
interdependence relates both to actually used and potential new
policy instruments. It is this actual and potential interdependence
which creates a main challenge to better integration of education
and intersectoral planning, which can be formulated as follows:
Increase effectiveness through reducing contradictions of policy
instruments applied to the same or interacting target populations;
increase effectiveness and efficiency through integrated use of
policy instruments functionally interdependent; increase innovative-
ness through new uses of policy instruments by their transfer from
one sector to other sectors and through stimulation of new alternatives by coherent and comprehensive consideration of policy
instruments of different sectors.

More operationally formulated, this leads to the following
recommendations:

a) Theoretic research recommendations:

a)8. A general theory of policy instruments in relation to
education and other sectors should be aimed at.

a)9. Research should be directed at invention of new policy
instruments potentially useful for education and related sectors.

b) <u>Field study recommendations</u>:

b)9. In the country studies, policy instruments that are actually used should be identified and their interdependencies should be studied.

b)10. The underlying processes leading to the selection of specific policy instruments should be explored, with special attention to alternative-search-reducing factors.

c) <u>Improvement recommendations</u>:

c)14. A comprehensive set of policy instruments actually used and proposed for education and related sectors should be prepared. This set should be analysed in terms of consistency in respect to different uses of the policy instruments, in terms of internal relations between the different policy instruments and in respect to possible cross-transfer of policy instruments and possible multi-sector uses of policy instruments.

IV.   SOME IMPROVEMENT PROPOSALS APPLIED TO THE PLANNING SYSTEM

To move on in the direction of the goals of intersectoral educational planning, somewhat more specified improvement proposals are in order here. Theoretic research and field studies are essential for elaboration of reliable improvement proposals in operational form. But, enough is known on the basis of available theories and research findings to justify some tentative improvement proposals in more general form. In particular, I want to try to outline a frame for searching for improvement proposals and then indicate some possible ideas located in the frame. These proposals should be judged in terms of "preferability", that is through comparing them with the realities of policymaking rather than some hypothetical "optimum". At the same time, the proposals are tentative, to be regarded as hypotheses to be examined, revised and worked out with the help of suitable theoretic and field research. Because of the nature of policy studies, a main method for improving the improvement proposals themselves is through experimentation: trying them out in reality. This is a further justification for trying to identify improvement proposals formulated operationally already now.

The model underlying my presentation of the improvement proposals is again a systems model, now applied to the policymaking (or planning) system itself. Proceeding along the main dimensions of that system, I will discuss various improvements under the following categories: 1) overall system dynamics; 2) structure; 3) process; 4) personnel. Based on a broader theory of policymaking-improvement (see, in particular my book <u>Public Policymaking Re-examined</u>), I will limit myself to presenting and discussing some selected issues which, I think, are sufficiently supported by available knowledge to serve as concrete recommendations ripe for a try-out in reality.

1. Overall system dynamics

Improvement of the relevant policymaking system through better integration of education and intersectoral planning can - as in all system improvement (see section II above) - proceed in principle along two, interconnected, roads: changes in the system dynamics, that is, the interaction processes between system components which produce the overall system output (or, in more exact theoretic terms, the "net probable real output"); and changes in the system components in a way influencing the system output in the desired direction. Clearly, these are but two aspects of closely related processes, as changes in system components constitute also a main way to influence system dynamics. Nevertheless, for the limited purposes of my present treatment, I distinguish analytically between these two, any danger of an over-artificial distinction being reduced by some repetition between the recommendations to be presented in respect to improvement of system dynamics and the recommendations to be presented in respect to system components; this repetition will further emphasize the overlap between these two approaches within the context of concrete recommendations.

Discarding in this part of the paper the general type of recommendation aiming to improve incentive structures, which at the present state of knowledge serve more as guides for research and alternative-search than as concrete proposals, the scope and significance of overall system dynamics improvement proposals will be demonstrated by a more detailed discussion of recommendations c.16 to c.19.

However, it shall first be mentioned that all the recommendations presented in this part of the paper should also serve as bases for theoretic and empiric work. Rather than pedantically repeat the same forms of recommendations over and over again, let me formulate this matter in the following three general recommendations:

a) Theoretic research recommendations:

a)10. Theoretic work should be oriented towards the assumptions underlying the various proposals and towards the proposals themselves. As a first step, literature surveys and processing of relevant experience in different countries should be undertaken.

b) Field study recommendations:

b)11. The country studies should be directed to examine, inter alia, all features relevant to the various recommendations - both to collect data permitting judgement on the worthwhileness of the recommendations and to gain information of the feasibility of these recommendations and their probable consequences under concrete country conditions.

c) Improvement recommendations:

c)15. Efforts should be made to introduce experimentally the various recommendations, so as to gain a better understanding of their problems and effects. Pilot-improvement-projects in selected OECD countries may constitute a preferable vehicle for doing so.

Following these general recommendations - which apply to every and each of the improvement recommendations presented in this part of the paper, let me proceed with some comments on each of the following recommendations:

c)16. Simultaneously introduce similar elements into different system components.

c)17. Reduce distance between components engaging in relevant planning activities.

c)18. Provide shared feedback to relevant system components.

c)19. Establish overall system direction units.

A main way to achieve better integration between planning activities in different units is to introduce into these different units similar elements, such as: data, goals, basic assumptions, decision doctrines, professionals, and images and preferences concerning the future. Therefore, as stated in improvement recommendation c.16, the various recommendations to be presented in respect to system components concerning improvements in process and personnel should be applied cross-sectorally. As already explained, the hypothetic danger of over-reducing diversity is not real in most discrete policymaking systems, though that danger should be borne in mind.

The distance between different system components influences their co-ordination. Therefore, as stated in improvement recommendation c.17, reduction of that distance between relevant units will often improve integration between education and intersectoral planning.

Possible ways to decrease that distance can be illustrated by the following sub-recommendations:

c.17.1 Try to put units in education and intersectoral planning into proximate physical facilities (on both the macro and micro levels).

c.17.2 Establish opportunities for interpersonal contact between the various groups and persons engaged in education and intersectoral planning, such as through common associations, clubs where they mix informally, conferences, etc.

c)17.3 Build a foundation for interpersonal contact between these groups and persons by some mixed activities during their training, both at professional schools in universities and, later, in-service training activities.

c)17.4 Set up shared communication media, such as professional periodicals devoted to social policy as a whole and appealing to different groups engaged in planning in the different sectors.

c)17.5 Establish rotation opportunities and even rotation-duty through suitable career planning.

Additional specific recommendations can be formulated to encourage distance-reduction in ways relevant to improve interaction between relevant units, and thus improve the integration of education and intersectoral planning. But I think the five illustrations given above suffice to concretise the contents and significance of improvement recommendation c.17 as a whole.

Shared feedback can be viewed as a specific version of the recommendation to introduce similar elements into different system components, applied to information on the state of the system as a whole and its changes. But this is so important an item as to justify formulation as a separate recommendation. The underlying idea here is, that by getting a dynamic picture of the results of various sectoral policies and of changes due to other causes, the interdependencies of the various policies in reality will be made plastically clear, increasing propensity at least to co-ordinate. This recommendation is technically difficult, tying in with the social indicator and social mapping problems. But some beginnings can be made, at least by establishing shared data banks for social problems. Therefore, the following sub-recommendation:

c)18.1 Establish data-banks for social policy issues as a whole, to be shared by education and other related sectors and to serve as one of the bases for intersectoral planning.

The data-bank is related to the general recommendation to establish overall system-direction units. Please let me emphasize the use of "units" in the plural form: the complexity of issues, multiplicity of useful approaches and variety of relevant interests and values require an abundance of such units which take different forms, such as: intersectoral planning units in central government; integrated service units on the field level; comprehensive social policy research units at universities; and policy research units of the Think Tank type in special relationships with various public agencies. This is a major issue, as overall system-direction units are, in my view, absolutely necessary in order to move significantly in the direction of better integration of education and intersectoral planning. Therefore, I recommend that the problems related to such units should constitute a main subject for an OECD intersectoral project. At the present state of this work, let me limit myself to the following preliminary observations:

- To achieve their main mission, overall system-direction units should not be diluted by imposing on them many additional functions, such as serving as a change-agent on the micro-level or changing the characteristics of sectoral personnel.
- Significant experience, both positive and negative, is available, but it has not been adequately studied and processed.
- More successes can be identified in respect to the strategic area than the social policy area. Reasons include the greater complexity of the latter, its higher political sensitivities, and less available knowledge. The latter point deserves emphasis: even a concept package for dealing adequately with social policy issues as a whole is sorely missing. Therefore, extensive theoretic work may well be a most practical way to advance significantly integration of education and inter-sectoral planning. It follows that some of the overall system-direction units will engage in what looks like highly abstract studies, while others will achieve relatively little until new knowledge becomes available.
- It is impossible to divorce overall system-direction in respect to social policy issues from policymaking as a whole, including its intensely political elements. Therefore, this recommendation should be handled as a part of even broader approaches to the improvement of policymaking, including the issues of relations between political institutions and new types of central policymaking units.

2. Structure

Recommendation c.19 belongs to structure as well as to overall system direction, well illustrating the overlap between different improvement dimensions. Recommendation c.18 also has clear structural implications. Therefore, instead of discussing additional structural improvements (which, surely, will serve as a main subject for the further phases of OECD work in this field), let me mention a few points dealing with the structural dimension of better integrating education and intersectoral planning, in general:

- Nothing is easier (relatively) than formally to establish new units (or new formal procedures). I think that new units are needed and can be useful; but the danger of escaping from the difficult reform needs of existing units by establishing new units which are not geared into the actual policymaking process is a very real one. Therefore whenever a new unit for integrated planning etc. is established, its interaction with the various units in charge of actual policymaking must be carefully considered and evaluated.

- New units often cannot fulfil their innovative missions in respect to intersectoral planning etc., in the absence of novel knowledge and new types of professionals. The capacity of new units to actually execute their nominal tasks must, therefore, be carefully assured.
- Recommendation c.16 applies to new units too, in the sense that new sub-units within existing policymaking components are important for influencing system outputs. For example: establishment of social policy analysis units within the main central agencies in charge of sectoral planning may be of critical importance in moving towards better intersectoral planning integration, as distinguished from leaving sectoral planning units as they are and only adding a central intersectoral planning unit.
- Structural innovations can become a closed road leading nowhere. But without new units and new sub-units it is impossible to achieve major system-output changes. Therefore establishment of new units in close relation with the introduction of other changes is a major strategy for getting better integration of education and intersectoral planning.

3. Process

"Planning", "policymaking", "decision-making" etc. are processes. Therefore changes in processes are mostly related to OECD work in this field and constitute a main dimension for improvement. It is largely correct to view new structures and personnel as a way to influence the planning process; they are therefore of special importance.

The improved integration of education and intersectoral planning is related to the improvement of the planning process as such. One fork of the improvement road leads, therefore, into the study and improvement of planning as a type of decision-making (or, to take a broader view, of policymaking as a form of societal self-direction). To speak of better integration of sectoral planning activities without going into the actual and preferable characteristics of those planning activities, leaves out an essential set of elements. But to go into planning theory and planning studies as a whole and their application to social sector planning in particular may push the project beyond its reasonable and feasible limits. This paper must be limited to mentioning this problem, which would have to be resolved in any further stages of the OECD work in this field.

Leaving aside the planning process as a whole and limiting myself to specific improvements in process directly related to integration between education and intersectoral planning, the following concrete recommendations are based on matters already discussed in this paper. They also serve to demonstrate the possibilities of improving such integration through concrete changes in process by introducing various analytical tools and methods throughout educational and intersectoral planning units:

c)20. Standard goal sets including the main goals of all related sectoral planning activities should be prepared and utilised as check-lists in all planning units, to consider alternatives. These goal sets should be open-ended, operational and widely disseminated. They should be prepared in co-operation by the overall system-direction units and the various units dealing with sectoral planning. Suitable versions of them should be utilised on the various levels of planning, macro as well as micro.

c)21. Standard sets of alternative comprehensive futures, including all related sectoral futures , should be prepared and utilised in all planning units. These standard alternative comprehensive futures should be prepared, revised and utilised in ways similar to the goal sets discussed in recommendation c.20 above.

c)22. On a more general level, shared policy analysis methods, methodologies and formats should be used in the different units engaged in educational and related sectoral planning.

Recommendation c.22 deserves additional discussion. Utilisation of identical or, at least, compatible planning and policy analysis methods, methodologies and formats is a main step towards better integration. Care must be taken not to enforce standardization in a way repressing truly unique features of the different sectors; but the shared characteristics of social policy sectors can, in part, serve as a basis for similar policymaking-formats. Much can be learnt from attempts in that direction with new budgeting methods, both for better and for worse. The trouble is that new process formats can easily become empty rituals, unless four conditions are simultaneously met: The methods must be good substantially; staff must be available that is familiar with the methods and knows how to use them; incentives must be provided and support given, to overcome resistance to innovations (which, however technically put, change power relations); and other features of policymaking must be adjusted to the new formats, such as new structures, different data bases, change in career patterns, etc.

An interesting illustration, less well known than budgetary methods, is the planning integration methods tried out by the Planning Staff of the Office of the Chancellor in the Federal Republic of Germany where a procedure evolved designed to provide shared data on possible cross-impacts between different decisions in various ministries. I mention this illustration to show the potentials of possible innovations in this direction; empiric study of the concrete case will also show many difficulties, pitfalls and possible counter-productive effects.

4. Personnel

Earlier recommendations already indicate the needs for changes in personnel as a requisite for any other changes in education and intersectoral planning. Leaving aside the general issue of introducing organisational change and related matters of motivation etc., which is not unique to this field, other than the special difficulties of dealing with highly and narrowly trained professionals, the following recommendations serve further to operationalise the needs for innovations in personnel:

c)23. A new type of "social policy planning" professional is needed and should be developed through suitable graduate university programmes.

c)24. Orientations towards integrated educational and intersectoral planning should be introduced into the advanced professional training of all relevant professionals at the university level.

c)25. Crash programmes should be undertaken to prepare social policy planning professionals on an ad hoc basis to staff new positions which depend on availability of such professionals.

c)26. Intensive workshops for senior staff engaged in educational, intersectoral and relevant sectoral planning should be held, to introduce a comprehensive view of integrated planning approaches.

All these proposals can be supported with available though inadequate field experience. The most far-reaching proposal, namely c.23, is closely related to new developments in the United States, especially to the various novel programmes in public policy, social policy planning, policy analysis, etc. The other proposals are less radical, though they depend conceptually on the first one. Because of the critical importance of personnel for all advances towards integration of education and intersectoral planning, the dimension of new training programmes should serve as another main focus for future work. This is a subject which may well suit active co-operation between OECD countries, in the form of a common Centre for experimenting with innovative training programmes in the areas of social policymaking.*

_____

*) See, Dror, Y., Design for Policy Sciences, Chapters 14-15, for a detailed treatment of this subject.

SOME THEORETICAL NOTES
FROM HISTORICAL ANALYSIS

by David Cohen

I.   INTRODUCTION

The idea of co-ordination among social services is no novelty.
Since the inception of social policy, social service workers in
industrialised societies have noticed that clients' problems often
elude the formal boundaries of service organisations. These observations regularly lead to pleas for eliminating the boundaries, or
inventing ways to bridge them. And almost as regularly the proposed
co-ordination seems either not to materialise, or not to achieve the
desired results.

The chief puzzle in this, of course, is why such a seemingly
obvious measure is so difficult to implement, or when implemented so
prone to failure. The purpose of this essay is to explore that
puzzle. Co-ordination, though, is not a simple phenomenon. In order
to think about influences on its success or failure, it is necessary
to have a decent sense of what co-ordination means. The first part
of the essay addresses this point. The second explores factors
relevant to its success.

II.   CO-ORDINATE WHAT?

If the idea of co-ordination of social services is common, the
idea of specialisation is no less familiar. In fact, one can easily
observe an ebb and flow between these two ideas in the development
of social policy. Housing programmes in the United States, for
example, began late in the 1930s as fairly specialised efforts to
provide housing for the poor. The experience with public housing
was not entirely reassuring, and partly in response the Model Cities
Programme sought a "co-ordinated" attack on the problems of low-
income neighbourhoods. Efforts were made to create local agencies
which could administer a broad range of social services in neighbourhood renewal - rather than just housing. The experiences with
Model Cities were also problematic, and in the last few years the

pendulum appears to have swung back from the idea of comprehensiveness and co-ordination, towards less ambitious and more specialised approaches to housing provision.

In a sense, of course, the tension between co-ordination and specialisation is timeless, like the tension between equality and liberty, or freedom and order. There has, however, been a general historical drift on this point. When social policy began to emerge as a formal concern of government in the middle and late nineteenth century, the emphasis in social services was chiefly on specialisation. One important reason for this was that the social welfare professions were then in their formative stages, emerging from private philanthropy, working men's associations, church work, and the like. There was, in consequence, considerable introspective concern with the professions' definition and the clarification of their competencies. Not surprisingly, there also was much defensive assertiveness about the importance of the particular special services each represented. Quite naturally, then, the social welfare professions placed a high priority on specialised service.

A second reason for this early emphasis was the fact that the history of social policy began with a struggle to achieve minimal standards in a few areas of welfare. A bit of education, certain basic aspects of public health, and minimal nutrition and clothing were chief among them. Efforts to achieve minimum decency in a few areas did not result in constant collision and overlap among social services. Quite the contrary, the problem seemed to be insufficient breadth and depth in each service. This naturally focused attention within each service's boundaries.

A final reason for the relative lack of early concern with co-ordination was the modest extent of government intervention. In the United Kingdom and the United States state involvement in social policy was quite limited, as was its interference in other economic and social activity. As a result, it hardly occurred to anyone to suggest that social policy should be improved by placing some social services in concert with others. The idea of such co-ordination simply was not suggested by what government did at the time. And the notion of co-ordinating social policy with other government action was even more remote.

As can easily be seen, these generalisations about the state of affairs half a century or more ago hardly apply now. For one thing, the professions concerned with social welfare have achieved greater stability and more status. Of course the exact basis of their separate specialities is in a state of continuing theoretical uncertainty. But as a practical matter teachers, social workers and others think they know their craft, and almost everyone else agrees. Because the social welfare professions are less defensive and insecure than they were a few generations ago, the emphasis on specialisation and internal craft development has somewhat lessened.

Equally important, the domain of social policy has grown. One reason for this is that even in the longest-established areas of social service, the conception of minimum standards has expanded greatly. There has been lateral expansion. Schooling (to take one example) is no longer focused on providing a few basic skills but on the "whole child". There also has been vertical expansion. Standards of minimum decency have risen, so that while a few basics in public health were thought sufficient two or three generations ago, now much more comprehensive health care seems necessary. A third reason for expansion in the domain of social policy is that the spheres of social relations thought central to welfare have grown. In addition to health, public assistance, and schooling, entire new areas - such as community development, social security, victimisation and accident insurance, etc. - are emerging as public responsibilities.(1)

A final reason for the growing territory of social policy has been changing standards of fairness. Not long ago rescue from severe crisis was the accepted criterion, but now we increasingly question this idea. One notion, especially current in educational policy, is that there is a public responsibility to make up for pre-existing inequality by providing better than equal services to those in need.(2) Another, which receives increasing attention now, is that society should create equal outcomes among groups differing in their initial social oppportunities.(3)

These developments suggest that ideas about the nature of welfare, and the extent of public responsibility for it, change regularly. They also reveal that the expansion of social policy itself has produced increasingly frequent boundary contacts among practitioners from different professions, greater awareness of overlap among services and redundancy among agencies, and a growing sense

---

1) Recently, for example, New Zealand has instituted a comprehensive national insurance plan, designed to protect citizens against the fiscal consequences of all accidents. See: Report of the Select Committee on Compensation for Personal Injury, Wellington, New Zealand, 1972; also, An Act to Make Provision for General Safety ... enacted by the General Assembly of New Zealand, 20th October, 1972 (commonly known as the Accident Compensation Act).

2) The chief example of this in the United States, recently, is Title I of the 1965 Elementary and Secondary Education Act (ESEA). In the United Kingdom there is a programme known as Educational Priority Areas, which roughly corresponds.

3) Coleman, James, "The Concept of Equality of Educational Opportunity", Harvard Educational Review, vol. 38, 1968, pp.7-22.

of the complexity and interrelatedness of social welfare. As social policy expands and grows more complex, neat divisions of responsibility among services seem increasingly hard to maintain. The rising concern with co-ordination among social services only reflects developments in the services themselves.

Finally, with the expansion of the welfare state, the legitimacy of government action and state involvement in the private sector have grown. It is now widely agreed, for example, that the United States' Government ought to consider social security (that is, problems of unemployment, retirement, and so on) in framing general economic policy. Policy debates which used to centre on whether these problems should be considered now centre on what form this consideration ought to take, and how extensive it should be. Co-ordination is therefore no longer a legitimate concern only within social policy. It is now thought important to co-ordinate social policy with other government action, and with private economic and social activity.

Thus, the notion of co-ordination, like the conception of social policy itself, is not fixed. It is a changing value. For example, ideas about what should be co-ordinated have changed. As the public responsibility for welfare grows, our sense of the areas which require rational and concerted effort also grow. In addition, strategies for co-ordination change. For example, when service gaps and boundary collisions among services call discontinuity and overlap to attention, it sometimes seems wise to solve the problem by consolidating existing agencies - thereby making administrative units larger and more comprehensive. This has been a classical approach in the last three or four decades. Presently, though, when the problems of bureaucratic oppressiveness and inefficiency in large agencies seem paramount (partly as a result of the earlier efforts at co-ordination), new strategies develop. Clients, it is argued, should be given the power to determine what should be co-ordinated, by whom, and for what ends. Community control of services, or individual vouchers are therefore advocated.

This discussion suggests quite a variety of ideas about co-ordination. In order to sort out the tangle, I think it may be useful to think first about what is being co-ordinated (sectors of co-ordination), and then about how it is to be co-ordinated (strategies for co-ordination).

1. Sectors for co-ordination

The historical developments in social policy sketched above suggest several ways of thinking about sectors for co-ordination. One centres on improving the articulation among social service

sectors. Another concerns co-ordination within one or more service
sectors - between policy and administration on one hand (especially
at the regional or national levels) and practice on the other. A
third concerns the relations between social welfare and other government action. And a fourth concerns the relation between social
policy and private action. Co-ordination has different meanings in
each context.

Historically, of course, the concern began with co-ordination
among social service sectors. The interrelations among health,
education, family stability, and the like have been a long-standing
concern of social service practitioners. With the growth of social
policy, this concern has grown. In United States social programmes,
for example, there has been a slowly growing effort, especially
marked in the last decade, to integrate education with other services.
This has been evident in the Model Cities Programme, in the nutritional and health aspects of Title I of the Elementary and Secondary
Education Act, and, of course, in Headstart and other programmes
managed by the Office of Child Development. Indeed, the growth of
social policy has made it increasingly difficult to separate the
idea that existing services should be co-ordinated from the idea
that all the needed services ought to be provided. Arguments for
service co-ordination have come to be almost indistinguishable from
arguments for comprehensiveness. The social programmes which seek
to co-ordinate services - Headstart and Model Cities, for example, -
often argue for this goal on the grounds that clients needed comprehensive services.(1) As the scope of social policy continues to
expand, it seems likely that the equation of co-ordination and comprehensiveness will become more pronounced.

But co-ordination is not just an issue at the point of service
delivery. More and more it seems to concern relations among various
administrative, political, and organisational entities. One such
entity is the profession. In industrialised societies these are
national organisations, with distinct institutional loyalties,
conceptions of service, and territories. Another is the government
agency - of various local, national and regional types. Each has
separate missions, distinct legislative constituencies, and different
catchment areas, problems, procedures, and remedies. Since the

---

1) One recent example of this tendency can be found in a new programme under development by the Federal Office of Child Development in the United States. The programme - called Project
   Development Continuity - is aimed at eliminating service discontinuities in the pre-school-school transition; the strategy
   for doing this seems to centre on providing comprehensive services
   for children. See: "Programme Guidelines for Project Developmental Continuity", issued by the Office of Child Development,
   May, 1974.

expansion of social policy has entailed the growth of large administrative agencies, new government jurisdictions and welfare professions, the barriers to co-ordination seem more and more to centre in
relations among these entities - rather than in gaps and overlaps
at the point of delivery. As social policy expands and the scope of
government and professional responsibility grow, it is reasonable to
expect that this trend will continue. It would not be surprising if
the problem of co-ordination drives social policy planners and analysts to reconsider government jurisdictions, administrative territories, and professional boundaries.

Third, the problem of co-ordination no longer refers simply to
relations among established social service sectors. The growth of
government action, and national economic and social integration mean
that social policy planners and analysts increasingly worry about
other sectors of government, such as employment, environment, or
trade. In effect, this really redefines the conception of co-
ordination. For one thing, from an organisational point of view,
co-ordinating public assistance with school policy involves some
different issues than co-ordinating public assistance and minimum
wage policy. Government economic agencies are different from social
welfare agencies; the interest groups outside the government are not
the same; the congressional constituencies are different, and operating methods vary as well. For another, value differences among
social welfare agencies are likely to be more modest than value
differences between social welfare and other government agencies.
Differences between the United States Treasury and the Office of
Economic Opportunity on such things as income maintenance or health
insurance ordinarily can be expected to be greater than the differences between the Office of Economic Opportunity (OEO) and the
Department of Health, Education and Welfare. These value differences
reflect different missions, constituencies and conceptions about the
responsibility for welfare. Third, linking social welfare and other
government agencies redefines the co-ordination problem, because it
really involves an extension of social policy - not simply a better
connection among agencies. Suppose, for example, that the United
States' Government decided to co-ordinate public assistance policy
with labour policy, by lowering federal apprenticeship programme
entry requirements so that welfare recipients could receive apprenticeship training leading to craft union jobs. Co-ordination would
have taken place, but in addition social policy would have been
extended to an area formerly dominated by a private sector force -
the craft unions. In such cases, co-ordination really means expansion of social policy. Acting in concert means drawing other areas
of government action into social policy.

This notion holds even more strongly in the case of co-ordination between government social agencies and the private sector - my fourth way of thinking about co-ordination. For example, working out arrangements between public assistance policy and industry hiring standards in order to get welfare recipients jobs for which they would not ordinarily be qualified is a form of co-ordination. But it is in many ways different from co-ordination among welfare agencies. There are different organisational issues involved, for industry is not centrally administered, or even much regulated in the United States. These imply different strategic approaches to co-ordination. There also are value differences between social welfare agencies and industrial firms. And most important, the chief barrier to co-ordination in such cases is not administrative but political - it is a problem of legitimacy. To co-ordinate public assistance with private industry hiring is to extend the web of government and the domain of social policy. It is less an effort to co-ordinate social policy than to co-ordinate society.

Thus, the expansion of the welfare state has not only brought the need for co-ordination more forcefully to our attention, it has multiplied the sectors concerned. In summary, this discussion suggests four different ways of regarding sectors for co-ordination:

- lateral co-ordination among social service sectors;
- vertical co-ordination within and among social service sectors, between direct practice on one hand and administrative, professional and governmental agencies on the other;
- co-ordination within government, between social policy and other areas of public responsibility;
- co-ordination between social policy and action in the private sector.

These distinctions among sectors are useful because they make the meaning of intersectoral planning a bit more concrete. They delineate the different elements of society which might be considered, they suggest the gradual historical expansion of the co-ordination concept, and they reveal the increasing difficulty of limiting co-ordination to social service sectors. The expansion of the welfare state, continued national economic integration, and the continuing trend toward corporate concentration all mean that co-ordination within social service sectors will become harder to separate, as a practical matter, either from a more general co-ordination within government or from co-ordination between public and private action. At least in the minds of social planners, these issues tend increasingly to merge.

90

2. Strategies for co-ordination

Another distinction among the meanings of co-ordination involves the different strategies which may be used to promote it. The classical difference is between bureaucratic and economic inducements for action. Both can be manipulated by government, but there are considerable differences in the assumptions and organisational consequences involved. Consider, for example, a policy of reducing public assistance and improving opportunity by getting welfare recipients mainstream jobs. One way of doing this might be to co-ordinate public assistance policy with education policy, by providing training in state-maintained institutions so that recipients emerged with the necessary skills or certification to qualify as workers; and to co-ordinate this training with existing government-run placement institutions, so trainees could find jobs. Another way of carrying out the same policy would be to offer tax incentives to industrial firms for hiring and training welfare recipients. The formal goal of the policy is the same in both cases, but the instrumentality for executing it, the sectors for co-ordination, and the means of co-ordination are really quite different.

Perhaps the best way to get at the differences between economic and bureaucratic approaches to co-ordination is to explore each by way of some concrete examples. Within each approach several different tactics have emerged. In the case of the bureaucratic approach to co-ordination, these seem to include: co-option of mixed services into one agency; creation of new consolidated service or administrative agencies; various linking devices designed to permit partial co-ordination; and oversight agencies which seek to insure that various government activities satisfy the values of social policy.

Service co-option: co-option of services has emerged slowly from experience, rather than having been deliberately invented. The best example in the United States is elementary and secondary education, which has gradually accumulated an increasing array of social services during the last three or four decades. Schools now often perform at least minimal health screening, and often other basic public health and dental services as well. Often they try to satisfy some nutritional needs. Increasingly they provide various psychological and counselling services, though these are more typically screening than treatment. The recent social programmes in education have added, at least for disadvantaged children, more nutritional and health services, as well as clothing in some cases. And some educational programmes now in the developmental stages

offer a broad range of family services, including household management, adult literacy, employment counselling, day care, and so on.(1)

The accumulation of these services in the public schools is
not the result of an explicit strategy. In some cases it has occurred because a particular social problem was seen as a deterrent to
good education. In other cases it occurred because the schools
were a convenient place to locate services which other agencies
wanted to have provided, but could not. And in still other cases it
occurred because the conception of necessary educational services
has grown. The result has been that schools increasingly resemble
a sort of two-tier multi-service agency, with other social services
clustered on the periphery of a class-room-oriented core programme.
Schooling seems to be the best example of this co-ordinating strategy,
though other agencies occasionally do something of the sort (hospitals which offer day care, for example). No sanctions are involved,
and there are no penalties for non-co-ordination. The services
simply accumulated, much in the way some historians imagine the
Roman Empire to have grown.

Agency consolidation: one of the most interesting features of
the service co-option approach is that it occurs only at the point
of service delivery. These are not cases of large-scale bureaucratic
or political merger, but rather of co-ordination undertaken by
direct service-providing agencies. This is in rather clear contrast
to the agency consolidation strategy (our second type). This was
invented rather than accumulated, and it originally had more to do
with administrative agencies than providers of services. The prime
examples in the United States have been the Federal Department of
Health, Education and Welfare, and various consolidated municipal
agencies which were sometimes created during the last several decades
recently culminating with the so-called "superagencies". Although
all of the consolidated administrative agencies govern or finance
social services, many of them appear to have no direct contact with
clients. The Human Resources Administration in New York, for
example (which may be abolished by a new Mayor with different administrative tastes), includes a broad range of established agencies
concerned with public assistance, training, and so on. But their
consolidation in HRA seems to have left the old separate delivery
mechanisms still largely intact; the HRA superstructure is in contact
only with other administrative agencies.

Two recent variants of service consolidation present a rather
different aspect. One is the multi-service centres which have
appeared in several United States cities during the last decade.

_____

1) McLaughlin, M, "Parent Involvement in Compensatory Education
   Programmes", unpublished paper, Harvard Graduate School of
   Education, 1971.

These do co-ordinate a broad range of social welfare services at the
point of delivery. Insofar as I have been able to determine, these
have been sponsored chiefly by the community action programme of OEO
(now more or less defunct) and operated by municipal anti-poverty
agencies. As a result, in many cases they have served less to draw
together existing agencies than to provide, in a co-ordinated way,
services hitherto unavailable in particular neighbourhoods.(1)   The
services seem to run the gamut from health care, to assistance in
coping with other public agencies (the Hunt's Point multi-service
centre in New York City has been active in local school politics
there), to public assistance, One such centre in Brockton, Massa-
chusetts is sponsored by a state government, as an experiment in the
consolidation of social services.(2)

A second non-traditional approach to consolidation involves
information rather than service delivery. The best example here is
the Boston "little city halls", which provide co-ordinated referral
and general problem-solving assistance at neighbourhood offices.
Informal evaluations suggest that their work centres on helping
individuals to find their way through bureaucratic mazes in central
city agencies, and sometimes on helping local groups to un-stick
bureaucratic or political jams. While a great deal of the little
city halls' work centres on the performance of a single public
service, they do involve an important form of consolidation. The
underlying idea is that if information feedback on services can be
drawn together at the neighbourhood level, the provision of those
services (co-ordinated or not) will be substantially improved.
Consolidating information on social services at the point of
delivery is seen as a way of improving the largely separate work of
central service agencies.

Bureaucratic linkage: perhaps the classical bureaucratic co-
ordination tactic is partial linkage between established agencies.
In some cases the links are informal - as in the instance of impro-
vised referral systems which often exist between schools and mental

---

1) The multi-service centres may disappear as a result of the slow
   death of the OEO and the related decrease in social programme
   funds. Because they often seem to involve the provision of
   services hitherto unavailable in a co-ordinated way - rather
   than the co-ordination of services already in place - these
   centres required considerable new funds. This has made them
   dependent on national political arguments.

2) It is also worth noting that in some cases these centres have
   pioneered in restructuring the governance of social services,
   because community boards control them. There seems to be no
   published evidence, however, on the extent to which lay control
   is nominal or actual, whether it has actually changed the nature
   of relations between clients and practitioners, or whether it has
   changed decision making about either services to be provided or
   their co-ordination.

health agencies, or between social workers and health or family service agencies. In other cases links are formal but restricted to service-providing agencies - as in collaborative arrangements between pre-school programmes and schools for the exchange of information on students, or in efforts to relate day care programmes and adult training or job placement programmes. In many other cases links are formal, but confined to administrative rather than service-providing agencies. Here there is a rich variety of bureaucratic inventions, which run the gamut from temporary task forces, to long-term liaison, to more or less permanent inter-agency working parties. In the United States, at any rate, formal administrative co-ordinating efforts are often intended to explore the possibility of more permanent arrangements, or to present a suitable appearance of co-ordination. As a result there is a short supply of impressive permanent inter-agency efforts. Even in the case where two agencies perform very similar functions (as with science education programmes in the National Science Foundation and the United States Office of Education) there typically is little contact, let alone co-ordination.

The last bureaucratic co-ordination tactic involves the establishment of supervisory bodies, to harmonize areas of social policy, or to co-ordinate social policy with action elsewhere in government. The office of Federal Contract Compliance (located in the Department of Labour) is supposed to make sure that government contractors observe nondiscriminatory hiring practices. But its chief role has been co-ordinating standards for contract compliance within the government - in order to assure that federal agencies speak with one voice. Not surprisingly OFCC has had mixed success in that role. Another example of efforts designed to harmonize social policy among government agencies is the Office of Management and Budget.(1) There is some evidence that planning and evaluation offices within the federal social agencies play a similar role to OMB. In both cases, the incentive lies in the co-ordinating agency's influence on budgetary decisions.

These co-ordination tactics have several elements in common. One is that the motivating force is more often administrative - to eliminate bureaucratic overlap, to reduce costs, to gain better information, etc. - than directly concerned with services. A second is that the implementing agent ordinarily is rules - that is, guidelines and regulations. Money is rarely involved. This is

---

1) For a study of the Office of Management and Budget (formerly Bureau of the Budget) see, U.S., Executive Office of the President Bureau of the Budget, Task Force Report on Inter-Governmental Programme Co-ordination, 2 vols.

natural enough for bureaucratic action. And a third, which can be
inferred from these two conditions, is that the incentives for action
tend to be relatively weak. Administrative inducements, after all,
are generally not compelling causes of action, save at times of
great social crisis. Certainly administrative rationality or
efficiency are not values with the same practical weight as political
survival, or professional independence. Ordinarily it is much easier
to fudge administrative rules than to avoid explicit political or
economic pressure. Finally, bureaucratic approaches to co-ordination
often produce new agencies or bureaux which are charged with new
responsibilities. Often this does not have a simplifying effect.
The result may be more co-ordination, but it certainly is increased
administrative complexity.

These attributes can be seen more clearly in comparison with
an economic strategy. One main tactic here is tax incentives or
operating subsidies to either private sector or government agencies,
as rewards for co-ordination. Another is the creation of public-
sector markets, by giving consumers either the political freedom to
choose within existing public monopolies or the economic power to
avail themselves of existing private service suppliers.

The first of these tactics is well established in government
action, but it has not been much used in social policy. Tax
subsidies to industrial firms are employed to encourage capital
development and natural resource exploitation, but I have been unable
to find cases in which subsidies have been employed affirmatively in
social policy.(1) There has been occasional discussion of using
such subsidies as an incentive for hiring public assistance recipients, or as a means of decreasing unemployment in periods of
recession, but there has not been action along these lines in the
United States. They could be used, of course, to reduce unemployment, to provide child care, to promote environmental improvement,
or in countless other areas. Ordinarily, however, administrative
instruments are chosen for such policies.

This paucity of experience is also acute in the case of public-
sector markets. There has been quite a bit of recent debate about
the idea, but very limited experimentation. Choice within public
monopolies is being explored on a limited scale in education, by
allowing consumers to select those variants of the service they
most prefer, and thus providing incentives for the service to diversify and become more responsive. Families are given vouchers
(cashable by schools) which are used to pay for tuition at schools

_____

1) There are lots of cases in which tax incentives are used in ways
   which have an adverse impact on social policy, of course.
   Federal tax subsidies for homeowners, for example, benefit more
   advantaged elements in the population.

of the parents' choice. Since the experiment with education vouchers
in the United States started (in Alum Rock, California), there also
have been efforts to design and mount experiments with consumer
entitlements in health and housing. In these cases, the strategies
involve tax subsidies for consumers to use in hitherto private
markets. If several of these approaches materialised, consumers
could be in a position to co-ordinate among services themselves to
some degree. Choices could be made about housing, for example, for
reasons of school location - or vice versa. The possibilities for
such co-ordination would depend partly on the rules by which such
public-sector markets were regulated, and partly on the extent to
which diversity actually existed within services.

Lacking experience with these market-oriented co-ordination
strategies, one can report nothing on their actual feasibility in
social policy. But it is possible to discern some important differences - at least in principle - between economic and bureaucratic
approaches to co-ordination. The economic approaches rest on fiscal
rather than bureaucratic motives for action: the instrument of
implementation is a financial incentive rather than an administrative
rule. It could therefore be argued that the market approaches would
provide a stronger stimulus for action - assuming the economic incentives were of a sufficient magnitude. It could also be that market-
based co-ordination strategies would be less likely to proliferate
bureaucracy in the process of encouraging co-operation. The last
point is almost surely the case in the case of tax subsidies, which
operate now with a minimum of administrative paraphernalia. But
these arguments are based on incomplete experience and evidence;
economic incentives might turn out to be no more compelling than
bureaucratic ones, and it is possible that they would have other undesirable consequences. In fact, the experience with other government grant-in-aid programmes in the United States suggests that
offering inter-governmental fiscal incentives is a rather weak
influence on the recipient agencies. In education, at least, there
is a good deal of evidence that the recipients manipulate such funds
to meet their own priorities, rather than satisfying the rules of
the granting agency.(1) If one were to go on the basis of past
United States experience, then, one would have to conclude that within government, at least, fiscal incentives for co-ordination would
not be terribly effective.

In spite of these caveats, there are good reasons to turn the
co-ordination problem on its head, and ask whether service consumers
ought not to be the agent of service co-ordination. The great difficulty with this notion, as Martin Rein has pointed out, is that most

---

1) Porter, D., et al. The Politics of Budgeting Federal Aid, Sage,
   Beverly Hills, California, 1973.

co-ordination efforts thus far have been aimed at increasing efficiency in social services, or at least decreasing unit cost by reducing overlap, redundancy, and the like. But increasing client choice
would require introducing more variety in social services, which
would inevitably lead to overlap and redundancy - without these,
choice would be meaningless. Thus, the idea of consumer choice as a
strategy of co-ordination is at cross-purposes with the cost-reducing
motives underlying much of the interest in co-ordination strategies.(1)

The contrast also is useful because it suggests a variety of
potential hybrid strategies for service co-ordination. The idea of
consumer choice, for example, could be taken beyond the forms discussed here. One could imagine a form of general social insurance
which guaranteed minimum protection in several areas of social
policy. If there were basic entitlements in health, education,
child-care, and unemployment, much co-ordination (relating child-
care leave to educational needs, or unemployment compensation to
educational opportunities) could be left to the decision of service
consumers. Such a scheme could be worked out within the framework
of existing social service monopolies, or by making these monopolies
private.

Finally, however, one must say that juxtaposing market and
bureaucratic approaches to co-ordination evokes a distinction between public and private sectors which is increasingly misleading in
the advanced industrial societies. These societies are marked more
and more by the development of what might be termed a quasi-public
or quasi-governmental sector, in which what seem to be private
organisations accomplish public purposes or shape public action.
This development is so pronounced in some respects that I am inclined
to advance quasi-government as an emerging third strategy of
co-ordination.

Some examples may help to make the point. In education, quasi-
governmental agencies serve a variety of functions. Private consulting firms plan, develop, and evaluate governmental programmes. Often
they provide operational assistance to public agencies in carrying
out programmes. In these roles such firms sometimes have a substantial impact on the content of policy, on the choice of criteria
for evaluating policy, and on the conclusions drawn, promulgated,
and believed. Thus they can affect the political climate and the
legislative process. But while such agencies are almost wholly
supported by public funds - they are, in effect, creatures of the
government - politically they are almost wholly invisible. They
are accountable only in a fiscal sense, and only to administrative
agencies.

---

1) Rein M., "Co-ordination of Social Services", pp. 103-137 in
   Rein M., Social Policy, Random House, New York, 1970.

Consulting firms, of course, serve few functions related to social service co-ordination. But other quasi-governmental organisations do more. In education, in the United States, for example, many important standard-setting functions for public agencies are performed by quasi-governmental organisations. One excellent example of this concerns standardized tests, which have come to be the chief instrument for evaluating student performance. They play a critical role in determining the allocation of students among programmes and schools, and as such, they are important in articulation among levels within the school system (i.e., between high schools and universities). Tests also help shape standards for recruiting and selecting workers, and thus are important in co-ordinating schools and work.

But while tests serve as a basis for co-ordination among elements of the educational system, and between education and elements of the private sector, their official standing is obscure. They have not been mandated by courts or legislatures, but rather were created by private agencies and gradually adopted by executive action until their usage became virtually universal. Test content and standards are not defined by any formal public body, but rather by private experts in consultation with various educational practitioners. Major test organisations have a quasi-governmental character not just because they often depend heavily on governmental contracts for their revenue, but because they devise and promulgate standards for public education without any formal public responsibility. In effect, private test organisations set standards for institutional practice and social policy - typically with official approval - even though they are not politically accountable.

There are more examples of quasi-governmental organisations in education and other social services - most accreditation and standard-setting agencies are of this sort - and this domain will almost surely continue to grow. Such agencies provide a convenient way to co-ordinate public policy with private sector activity without seeming to extend government control or multiply administrative agencies. They provide the opportunity to regularise informal decision-making systems involving stable interest groups, and they reflect the growing impact of national private organisations on standards for public action.

The distinguishing characteristic of quasi-governmental organisations, then, is not the use of some novel incentive for action. Rather, a mixture of bureaucratic and economic incentives are employed, in novel organisations which bridge the public and private sectors. Some such agencies are explicitly created to co-ordinate public policy with private action - the proposed new health insurance system, or Comsat, or the new railroad agency are all good

examples. Others have simply taken on such functions as a result
of developments in the society - such as the test agencies, or
accreditation groups. As a result what is unique in these organisations - the creation of a new institutional zone to co-ordinate or
mediate public and private action - is also their greatest problem,
because of unclarity about accountability. At this point it is
unclear whether this new zone will expand, or whether it will diminish
or be absorbed into government because of the desire for
accountability.

Thus, there are three main approaches to co-ordination, and
each involves several distinct tactics. These differences do not
only have tactical content. For example, the choice between state-
maintained institutions and tax incentives as agents of co-ordination
is a matter of implementation, but it is also a choice between two
philosophies of government action, and two notions about the motives
for collective action. There is, to take another case, a strategic
difference between consumer and agency initiated co-ordination, but
they also rest on different political assumptions about what the
relative power of service consumers and producers ought to be.

The first part of this paper has had one central theme - that
co-ordination is a diverse and evolving idea in social policy. One
notion has been the idea that co-ordination has become more important
as a result of the growth of social policy. Another has been the
notion that it is important to distinguish different sectors for
co-ordination, because of the great differences between co-ordinating within the social service sector, between social services and
other parts of government, or between social services and the
private sector. And a third has been the idea that there are varied
strategies for co-ordination, distinguished partly by differences in
organisational inducements and partly by differences in how organisational territory is defined.

One point in all this has been to get a preliminary grasp on
the meanings of intersectoralism by mapping its development and
varied meanings. Another was the expectation that by delineating
the meanings of co-ordination, understanding the factors which
influence its success might be improved. This is our next concern.

III. INFLUENCES ON CO-ORDINATION

This section will consider factors which seem relevant to the
success of co-ordination efforts. My purpose is to develop a conception of those influences likely to be generally relevant to inter-
sectoralism for education, and to briefly explore each one. My aim
is not to offer an explanation of why particular co-ordination efforts

have succeeded or failed but to suggest a suitable analytic framework for assessing the prospects of various co-ordination strategies.

In my view, considering the influences on intersectoral co-ordination requires that we conceive social service systems as something more than administrative conveniences, to be rearranged more or less at will. They ought instead to be understood as complex social systems which involve several crucial elements:

- diagnoses of social problems and parallel conceptions of social service;
- theories, evidence, and assumptions about the operation of society in general, and of a social service in particular;
- gradually accumulated decision-making habits, involving organisational culture, institutional forms, configurations of interest groups, and so on;
- formal and informal incentives for providing services in particular ways.

This is hardly a great theoretical novelty. But it is important to bear in mind that whatever the units for co-ordination may be, they will rest on a combination of values and beliefs, knowledge and theory, history, political culture and tradition, and inducements for action. Unless we try to understand them as complex systems of values and action, we will always be puzzled at the problems of trying to rearrange them.

1. Decision networks

Among other things, social service sectors and organisations within them are systems for making decisions about the allocation of welfare, the delivery of particular services, the internal allocation of resources, and the nature of social problems. These systems have many components and are subject to influence from a variety of sources. While one useful way to think about decision making is to focus on formal and explicit procedures, decision making involves more than explicit procedures. Co-ordination among institutions touches on more than the formal aspects of organisations. For example, the formal United States education decision process involves voters, elected boards, and an explicit chain of command reaching down to the classroom. While these are all quite important, other less formal factors also count for a good deal. The political culture of organisations, for example, often is critical. In some local systems there is extensive consultation with citizens on important issues, while in others there is none. In some systems school board elections are informally a part of local party politics, while in others they are dominated by strong civic associations. In many districts there are more or less stable interest groups, with

ongoing connections to the official decision system - teacher organisations and civic groups, for example. And a final non-formal
influence on decisions are those non-public organisations which set
standards or influence curriculum content. These are increasingly
national in character. Testing organisations, textbook and curriculum publishing and reform organisations, and professional associations are the chief examples.

While these non-formal influences are not equally important to
every decision, they do affect educational policy and practice at all
levels of government. They do not compose a decision-making system
which is either formal, politically, legitimate, or explicit. Nonetheless, they add up to a loose, reasonably stable and extremely
important set of informal networks. These networks penetrate into
the public and private sectors and various levels of government with
little regard for formal legal or political boundaries. The logic
of decision networks in education is not the logic of formal political
organisations.

This makes many forms of co-ordination difficult. For one thing,
the formal mechanisms through which co-ordination efforts are undertaken - administrative agencies - are not the only influence on
policy, and often are not the most important. Many administratively
oriented co-ordination schemes have foundered on problems which arise
from policy systems not controlled by the administrative agencies.
The fact that education policy is made in a loose grouping of
decision networks means that it is often difficult for governmental
organisations to exert the control necessary for intersectoral co-
ordination. The history of federally sponsored reform in the
United States' education, for example, suggests that even co-
ordination within the school systems' various parts is extremely
difficult to achieve.(1) Such diffuseness in decision making has
many advantages, but concerted action is not among them.

This feature of policy making in education bears on co-ordination
with other service sectors. As things now stand there is very little
congruence between the ways in which decisions are made about education, as compared to other social policy sectors. There is a good
deal of overlap in the territorial jurisdictions between (for
example) health, welfare, and schooling at the local level. But
the similarity ends there. Catchment areas for the three services
ordinarily differ within local jurisdictions, and problems, eligibility, and procedures also are defined differently. In addition,
the formal decision processes vary widely. They are local and
electoral in the case of schools, completely administrative and
dominated by state and federal agencies in the case of public assistance, and a mixture of state and federal administration in the case

1) See, for example, Murphy, J., Grease the Squeaky Wheel,
   Lexington Books, Boston, 1974.

101

of health. The role of quasi-governmental organisations also varies widely from one sector to another. In education standard setting is carried out by a variety of national testing, curriculum and professional organisations. In public assistance, however, standards are more centrally affected by the federal government, with some influence from professional groups, clients and the courts. Finally, clients' decision-making roles vary a good deal from one sector to another. In education their formal governance role as electorate is supreme in theory, but as clients and consumers of the service they have little room to manoeuvre within a sector dominated by administration and professionals. In health, though, consumers have little or no control over the governance of the service. They do have plenty of room to manoeuvre among service providers though - unless they are workers or poor people. And in the case of public assistance there is little role for clients at all, save legal action designed to change national regulations.

These differences among policy systems in various social service sectors explain why administrative co-ordination or consolidation among services is so difficult, and why service co-option has been a relatively successful approach to co-ordination in education. In the United States, extensive administrative and political changes are required for administrative co-ordination or consolidation, because of the great differences among social services. Co-option, however, avoids some of these problems. This, in turn, helps to explain the attractiveness of proposals designed to allow service consumers to achieve co-ordination themselves. Because of the large political barriers to co-ordination among existing service systems, the search for administrative rationality often seems less sensible than consumer entitlement as an avenue to greater coherence in social services.

Finally, these differences among decision networks for social services remind us that the services are not simply administrative units. They are really quite complicated social systems - with distinct traditions, social territories, role definitions, decision systems and allocations of power. In many respects they are social icebergs, for the exposed and publically administered portions are typically less substantial and less important than those larger portions which are neither clearly visible nor easily subject to public control.

2. Inducements to co-ordination

Typically, co-ordination is supposed either to reduce administrative overlap or to improve service delivery. Both are sensible rationales, but the United States experience suggests that co-ordination is not brought about by sensible rationales. In fact, many approaches to co-ordination are essentially hortatory - the rhetoric seems appealing, but the inducements are weak. Earlier in the essay I mentioned three sorts of incentives - economic, political, and bureaucratic - but pointed out that most inducements for co-ordinated action in education were bureaucratic and weak. Most co-ordination efforts in education, in the United States, have been marginal to ongoing enterprises, and outside of those few cases which involved total consolidation (the Office of Child Development, for example) rules have been promulgated within separate organisations, under conditions in which participation produced no serious consequences for the constituent agencies. Co-ordination of education services in Model Cities, for example, seems generally to have involved little more than arranging administrative evidence that joint agency approval of existing programmes had been secured. Roughly the same result appeared in various antipoverty programme efforts at co-ordination. Thus, even when programme funding depended on evidence of co-ordination, mostly this seems to have been achieved by a form of organisational détente, in which agency turfs were left intact and the evidence of co-ordination was purely formal.

One alternative might be to arrange the governance of social services in such a way that various interested parties, including clients, could express preferences. Thus, if there were real demands for co-ordination, governing agencies could transmit the pressures to service administrations. Such an approach is technically feasible at the local level in the United States, simply by establishing neighbourhood community service corporations governed by elected local boards. Organisations of this sort have been established in several places.

There is, however, no reason to expect that much co-ordination would result from such a governance scheme. A neighbourhood agency would be subject to considerable counter pressure from established agencies, professional groups and local governments, and could not reasonably be expected to overcome these forces for separation. At most they could provide pressure for marginal changes in the configuration of services, for the structure of social service organisations offers powerful inducements for isolated action.

I think this would be true even if intergovernmental grants were used to offer economic incentives for programme co-ordination. Evidence from Model Cities and Community Action Programmes (CAP) - as well as from recent education programmes - makes me dubious about the prospect of achieving co-ordination by way of fiscal incentives to administrative agencies. At least when the incentive is approval of programme monies, experience suggests that agencies will co-ordinate paperwork, but will not seriously collaborate in service provision or planning.

If incentive grants for co-ordination were combined with client political power and pressure for co-ordination, this situation might be different. There is, however, no evidence of any such spontaneous pressure, nor is it likely to exist unless service consumers are more deeply involved in service management. One device which might accomplish this would be to establish neighbourhood service corporations and provide them with funds to offer incentive grants for service co-ordination. Such a combination of local governance and direct fiscal incentives seems attractive, but it would not be easy. It would require either federal legislation which would mandate that municipal services now centrally administered be radically de-centralised (an unlikely step for the federal legislature), or a system of federal grants with which such neighbourhood corporations could offer inducements to central municipal agencies or private suppliers to deliver services through such centres. Either way, the political and bureaucratic prospects are a bit intimidating.

The alternative - some form of consumer-based co-ordination system - is no less improbable. The idea of making consumers rather than agencies the pivotal unit of social service administration seems unlikely to sweep social policy by storm even though it offers an interesting way to shift incentives for co-ordinated action. The great appeal of this approach, of course, is that it would permit service consumers to make judgements about co-ordination, and would offer them some means of effecting the desired result. But one of the most formidable barriers is opposition to granting low-income citizens autonomy in the management of whatever state assistance they receive. Typically in the United States one purpose of such assistance has been to manage poor people, on the assumption that they are untrustworthy deviants. Another problem is uncertainty about the exact effects of providing such individual entitlements to consumers. It is by no means certain, for example, that the quality of services would be improved under such schemes - false advertising might be an alternative, or inflation. Nor is it clear that providers would respond to the economic incentive and offer services in neigh-bourhoods where they now are minimal or absent. In addition, such entitlements are appealing as a co-ordination strategy in direct relation to the number of service areas they cover. Co-ordination between education and housing by the low-income consumer might be better than nothing, but it is a limited approach to service co-ordination.

Thus there is some appeal in the notion of entitling service recipients to define their needs for co-ordination and empowering them to execute matters. There is even some reason to think arming consumers with cash (or vouchers) would be a sufficient inducement to service providers to make such schemes work. But political

resistance to such systems makes it quite unlikely that they will
soon be widely employed in the United States. And at this distance
it is difficult to see exactly what the elements in a consumer-
based system would be, even though one can discern the need for such
things as service regulation to prevent gouging or persistent
inequality due to higher ceiling costs, fair information, and so on.

3. Values and knowledge concerning services

Social services are provided by organisations, but they are
more than institutional phenomena. Each service rests on diagnoses
of client needs, or ideas about social or individual pathology.
Each involves assumptions about remedy. And each is underlaid by a
mixture of scientific knowledge and practical experience concerning
the links between needs on one hand and remedies on the other.
Social services are thus not just formal organisational systems -
they are also complicated intellectual and moral systems, and co-
ordination among them is likely to depend as much on values as on
organisation. It is possible to separate two important threads -
conceptions of service and formal knowledge - which probably influence
co-ordination efforts.

Conceptions of service: every social service is the embodiment
of diverse values and experience, accumulated over the course of
several generations. These values have many important aspects but
for our purposes it is most important to highlight assumptions about
the responsibility for social problems, ideologies of problem-
solving, and conceptions of client and professional roles. To vary
these assumptions is to vary entire world-views of how society works,
how problems arise, and how they ought to be solved. It is, more
often than not, to vary ideas about what should be co-ordinated,
and by whom.

In the case of public assistance in the United States, for
example, it was long assumed that those who qualified did so because
individual character defects for which they bore personal responsibility made self-support impossible. This made it almost impossible
to avoid the idea that society's responsibility should be limited
and aimed at returning recipients to work. It cast welfare as an
aspect of social policy concerned with eliminating individual defiance,
rather than solving socially-induced problems or meeting public
responsibilities for fairness. These ideas helped shape an approach
to problem-solving which was punitive, minimalist, and focused on
getting undeserving recipients back into the labour force. It
produced programmes which encouraged dependency and family instability,
and it made it hard to see beyond the welfare-work connection (to
health or child care, or training, for example) as areas for improved

service and co-ordination. Because of the idea that welfare recipients are personally defective and undisciplined, the "problem" of
welfare policy has been providing discipline and getting people to
work. This has tended to direct attention away from the complex and
societal problems which often bring people to welfare. It has also
made it intellectually and politically difficult to frame more
coherent policies.

Assumptions of this sort have an equally important effect in
thinking about co-ordination of services for education. Schooling
has never been conceived in nearly as single-purpose a way as public
assistance, but the shape of United States public education has been
strongly influenced by the notion that it could eliminate various
forms of deviance.(1) These motives contributed to a conception of
schooling as a form of remedial discipline - a sort of moral anti-
dote to the social pathologies found in cities. As a result the
profession was cast in a role which emphasised the responsibility
for disciplining what were seen as pathological groups, which stressed dependency and weakness in clients, and which generally cast
education more as a mechanism of social control than as an agency
for personal liberation. It is in part as a result of these ideas
about social reality - and the social reality they have produced -
that co-ordination for education is seen as a problem of relating
administrative agencies from above, rather than of constructing
coherent relations among social services from below.

Another way in which conceptions of service affect ideas about
co-ordination centres on ideas about what social services are supposed to accomplish. In the middle and late 19th century education
was conceived as a form of social control in a society increasingly
populated by deviants and marked by disorder. These notions were
overlaid on earlier ideas that education was an essential element
in making democracy work. By the early twentieth century, however,
education had become quite firmly established in the public mind as
an important prerequisite for economic success and occupational advancement. The schools' present organisation was strongly influenced
by the idea that they were society's central occupational selection
mechanism. Since mid-century, though, there has been a growing
tendency to regard schooling as an avenue to personal discovery,
liberation, or cultural development. The economic and political
effects of schooling have been de-emphasized in favour of its cultural and intellectual benefits.

---

1) An elegant study which documents this line of thought in social
   policy concerning education is Schultz, S., The Culture Factory,
   Boston Public Schools, 1789-1860, Oxford, N.Y. 1973.

These ideas about the purposes of education and the nature of schooling presently co-exist, of course, but each leads in a different direction. And each has different implications for co-ordination. Suppose schooling is thought to be principally an economic good, of value to individuals for its income and occupational effects and to society for its effect on economic growth and development. The critical co-ordination issues thus seem to centre on the relations between training and work (ordinarily a problem of co-ordination between schooling, other training, and private firms), and on ways in which the school system seems economically ineffective - as in the case of children from disadvantaged families. On the other hand, schooling might be conceived chiefly as a consumer good, of use to individuals in their search for self-realisation. Co-ordination would then seem a less important issue, and would tend to centre on connections between schools and other cultural organisations.

Such differences in conceptions of a social service affect not only ideas about sectors for co-ordination, but they also suggest different strategies. Because they involve different assumptions about professional client relations and the aims of education, they imply different approaches to co-ordination. The idea that education is an economic good of importance to individuals and society leads more or less naturally to increasing state involvement in educational planning, in the allocation of school resources, and in the relations between education, training, and the private sector. It leads, in other words, to the assertion of a strong state interest in co-ordination, and to a top-down administrative approach to co-ordination. This is evident in most discussions of national planning for education. By contrast, the idea that education is an intellectual and cultural good of interest chiefly to consumers leads more or less naturally to the idea that individual consumers, not the state, have a controlling interest in how schooling is arranged. This, in turn, suggests consumer-based approaches to co-ordination.

Conceptions of service, then, have a considerable impact on both priorities and strategies for co-ordination. Many definitions of social problems are possible, and there are alternative conceptions of remedies, professional responsibility, and client roles. In every social service ideas of this sort have shaped our perception of social reality and the reality itself - by way of specific definitions of problems posed, remedies delivered, and professional-client relations established. Although empirical evidence is relevant here, conceptions of social service and the ideas about co-ordination flowing from them are in good measure moral and political judgements. By and large, in the United States these ideas have

defined reality in such a way as to place a priority only on administrative co-ordination, and to de-emphasize clients' ability to define
and solve problems.

Knowledge about services: formal knowledge probably does not
have the same power to shape services as do beliefs. Nonetheless,
such knowledge is important to calculations about co-ordination.
The reliability of knowledge about solving social problems varies
among service sectors and within them, and this can affect the results
of co-ordination efforts.

One important source of variability in knowledge is policy or
programme outcomes. Most social programmes and policies contain
both unclear and reasonably specific goals, but the ratio of the two
varies a good deal. Programmes designed to provide educational
certification for paraprofessionals so they can qualify for better
jobs, involve some broad and hard-to-define goals - equality or
mobility, for example. On the other hand, it is relatively easy to
observe and measure the achievement of educational certification or
the attainment of jobs. By contrast, programmes for training pre-
school children to increase their social competency so they will not
fail in school and adult life are more than a little harder to deal
with. The broad social goals of such programmes are no easier to
define than in the case of paraprofessionals, and the short-range
out-comes are much harder. No one knows what social competency is,
and there are various notions about how to measure it. We know even
less about whether it affects performance in school or later life,
and if it does, how.

Now, it may not be harder - in a purely administrative sense -
to co-ordinate programmes with broad and fuzzy aims than programmes
with narrow and clear aims. But it certainly is harder to distinguish
effective from ineffective action in the first case than in the
second. One does not know that co-ordinating educational, health,
and family support services will actually produce more social competency in children. Nor, if it succeeds or fails, does one know
why. As a result, the co-ordination work occurs in a less organised
and intelligible environment. This makes the circumstances of such
efforts more difficult, because it is never clear whether a particular approach will have the desired effect, or just what the desired
effect is. Co-ordination is more an exploratory venture than anything
else.

These are not insuperable difficulties - experience with education and other services shows that most co-ordination efforts occur
under just such circumstances. Indeed, knowledge in education
generally is such that unless the goal of programmes and policies is
delivering resources (which includes everything from getting money
and services to schools to getting students certificates), it is very

108

difficult to speak with much confidence either about the appropriate-
ness of outcome measures or the nature of underlying processes.(1)
But this situation produces a particularly pathological phenomenon
in efforts at co-ordination. Because we have such a relatively
modest understanding of how education occurs, unsuccessful experiences
with co-ordination are generally interpreted as evidence that not
enough co-ordination occurred. Because there is no relatively clear
criterion of policy outcome or programme effectiveness, it is easy
for social service workers and administrators to interpret the frequently negative results of co-ordination efforts as nothing more
than evidence that not enough co-ordination was achieved. This may
be either self-serving, or the result of a humanitarian concern
that clients receive an adequate range of services in a convenient
way irrespective of evaluative criteria. But in either event, it
makes the task of planning, interpreting, and evaluating efforts at
co-ordination between education and other social services much more
difficult.

While this suggests some general cautions, it does not mean that
the uncertainty of existing knowledge is prohibitive. In large
areas of education the knowledge base is remarkably uncertain, and
not likely to improve rapidly. In these areas - which can be roughly
summarised as the acquisition of broad social and intellectual competencies - co-ordination efforts will continue to be explorations
of the unknown. On the other hand, there are more specific skills
which are more or less rationally related to training (teaching
executives new budgeting systems, or workers new production techniques), and there is a considerable realm concerned with service
delivery. Here the base of knowledge is noticeably more substantial,
and efforts at co-ordination could be expected to proceed on a somewhat firmer footing.

This section has enumerated and briefly discussed the factors
which seem likely to influence the results of co-ordination efforts.
These are factors which might be borne in mind when considering
sectors for co-ordination or weighing alternative co-ordination
strategies, and they might be useful points of reference in efforts
to learn from co-ordination efforts mounted in the future. But the
chief point of this discussion of course, is the conclusion it
suggests about co-ordination itself: wherever we turn, there are
substantial barriers. The incentives for such action are weak, the
administrative and political structures involved typically are not
congruent, belief and custom predispose us to a particularly narrow

---

1) Bissel, J., White, S., and Golenski, J., "Knowledge in Education".
   Paper presented at the National Institute for Education Symposium
   on Educational Research and Development, Washington D.C., 11th-12th
   December, 1972.

view of co-ordination, and large segments of our knowledge are very weak. While there are some areas in which efforts might proceed with a decent prospect of success, these are not likely to be high on national priority lists.

IV. CONCLUSION

This paper highlights a paradox which lies close to the heart of the co-ordination issue. I began by arguing that co-ordination became an increasingly important problem in social policy because of an increasing awareness of service overlaps, boundary collisions, and shared territory. I then argued that the chief barriers to effective co-ordination arise from distinctive organisational networks within each service sector, from the absence of incentives for action out of channels, and from beliefs about social problems and solutions which reinforce sectoral thinking and administrative approaches to co-ordination. Ironically, though, these different developments have a common root. The expansion of social policy and the growth of the welfare state caused the overlaps and collisions which seem to make co-ordination necessary. They also are the source of the beliefs and organisations which appear to stand in the way of co-ordination.

This does not mean that co-ordination efforts will inevitably come to grief. But it does mean that the continued growth of social service administration, and the persistence of ideas about social policy which tend to collect responsibility in agencies rather than locating it in clients, are among the most important barriers to co-ordination. It also suggests that continuing a purely adminis- trative approach to co-ordination of services will probably produce - in the United States at least - the same marginal results as reported here. If this analysis is roughly correct, it might be wise to explore approaches to co-ordination which would offer consumers more control over the definition of social problems and the construction of remedies. This would be a difficult path, because of existing power, uncertainty about the impact of such efforts, and the greater costs of providing choice in social services. There is little evidence that in the short run, at any rate, such approaches will succeed. But it might be a way to promote co-ordination between education and other social services in the United States without compounding the problems previous efforts have produced.

ANALYSIS OF OBSTACLES AT THE
INSTITUTIONAL LEVEL

by Maurice Kogan

I. INTRODUCTION

In this paper, Social Planning is taken to mean systematic social intervention. It is thus a form of inter-sectoral planning between the social service areas of education, health, personal welfare services (or social services), housing, town planning and social security. The examples used in this paper are derived from British experience of these areas but it would be surprising if some of the generalisations did not also apply to other OECD countries.

The underlying assumptions of this paper are that while social problems present themselves in a complex skein of deficiencies, deprivations and alienations, they ultimately focus on discernible groups - communities, families and individuals - and that the responses to them must, therefore, be focused and comprehensive. The need for integration is accepted, at least in theory, by British social welfare administrators and observers. So far, the scepticism of say, Wildavsky[1] or Lindblom and Braybrooke[2] about the ability of government to predict social futures synoptically, or the dangers to democracy and individual rights of reinforcing labelling, or technocractically prescribing community futures, have hardly become translated into the British context; the difficulties are seen more to be that British social provision is benign but muddled so that it is to be sharpened up and improved rather than reduced in power.

---

1) Aaron Wildavsky, "The Political Economy of Efficiency: Cost Benefit Analysis, Systems Analysis and Program Budgeting", Public Administration Review, December 1966.

2) David Braybrooke and Charles E. Lindblom, A Strategy of Decision. Policy Evaluation of the Social Process, The Free Press, New York, 1963.

and

Charles E. Lindblom, The Intelligence of Democracy: Decision Making Through Mutual Adjustment, The Free Press, New York, Collier-Macmillan Ltd., London, 1965.

Opposition to synoptic planning is sporadic and on a fairly narrow set of issues.(1)

The precise issues discussed here are, therefore, the obstacles which stand in the way of connecting principal social and welfare services provided by three separate sets of public authorities: local government, the health authorities and the Ministry of Social Security. The paper attempts to show that the different services have identifiably different value emphases and that these, together with other institutional characteristics, make inter-sectoralism difficult to achieve. It is further assumed that the difficulties do not all result from bureaucratic separatism but may derive, in part, from the needs of different areas to present different points of view, different expertise, and, indeed, some choice for recipients, as between different services at the same time as they usefully connect with other areas. Thus even if differences are conflictual, they may be fruitfully so. One service might have the function of testing, as an adversary, the policies of another.

The issues discussed in the paper are as follows:

a) the ways in which assumptions about social planning are revealing themselves in British institutions (Part II);
b) related aspects of British central government organisation (Part III);
c) the questions arising from conflicts, congruencies and parallelisms of values in different institutions (Part IV);
d) disjunctions caused by different institutional structures (Part V);
e) ways towards inter-sectoralism (Part VI).

II. THE TREND TOWARDS SOCIAL PLANNING

There are several themes in the present development of social planning. Perhaps the strongest drive towards integration has come from physical land planning although it has often been arbitary and coercive in its assumptions and methods. Town planners increasingly perceive development as concerning whole areas and assume consensus about the constituents of, and arrangements for, total environments which too quickly cease to exist merely in the planners' minds and become incorporated in cement and aluminium. While, however, planners are strongly oriented towards spatial aspects of planning, and

---

1) For example, the objections raised to the various proposals for the siting of the third London Airport. Such leading British policy analysts as David Donnison or Peter Self have pointed out the impossibility of making decisions such as this without synoptic decision making.

their education is not concerned sufficiently with decision making, organisational issues, human behaviour and value systems, there is some movement towards making them more sensitive towards community structure and related social services.(1) A further contribution towards social planning is embodied in the somewhat vague schemes known as "community development".(2) Thirdly, the development of corporate management in local government and other public agencies is directed towards ensuring that complex organisations can pursue more than one objective simultaneously but that there will be cross-over points within organisations where priorities between potentially conflicting objectives can be decided.

So there are strong trends towards inter-sectoral planning but they are somewhat unsystematic and insufficient thought has been given to the purpose, nor has there been enough work on detailed consequences.

III. DEVELOPMENTS IN CENTRAL GOVERNMENT

British central government has increasingly placed more emphasis on co-ordination among areas and on the analysis of objectives, and of the programmes pursuing them, in different areas, so that options can be set up for ministerial decision.(3) But the developments have been superficial because concerned mainly with super-structural organisation. The following points can be observed within the British context:

    a)   at central government level, inter-sectoral planning has related more successfully to resources control and programming than to creative development of services. To some extent this emphasis is inevitable, because in multi-level organisations the higher levels necessarily exercise control through resource allocations and leave the substantive content of services to be created by professionals at the subordinate levels. But the higher levels also create the organisational patterns, without, perhaps, enough thought about the non-resource aspects of inter-sectoralism. The

---

1) Report of a Working Group at the Centre for Environmental Studies, London, "The Development of Knowledge and Capability for Urban Governments", Pergamon Press, 1973.

2) There is no sustained literature on "community development" as yet. But the British Home Office has financed several community development projects which are now recognised as relating to uncertain objectives and working through indeterminate methodologies.

3) The Reorganisation of Central Government (White Paper: Cmnd.4506), HMSO, 1970.

changes in organisational patterns have been centred on the Treasury in spite of important competition as in the Central Policy Review Staff (located in the Cabinet Office). So the most powerful integrative creations have been in forward expenditure survey through a Treasury-led Public Expenditure Survey Committee, the creation of Programme Analysis Review machinery in the departments which relates to a central unit within the Treasury. The Central Policy Review Staff (the "Capability Unit"), located in the Cabinet Office, reports to the Prime Minister and has exceedingly eclectic terms of reference ranging from the organisation and funding of government research and development to problems of immigrants. These developments are more related to establishing resource flexibility and control than to ways in which integrated patterns of social policy might be built up;

b) mega-ministries have been created. They are evidence of government organisation planners' belief that government must be co-ordinated and unitary if it is to be effective in the fields of public policy, including social intervention. Since the mid-60s there has been the combination of, for example, departments responsible for lower and higher education, and science, into a single Department of Education and Science. The Department of the Environment now contains what was hitherto managed by the Ministry of Housing and Local Government (itself a large amalgam of previous ministerial independencies), the Ministry of Transport and the Ministry of Public Buildings and Works. At a recent count it had nine Deputy Secretaries, 87 Under Secretaries, and 289 Assistant Secretaries. The Department of Health took over most of the personal social service work of the Home Office, and also added social security. This has not of itself made central government more systematic in its treatment of such problems as urban deprivation, which is still tackled by two units in the Home Office, by the Department of Education and Science, the Department of Health and Social Security, and the Department of the Environment;

c) at the more local level, there have been equivalent movements towards integration in local government and health service organisation. The former Children's, Welfare and Health Departments have been combined into single Social Service Departments or, in Scotland, into Social Work Departments (which include probation as well). The three parts of the National Health Service - hospitals, family practitioner services and local authority health services - have been united into a single service. Attempts are being made to co-ordinate the separate health and local authority services with overlapping membership of joint consultative committees of the authorities themselves, and by the creation of roles jointly accountable to both sets of authorities;

d) at the same time, units of local and health service government have become larger so as to ensure that authorities will be both economically powerful as well as unitary. (Only in one major respect has the trend towards unitaryness been frustrated: the government rejected the proposals of the Royal Commission on Local Government(1) that all personal social services should be administered at one tier. In large parts of the country, housing and physical planning will be separate from education and social services).

The "horizontality" or integration theme described above has not, however, been carried far enough to meet the objectives set for it:

a) the movements in organisation make no real difference because connections are made at too high a point to resolve problems in the field. The single Secretary of State, with unified financial, planning, research and development divisions may ensure that priorities can be established over a wider field, but cannot take account of the detailed fabric of the institutions, and of the values and policies which need to be stitched together if effective social planning is to result. This generalisation can be supported not only by the example of British government but also by the difficulties encountered by the American Department of Health, Education and Welfare in making adequate connections between the programmes in different spheres which are effectively controlled at the political level by separate commissioners under a somewhat distant Secretary;(2)

b) national policies are unrelated at the delivery point, as well as at the centre. A single local authority has to relate to several government departments for education, health, social services, housing, local government matters, transport and police because local authorities have to seek

_____

1) Report of the Examiners, OECD Reviews of National Policies for Education, United States. OECD, Paris, 1971.

2) T.H. Marshall, Social Policy in the Twentieth Century, Hutchinson, 1970. (Revised edition).

approval on many issues from the Secretaries of State for
Education and Science, Health, Environment, and Home
Secretary. While they receive finance from unified sources
(rate support grants from the centre, and local land taxes
"rates"), the legal routes of approval are diverse, complicated and require large efforts of planning to bring into
a single process. Government is thus disjointed in the way
in which it faces some of the main agents of social
intervention;

c) at the local level it is difficult not only to integrate
    departments within unitary local authorities but also to
    relate their work to that of the separate health and income
    support agencies;

d) at both the central and local levels the professional
    advisory and inspectorial services are not well connected.
    For example, there are 500 central government inspectors
    (HMIs) and 3,000 local government inspectors in education,
    but only 70 social work advisers at central level in social
    work. There are no equivalent advisory and inspectorial
    systems for housing or planning, and there is a newly
    formed and somewhat specialist Hospital Advisory Service
    which does not carry the same breadth of functions as do
    the inspectorates in education and health. It is not at
    all clear that these central government professional groups
    relate strongly with each other on matters of common concern.
    They have, too, their own patterns and suffer from role
    conflict between advisory and monitoring or inspectorial
    aspects of their work;

e) there is also great unevenness in the extent to which cen-
    tral government calls upon external research and development.

The trend towards social planning is thus strong but not well
defined or made operational at the centre. But the difficulties are
greatest at the working level and the remaining paragraphs of this
paper are concerned with social planning at the institutional level,
and at the governing levels below those of central government, except
when we return to discuss possible future action and studies in
Britain, at the end of the paper. The discussion will be related
to each of the following services: education, housing, health, social
welfare (social services), and social security.

IV. AN OUTLINE OF ANALYSIS FOR SOCIAL SERVICE INSTITUTIONS

From the point of view of systematic social intervention at the
institutional level, it is necessary to identify those aspects of

116

each service which give it distinctive identity and which affect its
ability to work fruitfully with other services. The main differen-
tiators can be listed as follows:

a) the underlying or basic values present in each service;
the extent to which they are common to other services or
distinctive to the individual service; the extent to which
they are presented to other services as adversarial or conflictual, or congruent or additive; the extent to which
they are intrinsic to the work that must be done or volatile
as to time and fashion;

b) the objectives or intended outputs and the activities or
intended inputs of each service, and the degrees of congruence and conflict with other services;

c) the client base of each service as it affects values,
objectives and activities;

d) the patterns and content of training and recruitment for
each service;

e) institutional and organisational factors of each service,
such as:

   i)   patterns of delegation, particularly to the "prime"
        institutions;

   ii) the sizes of institutions;

   iii) the effects of building stocks on the development
        of each service;

f) the different statuses of professional groups in each
service.

All of the points listed in the above paragraph relate to each
other. Thus values may relate to the technology of a sector. For
example, the housing manager may want to prescribe for individual
clients but the technology of house design, production, and maintenance, impels him to make mass prescriptions as to standards of
service and control of tenancies. By contrast, doctors can hardly
ever prescribe "en masse" (except in certain aspects of public and
preventative medicine such as immunisation procedures).

V . VALUES

The main social and welfare agencies present varied and changing
ranges of social values. The statements of the founding fathers of
social administrative studies in the United Kingdom reveal some of
the differences in emphasis. They refer variously to "having a
direct impact on the welfare of the citizens, by providing them with
a service or income",(1) or "which reduce(s) alienation or enhances

---

1) R.H. Titmuss, Commitment to Welfare, Allen and Unwin, 1968.

a sense of community",(1) or "the integrative system,(2) or "a service rendered by, or on behalf of, the community, and individuals or at most a family, for its exclusive use and contains an element of re-distribution",(3) or as policy having economic growth and the dis-tribution of resources as the two predominant themes.(4)

It is possible to extend such assumptions into a list of basic values which underlie British social policies. Basic values should be differentiated from their instrumental consequences. Thus, the universality and selectivity argument is not about basic values but about such corollaries as the extent to which the educational priority area policy is both selective and egalitarian or the granting of tax relief on mortgage interest is non-selective and non-egalitarian.

Basic values are subject to changes of terminology and of status. For example, it is assumed in British social legislation that the notion of protecting and maintaining the family does not require further argument because "the family" is a basic value in itself. Plainly, however, in other cultures it could be an instrumental con-sequence of such basic values as the preservation of inter-personal values, or of the defence of society.

From a study of British welfare state provision and from inter-views with specialists in different fields, the following list of basic social policy values, which seem to underlie British social legislation, has been derived:

1. Helping the inadequate.
2. Equality.
3. Equity.
4. Worth of the unique individual.
5. Individual effort.
6. Self-determination.
7. Freedom.
8. Choice of life style.
9. Sense of community.
10. Family.
11. Inter-personal values.
12. Minimum living standards.
13. Economic growth.
14. Progress and change.
15. Defence of society.
16. Retribution.

1) Kenneth Boulding, "The Boundaries of Social Policy", Social Work, Vol. 12, 1967.

2) I. McLeod and E. Powell, The Social Services, Needs and Means, Conservative Political Centre, 1954.

3) David Donnison, "Ideologies and Policies", Journal of Social Policy, Vol. 1, Part 2, April, 1972.

4) "The Development of Knowledge and Capability for Urban Governments", op. cit.

Basic Values in the Different Services

To some extent, all social services are party to all or most of the values listed in paragraph 15. Their practitioners have more in common than with leaders of the private sector. No town planner or housing manager would accept that he is not concerned with helping the inadequate, or, to some degree at least, with egalitarianism or of enabling individuals to be free, self-determining or to choose their own life styles, though observers would impute more strongly other basic values to housing and planning policies. Doctors, teachers and social workers are concerned with social control and socialisation processes which, willing or not, make them party to the defence of society though they themselves would claim that personal autonomy and self-sufficiency is their prime aim for their clients. Perhaps only retribution would have no backers at all.

Moreover, as succeeding paragraphs will demonstrate, values are volatile in that they change over time in the different services and, at any one time, different layers of values pile on to each other, with individual practitioners emphasizing one and simultaneously others emphasizing another group of values. It is not, therefore, easy to see which values are intrinsic to the processes or services being administered and which are subject to changes in wider social or economic philosophy.

With all these reservations, then, we can only approximately attribute values differentially and then in the knowledge that they change, and, hopefully from our point of view, can be changed by reorientation in training and other patterns. Having said this, what differentiations can be made? Here are some:

a) doctors are trained to be concerned with the prescription, by them as individuals, for individual patients. They are also trained, as are nurses and other para-medical workers, to be coldly "scientific", and non-involved with individual patients. This is, it is argued, the predominant ethic in the health services. It is clearly changing as community health services and such social medical specialities as mental health or geriatrics become stronger. It was also not always thus: public health led British medical science in the nineteenth century. But the present interest in the development of community for its own sake is likely to come from education or social service rather than health practitioners;

b) doctors emphasize individual relationships for technological and ethical reasons. Teachers and social workers in the most recent British tradition advance individualistic and libertarian assumptions (the worth of the unique individual,

of individual effort, or self-determination, of personal
freedom, of a choice of life style - "all human behaviour
is explainable") as values in their own right. There is
also a technological justification: that children learn
best if they follow their own interests, that deviants are
best helped back to "normality" by a display of respect for
their own needs. Again, however, this essentially individualistic approach, deriving as it does from psycho-analytic
models in social work, is overlaid by virtually every other
social policy value. The community school, community development are regarded as hoped for but difficult to achieve
objectives but relate well to such anti-alienation values
as the preservation of the family, and development of good
inter-personal relations. And other "harder values" -
defence of society, economic growth or maintenance are also
there. If the order of preference is as stated here it
could be said that education and social services are both
the most ambitious of the services and the most volatile
because, more than any other service, they are concerned
with values relating to concept of the whole man, and his
potential perfectibility through benign human relationships.
But emphasis on the individual first, and society and the
economy last, is essentially an artefact of British social
thinking in the 1960s and 1970s. That they are volatile as
to time and place and not intrinsic to education and social
services as such is plain from comparison with other far
more prescriptive and collectively orientated societies.

Social security provision is ambiguous in its values. It takes
its overriding precepts from clearly stated norms of the income that
clients will need, at the minimum, to sustain them. But increasingly,
supplementary benefits officers in the 500 offices of the Supplementary Benefits Commission are given discretion to view individual
needs within broader social contexts and in relation to provision
made by local authority housing, social services and education
departments. But notwithstanding a widening of parameters, it is
still largely concerned with the individualistic values as well as
the minimum living standards, helping the inadequate values range.

Housing authorities are concerned with individual needs as has
been described in paragraph 11, perhaps because of the technology of
what they provide, perhaps because housing is so prevalently tied
up with ascribed social statuses as much as with the defence of
society, or at least the defence of social assets, of minimum living
standards, of individual effort, or helping the inadequate rather
than with the more libertarian of the individualistic values such
as promotion of freedom or choice of life style, or with the

anti-alienation and community values. Housing managers are concerned
with the defence of public assets and other "hard concepts" of public
utility. Their values lie as much in accountability towards those
who pay for public housing as to those who use it. Hence, there is
room for conflict between them and social workers on rent arrears,
and with education authorities on how basic housing developments
should be planned. But, again, they could be educated to change.

Similarly, <u>planning authorities</u> might well declare that they
act in favour of individual choice. Their values are, however, more
related to the "hard" policies of ensuring that social arrangements
are defended though appropriate physical planning flows freely.
Town planners are primarily concerned with a kind of social hygiene
which ensures that spatial relationships function well, that traffic
flows freely, and that there shall not be an undue mix up between
different categories of users. "The principal means of implementation of development plans still remains first, the nature and location of capital projects of the local authority itself and second,
development control regarding use of land or buildings by agencies,
public and private...... The structure plan...... is not a policy
plan for the community inhabiting that area and the local authority's
many roles in the community other than those affecting his environment."(1) So teachers and social workers might spend quite a deal of
time in building up community networks within a quite small catchment only to find that planners are concerned to break up those
communities in the interests of flow and mobility.

Changes in Values

The statements about values in different services above imply
that values change over time. Technology develops over time. In
the most personal of services - mental health, teaching-learning
processes, social welfare - the modern practitioner expects to use
techniques varying from person to person - casework to wide-scale
community action. Housing managers are beginning to accept social
scientific perceptions as part of some of their advanced training
courses. Social security officers increasingly exercise their discretion in relation to social service perceptions.

So values are sometimes additive to the point where a change of
overall orientation takes place in a service. Historical analysis
might show, for example, that:

    a) in social welfare services, the retributive and control
       values were dominant until the legislation of the 1930s.
       At that time personal autonomy values began to be more
       strongly established. In the 1960s and early 1970s

1) P. Blau and W. Scott, <u>Formal Organisations</u>, Routledge & Kegan
    Paul, 1963.

egalitarian and integrative values have become obvious. All
strands are present in social welfare work, and cause ambig-
uity for the social workers;

b) in education, the control and economic well-being values
have always been present. In Britain, however, personal
development and autonomy have been proclaimed purposes of
schooling. The "payment by results" system was disbanded
in 1898. Successive reports of the Consultative Committees
and Central Advisory Councils (the Hadow Report in 1926 to
Plowden in 1967) celebrated doctrines of individual child
development. A sense of community and inter-personal relations were exemplified in the Cambridgeshire village colleges
in the 1930s and are now evident in sporadic attempts to
devise community schools. Egalitarian and redistributive
doctrines have changed from the "soft" to the "hard" concept of equality as in proposals for educational priority
areas in the mid-1960s;

c) in health provision, egalitarian concepts were most strongly
present in the 1946 Act which established the National Health
Service with its emphasis on free and universal provision.
The personal autonomy values are implicit in the view of
clinical non-judgemental treatment. They have always been
present. Historically there may have been a missionary or
even evangelical values in health service. But the integrative or inter-personal values are now not strongly present in the health service, although the "good" general
practitioner always emphasized the family. There may,
moreover, be a move to community values, evinced in the
development of the community physician, of community health
councils, and current emphases on the treatment of the
mentally ill and handicapped and of the elderly. Adequate
personal functioning could be regarded as reducing other
charges on the economy. The defence of society or control
values are present in mental health legislation;

d) in the field of town planning, there have been major changes
from detailed defence of society values (not placing a
crematorium next to a primary school, for example) or controlling the inconsistent uses of land to far more sensitive anxieties about integration of communities, whilst
personal autonomy values are safeguarded.

Reversibility

Policies are presented in a complex public authority not only
as having positive merits but also in reaction to policies being
presented elsewhere. Sometimes there is open conflict and no

possible accommodation between obviously divergent values and professional practices. At that point the public authority must either act inconsistently or make a choice between two different sets of advice or practice. But divergence need not always lead to crude and simple conflict but might take more constructive forms. So values are operationally "reversible". A basic value is one which is proposed as self-evidently valid and defensible. Thus, a social service department might argue that freedom to choose individual life styles, or assisting self-determination and helping the inadequate are values which should lead them to support a "bad" housing tenant. These positive values are reversed when presented to the housing department who regard them as reservations or prescriptions affecting <u>their</u> basic values which are concerned with the defence of society, the defence of the economy, the worth of individual effort. The concept of reversibility, of a positive value becoming restrictive seems to get over the danger of crudely asserting that values are <u>necessarily</u> in conflict when, in fact, they might be in a parallel, or in a controlling, or limiting, relationship with the positive statement of basic values. This does not mean that all conflict goes. It might mean that conflict can become part of an authorised and ascribed role when different professionalisms have to work together.

The concept of reversibility relates to a positive function which might be called "adversarial". It is, for example, the task of one department to test the values and policies of another related department in such a way as to ensure that housing takes note of social services and education of health considerations.

This must be the type of inter-departmental transaction implied by corporate management or matrix organisation. Case conferences between services, matrix forms of administration in which integrated projects can be planned, are known in Britain and are becoming increasingly used. But it may be questioned whether pluralism of values, as displayed in the activities stipulated for the different departments, is not both inevitable and natural. It may well be that in displaying this range of values, and in working according to these different lights, the departments are expressing a fuller range of human needs and attitudes. The control and safeguarding of resources by housing managers, the social controls employed by teachers and social workers, the clinical detachment of a doctor who should not lose his cool in the face of human misery, may have no less legitimacy than the more obviously altruistic motives of the teacher and social worker and health visitor. And pluralism and conflict can be part of the dynamics of change and a means of clarifying objectives more realistically.

Objectives and Activities

From the volatile and uncertain complexes of values we can turn to somewhat more prescriptive statements of values in action, of what is now put into the services in terms of sanctioned activities and what are the intended outputs, or sanctioned objectives. The status of these statements should be made clear. They are the activities as they can be analysed in the institutions in Britain in 1974, and the objectives as they can be derived indirectly, again, since British legislation and other official statements are extremely unexplicit as to the purposes or hoped-for outcome.

The attached charts contain statements of activities, and objectives, and the values to which they might be related. But it will be seen, immediately, that there is no easily discernible relationship between the three separate sets of statements. Whilst objectives of the services relate to basic values (possibly because assumptions about values have been derived, in this paper, from what is known about the objectives of the services), the activities and statements of inputs cannot thus be related. They are essentially statements of resource inputs rather than statements of intention related to purposes. Moreover, there is the usual problem of establishing the viewpoint of objectives and activities in terms of the levels from which they are being viewed: a statement of a school teacher's objectives is bound to be different from those of the Secretary of State for Education and Science. And, indeed, although both of these are engaged in "educational" activities, job descriptions would show very different contributions towards the teaching-learning process or contributions to concepts of educational equality.

The statements of activities are, perhaps, most useful inasmuch as they show the possibility of working connections between the different services. This, again, is shown in the chart.

The activities shown in the charts are lists agreed in various field studies undertaken by Brunel University teams in health, social services and education research. The housing activities have also been worked out with a seminar largely consisting of housing managers and practitioners. The planning functions have been taken from the Bains Report on Local Government. No equivalent list is available for social security. It should be noted that the activities have been created unsystematically and without conscious reference to objectives, let alone basic values. It should also be noted that they are maximum statements of activities. There are, for example, few housing departments that have so wide a range of functions as is implied in the chart.

Client Bases

Clients differ in type, expectations and catchment areas and sizes. These differences affect organisational patterns(1) as well as values, objectives and activities. All of the services discussed in this paper are theoretically accountable for serving the whole community. But as the following notes show, the relationships with clients are varied:

a) Education is the only service which is compulsory for the whole population throughout substantive periods of their life. It has the largest number of institutions (some thirty thousand schools in England and Wales) at neighbourhood level. The relationship is usually to the school rather than to the teacher (in contrast to health or social services). The non-compulsory areas of education such as nursery or further or higher education, take on somewhat different institutional characteristics;

b) Health. Relationships with health service clients vary greatly between such different specialities as surgery, mental health, physical medicine. But the predominant assumption is of technical and esoteric services given to clients who can help themselves by collaborating with the health service practitioners, and whose views on the nature of the service given might contribute towards service but will not improve their substantive concepts. This assumption will become increasingly tested as community health councils become established under the law in Britain. There is not, except in the case of long stay hospitals, a continuous relationship, or, except in a minority of mental health cases, a mandatory relationship;

c) Housing clients are predominantly those in need with whom a relationship of control or "support" is sustained to ensure that tenants maintain public property and pay rent, as well as giving services to tenants. On this basis, there is no obvious way of achieving reciprocity between clients and administration. Other and new housing functions are projected towards providing advisory services to private tenants and landlords, housing associations, and so on. This may make for a broader, community relationship with clientele;

d) Planning. Theoretically the whole community is the town planner's client. Increasingly, town planning procedures

---

1) Adrian Webb, "Social Service Administration: A Typology for Research", Public Administration, Autumn 1971, Vol. 49.

have been designed to become more reciprocal with public
demands and criticisms (the Skeffington Report of 1969
proposed public forums and displays, some of which have
been put into use in local authority areas). The work of
town planners is, however, still considered to be remote
and difficult for citizens to comprehend:

e) Social Services. Relationships with clients are volatile.
Many procedures are still those of individual or family
casework often starting from a point of distress or control
activity. But probably 75 per cent or so of specific services given are not casework. Increasingly, however, community development and egalitarian assumptions in social
work are in conflict with case work. Concepts of community
power lead to stronger demands for reciprocity with clients
by detecting their feelings about needs and provisions;

f) Social Security clients are those definably in need.

The differences in client bases, in the attitudes of the professionals and administrators towards the different client groups,
are yet another difficulty in the way of social planning. These
differences are becoming all the clearer as review and criticism
machinery is created piecemeal: Ombudsmen for government administered services such as health and social security, community health
councils, governing bodies for schools, and open forum procedures for
planning.

Training Patterns

The patterns of training vary widely in relation to technological and value assumptions. Social work and teacher training have
many similarities with their emphasis on personal relationships and
the development of individual skills or self-dependence and these are
in strong contrast to far "harder" and more impersonal assumptions
in medicine, housing and planning.

The cost and status of training also vary widely. In Britain,
the order of status is: medical, town planners, teachers, social
workers, housing administrators, non-medical health services. Of
these, at present, only medical education automatically carries with
it graduate status although all of the others, roughly in the order
listed here, are beginning to provide full degree or postgraduate
courses. These differences in educational admissions qualifications,
and status of qualification acquired, undoubtedly make for status
differences within or between authorities.

There are historical differences in training patterns which
relate to differences in the build up of different services. Thus,
medical education has had a flow of finance and manpower to keep
up with demand (although notions of demand and the ability of the

system to meet it have been variable). Teacher training underwent
a dramatic expansion in the late 1950s and 1960s. Social work
began its largest expansion at the beginning of the 1970s; two
smaller expansions followed legislation in 1948 and 1962. Education
for housing management has hardly begun. The significance of these
differences lies in the fact that there are opportunity waves and
troughs in the different services which create generations of
leaders who carry with them the assumptions of their generations.
So education is "open", liberal and progressive in its assumptions
and is likely to remain so against severe criticism from the new
psychological rigourists and political conservatives; its leadership was recruited between 1945 and 1965. By contrast, social work
has hitherto been conditioned by the psycho-analytic approach of
the early child care officers and training for psychiatric social
workers and, at the same time, by the somewhat more traditional views
of the welfare and mental health officers. The psycho-analytic model
faded from 1960 onwards in many courses; by 1965 the balance was
fairly even between psychology and sociology and much of the teaching
moved from psycho-analysis to behaviourist, learning theory approaches.
The expansion in the 1970s will probably bring with it a new generation of whom half will be graduates and whose basic orientation may
well be sociological rather than psychological and who are critical
of present public service values. Housing managers are essentially
trained in concepts of public utility rather than those arising from
psychology and sociology. Town planning education has not yet
caught up with the full range of sociological, psychological and
organisational disciplines although attempts are being made to influence syllabuses (as in the Amos Working Party Report, 1973).
When these different groups of professionals meet in a corporate
planning network they will start with pre-suppositions derived from
different generations of training and education.

VI. INSTITUTIONAL FACTORS

The Prime Institutions

Values, client base, training are all important determiners of
relationships between the sectors. But other institutional factors
are also important. It is thus possible to view a typical administrative area as containing a range of different size and different
values-oriented institutions: a large hospital, 200 schoool, 10
social work area teams, a planning and a housing department, a social
security office. What are the prime units between which connections
must be made? What is the "prime" institution? By prime institution
is meant an institution to which enough authority is delegated for
it to produce a reasonably coherent and viable set of services.

Examination of the main social welfare institutions will show that such authority and competence are to be found at very different levels in the different services. The following characteristics might be noted:

a) in education, the British school or college is an institution to which adequate authority is delegated for it to be a comprehensible and clearly identified point of service delivery. It has a distinct catchment area. Its head is an identified public person, his name appears on the notepaper and on the board outside the school. It is received wisdom in the British education service that schools are largely responsible for their curriculum and for their internal organisation. The school contains a full enough range of professional workers and services under the management of the head, including the school meals service, the maintenance of plant and, where they are available, counselling services, for the main operational activities of the education service to be provided through its agency. It is thus a prime institution;

b) in the social services departments, the question arises as to whether the whole department is the prime institution of whether sufficient authority and resources are delegated to the area team or to residential institutions. Residential institutions are probably prime institutions. Area teams, however, fall short of this because they do not control the full range of services which they need - home helps, homelessness units, specialist teaching and therapists and so on, and because as a matter of organisational development, the area team leader is not delegated control over social workers without supervision or management from above in the way that is a head teacher in relationship to a Chief Education Officer. Nor have the teams acquired the public personality which is an important feature of the educational system;

c) in health services, a general practitioner has authority to provide what is in effect a comprehensive set of services and can prescribe services such as chiropody or drugs which are provided, on his prescription, by others. Equally, a comprehensive district general hospital is a prime institution with its own personality, range of resources, and authority to provide virtually the whole range of medical care and treatment. One, however, operates at the community and the other at the district level. But it is increasingly felt that some of this freedom should give way to more integrated administration under the new area health authorities;

d) in housing and planning, however, the prime institution seems to be the whole of the local authority department. Authority is not really delegated from the central office on any of the main provisions required by clientèle;

e) discretion is increasingly being asserted in the 500 social security offices.

There is, thus, a range of institutional patterns which, of themselves, present obstacles to effective social planning. The problem may not be willingness but of perceived authority and relationships. Thus, a head trying to create a community school, or an area team leader anxious to develop a sense of community, cannot easily in terms of the distribution of authority relate to those who are replanning a town centre. Heads and area team leaders may well work together, and both would then find that many of their basic values are common - both professions believe in individual development, for example. But it may well be that the area team leader has not the discretion to develop "style" as does the head of the school. And the point of address in housing departments may be quite high up and not local.

VII. OTHER INSTITUTIONAL FACTORS

The degree of delegation within the services is, therefore, an important variable in determining the ability of institutions to relate to each other inter-sectorally. This variable, however, relates to those that have already been discussed with others: the size of institutions, the prescriptions embodied in permanent buildings and the general social status of the different institutions.

Size of Institution

The catchment areas and size of institutions vary widely. The recommended average size of a primary school is 240 pupils.(1) A district general hospital is supposed to serve a population of a quarter of a million.(2) The catchment area for housing or planning is likely to be a whole local authority of between more than a quarter of a million and a million people. An area team of social workers is likely to serve a larger catchment but is not far different in size from a small school. But the area team is dependent on the

---

1) The Plowden Report on Primary Schools, Report of the Central Advisory Council for Education (England): "Children and their Primary Schools", HMSO, 1967, Chapter XIII.

2) Functions of the District General Hospital, DHSS, Welsh Office and Central Health Services Council, HMSO, 1969.

larger institution of the whole social services department for many
of its services. The size variable has two important effects.
First there is a difference in "feel" and status so that those responsible for the smaller institutions may find it difficult to make
much impact on those responsible for the larger institutions.
Secondly, the formal lines of relationships become more complicated
since the larger institutions will have more levels of decision
making than the smaller institutions. These problems are already
becoming apparent in the detailed working out of relationships between district management teams in the health service and departmental structures in the social service departments.(1)

Inherited Buildings

All social service institutions bear out Lord Franks' dictum
"if you want to find policy making in the University of Oxford, go
to the buildings committee". The buildings carry with them the
suppositions of the time in which they were built, and the differential allocation of resources at different points of development
in the services. Thus, British school building came in three waves:
three-decker town buildings (from the 1900s), which assumed differentiation between boys and girls, seniors and juniors, and teaching groups in self-contained class rooms. The buildings of the
1930s and late 1940s were largely on a "finger plan" in which only
some of these suppositions had been removed. From the early 1950s
perhaps two schools a day were opened in England and Wales and most
of these embodied assumptions about a far greater flow of pupils
and the removal of time and classification barriers. But this
movement was largely within the primary schools and educators who
would want to see more flexible forms of education in secondary
education will be confronted with buildings which will make this
difficult. The other social services also inherit buildings which
prescribe practice and therefore make it difficult for services
to move in line with each other. Old psychiatric hospitals and
wards assume strong control procedures rather than group and participative therapy. Old-fashioned old peoples' and children's homes
make it difficult (although difficulties are now largely overcome)
for individual attention and autonomous life styles to be pursued.

Social Status

There are also differences in general social status. From the
1950s onwards, for example, the education service received a perhaps

---

1) R. Rowbottom and A. Hey, "Collaboration between Area Health and
Social Service Authority", Health and Social Service Journal,
9th and 16th February, 1974.

disproportionate amount of recognition in such idiosyncratically
British forms as places in the honours list. No housing manager
or director of social services has ever received a knighthood.
Prominent chief education officers do, and so have a few prominent
heads of schools. There is a very wide and strong educational in-
telligentsia of perhaps 50 full time educational journalists. They
both criticise and reinforce the premium given to the education
service. But this is not evident in the other services.

Within the local authorities, too, education has always been
the leading service. It takes more resources than any other single
area. It has preserved its right to have its own committee, which
is required by law, its own chief officer (whose appointment may be
vetoed by the Department of Education and Science), and generally
to have a series of exemptions from corporate control which is resented by its chief executives.

VIII. WAYS TOWARDS INTER-SECTORALISM

In this paper, attempts have been made to show why it is difficult for education to relate to the other personal services at both
the central and at the local levels. Some of the differences may be
intrinsic to the processes administered by the different services.
Others relate to differences in values which may conflict with each
other but which may be evidence of the way in which the services
reflect a full range of human needs and characteristics. Others
relate to institutional factors. If connections are desirable, the
following is a brief list of possible ways through the difficulties:

a) it should be possible to link together activities of different departments. Heads of departments increasingly meet
   in coalition arrangements such as management teams under a
   chief executive. Committee structures in local government
   have been streamlined and more authority given to committees
   and officers who are concerned with synoptic and inter-
   service development and control. The dangers of strong
   corporate management are that it can restrict the creative
   use of discretion by practitioners, and subject client
   needs and demands to over-rational and over-systematised
   vetting so that, as with central government, the emphasis
   might be on control and priority setting, rather than development of services;

b) there have always been activities of public authorities
   which co-ordinate for purposes of control - Finance, Establishments and Organisation and Legal Department. Increasingly, however, such "new" activities as Research and Evaluation

and Strategic Planning make it possible for across-the-board work to relate to development, if they are accorded enough authority within the corporate planning systems;

c) inter-service work at the prime institution level is more difficult to achieve for the reasons given in this paper. But it could take two useful forms. First, the adversarial and advisory role, in which one service or practitioner is sanctioned to vet, criticise and propose developments in a neighbouring service needs to be explicitly recognised and sanctioned. (Medical officers have long had these functions in local authorities.) Secondly, analysis of tasks could show the possibilities of joint work between GPs, teachers and social workers in such areas as nursery education (which could also be a counselling service for parents) or adult education. Indeed, if common elements of training were identified, hybrid professions could usefully be developed. Small starts in this direction have been made.

Future Studies

In the opinion of the author of this paper, the major changes taking place in the organisation of the social services in England and Wales from April 1974, and in Scotland for 1975, make it an opportune time for studies of ways towards inter-sectoralism to be launched. The public services face a lot of criticism but there is not a strong anti-government mood in Britain so it should be possible for studies to be made collaboratively so as to establish how far values, objectives, activities and cognate institutional factors are inherently conflictual and how far, and with what benefits, congruence and mutual monitoring could be specified. Such studies could be fruitfully made at both central and local levels.

APPENDIX

ACTIVITIES, OBJECTIVES, VALUES AND LINKAGES OF MAIN DEPARTMENTS

EDUCATION

(1) OBJECTIVES (OUTPUTS)	(2) ACTIVITIES (INPUTS)	(3) INTER-SECTORAL ASPECTS	(4) VALUES
1. Providing compulsory schooling from 5-16 years.	1. Assessment of needs.	*1.&2. Screening and detection of needs in SSD, Housing and Health relate to same populations and needs.	*1.-4. Hardly a basic value except for retribution, that might not be involved here with different intensities.
2. Providing voluntary education for children before 5 and over 16 years.	2. Development and specification of educational services.		
3. A custodial objective for children under 16.	3. Provision of teaching-learning processes.		
4. Socialisation of population (e.g. as stated in Ch. XV Plowden Report).	4. Physical training and recreation (including assistance to local community bodies).		
5. Development of community (colleges, adult education, nursery education).	5. Providing practical elements of teacher training.		
6. Developing intellectual and other capabilities of individual children.	6. Ascertainment of pupils' handicaps.	Health and SSDs.	6. Helping the inadequate, equality, personal autonomy. Equality, equity, personal autonomy. Defence of society.
7. Strengthening the economy of the country (as stated in several official documents from the 1956 White Paper on technical education).	7. Awards to students.	7. Income maintenance and national taxes.	
8. Selection for differential education and employment of pupils.	8. Enforcement of attendance.	Truancy, SSDs.	
	9. School medical service.	Health services.	9.-11. Helping the inadequate.
	10. School milk and meals.		
	11. School transport.		
	12. Careers advisory services.	12.&13. Department of Employment services.	Self-sufficiency.
	13. Youth employment service.		
	14. Religious education and collective worship.		Family, inter-personal relationships, defence of society.
	15. Commissioning, replacing and maintaining buildings and equipment.	Planning and housing departments.	

* Numbers refer to Activities in Column (2).

SOCIAL SERVICES

(1) OBJECTIVES (OUTPUTS)	(2) ACTIVITIES (INPUTS)	(3) INTER-SECTORAL ASPECTS	(4) VALUES
As in para. 516 of the Seebohm Report: "To promote an environment positively conducive to the growth and development of all individuals; to detect social needs both potential and actual and, where necessary, to ensure the provision of services designed to promote the welfare of those involved through a family and community base approach."	1. Assessment of social service needs. 2. Development and specification of services. Community Work 3. Voluntary welfare activity. 4. Stimulating self-help groups.	*1.-4. All of these activities can be related to similar work in education (e.g. counselling to parents of children in nurseries or in adult education).	*1.&2. Hardly a basic value except for retribution, that might not be involved here without different intensities. Inter-personal relations, personal autonomy, community. 4. Personal autonomy, community inter-personal relationships.
Control of deviancy.	5. Registration and inspection of private and voluntary groups. 6. Creating public knowledge of services.		Defence of society. Sense of community, equity.
	Work with Individuals or Families 7. Basic social work (providing advice, monitoring and supervision, referring to specific services and casework). 8. Provision of specific services (money and goods, meals, aids and adaptations, personal domestic services, accommodation, recreation, outings, holidays; occupational training and sheltered employment, systematic psychotherapy and re-education, medical and para-medical treatment, formal education, misc.; burials, management of property). 9. Educational facilities for student social workers.	7. Relates to work of homeless, or rent rebates, or rent collection etc. in housing, truancy cases in education. Close connections with educational, housing, health and social security.	Full range of values, but with emphasis on inter-personal relationships, personal autonomy and defence of society rather than equality. Equity, equality, helping the inadequate, personal autonomy, freedom of life-style.

* Numbers refer to Activities in Column (2).

134

HEALTH

(1) OBJECTIVES (OUTPUTS)	(2) ACTIVITIES (INPUTS)	(3) INTER-SECTORAL ASPECTS	(4) VALUES
1. To detect general pattern of disease.	**Preventive Medicine**		
2. To diagnose disease in individuals.	1. School medical and dental services.	1.&2. Schools.*	
3. To take corrective action towards their reduction or elimination.	2. Health education.		
4. To enhance physical and mental well-being through preventive medical resources in individuals and groups of individuals.	3. Advice on health to other agencies.	Education, housing, social services, health departments.	
	4. Screening.	Relates to screening by LAs, SSDs and Education.	Most health authorities are concerned with adequate personal functioning, and only partly concerned with inter-personal relationships and sense of community.
	5. Preventive care for mothers and young children.	Social workers, housing, education.	
	Primary Care		
	6. General medical services.		
	7. General dental services.	Education.	
	8. Accident and emergency services.		
	Specialist Care		
	9. Medical care by specialists.	Social workers, housing.	
	10. Medical care by para-medicals.	Social workers, housing.	
	11. Nursery and midwifery.	SSDs.	
	12. Hospital admission and discharge facilities.	SSDs.	
	13. Ward and theatre facilities (including meals).		
	14. Health centre and clinic facilities (diagnosis and treatment).	SSDs and Education.	
	15. Ambulances.		
	16. Clinical teaching and research facilities.		
	17. Training for nurses and para-medicals.	SSDs and Education.	

* Numbers refer to Activities in Column (2).

135

HOUSING

(1) OBJECTIVES (OUTPUTS)	(2) ACTIVITIES (INPUTS)	(3) INTER-SECTORAL ASPECTS	(4) VALUES
1. The provision of housing to all of those who cannot provide it from their own resources.	1. Assessment of housing needs.	* 1.&2. Screening and evaluation of need in education, social services and health relate to same pops. & need SSDs, health, town planning.	* 1.&2. Community, economic well-being.
2. Providing advisory and control services in the field of private housing.	2. Specification of development and location.		Volatile, ranges from helping the inadequate to individual effort.
	3. Design of new housing.		Helping the inadequate.
	4. Giving housing advice (to buyers, developers, tenants & landlords in dispute).	Relate to advice given to clients by other departments. (SSDs and town planning.)	Helping the inadequate, sense of community.
	5. Prevention of homelessness.	Inter-changeable with SSDs and social security.	Largely progress and change, economic growth.
	6. Provision of special accommodation, sheltered housing schemes, and for disabled.	SSDs and health authorities.	Sense of community, minimum living standards, econ. main. Defence of society. Equality, defence of society, individual effort, retribution.
	7. Clearance for redevelopment (partly or wholly for housing purposes).	Town planning and all public users of land.	
	8. Maintenance of stock of public housing.	SSDs and social security.	Helping the inadequate, equity, individual effort, minimum living standards.
	9. Management of housing.	On whose prescription? Their own? SSDs or health?	
	10. Rent collection and rebates (tenants).		12. Individual effort, self-determination, defence of society.
	11. Allocation of housing.		13. Individual effort and self-determination.
	12. Selling council houses.		
	13. Giving mortgages.		

* Numbers refer to Activities in Column (2).

PLANNING

OBJECTIVES (OUTPUTS) (1)	ACTIVITIES (INPUTS) (2)	INTER-SECTORAL ASPECTS (3)	VALUES (4)
(As stated by the development corporation of a new town):-	1. Structure plans.	Almost all of these activities are strongly interrelated with the activities of other welfare state institutions.	The emphasis in decisions made is on the defence of society and economic well-being (as with ensuring good location for industry and transportation flows). Such considerations as, however, personal autonomy, self-determination, are also present. Increasing emphasis on community and inter-personal values is being proposed.
1. Opportunity and freedom of choice.	2. Local plans (in special cases).		
2. Easy movement and access, and good communications.	3. Development control (strategic and reserved decisions).		
3. Balance and variety.	4. Acquisition and disposal of land for planning purposes, developments or redevelopment.		
4. Attractive city.	5. Clearance of derelict land.		
5. Public access.	6. National parks (subject to existence of boards).		
6. Efficiency and imaginativeness of resources.	7. Country parks.		
	8. Footpaths and bridleways.		
	9. Commons - registration.		
	10. Caravan sites - provision.		
	11. Gipsy sites - provision.		
	12. Small holdings and cottage holdings.		

137

SOCIAL SECURITY

(1) OBJECTIVES (OUTPUTS)	(2) ACTIVITIES (INPUTS)	(3) INTER-SECTORAL ASPECTS	(4) VALUES
1. To give income support to those unable to provide wholly or partly for themselves. 2. To avoid creating disincentives to individual self-help and work. 3. To give casework help.	No empirical analysis undertaken.	Social security officers sometimes relate closely to social service departments which are able to give help in cash or in kind and who counsel clients on entitlement to benefit and to ways of becoming in-dependent of social security through work and other means. They have a similar relationship with housing and health authorities. There are some unacknowledged rela-tionships with the education service which has powers to help pupils with free meals, clothing allowances, school maintenance grant, etc.	Helping the inadequate. Equality. Equity. Individual effort. Self-determination. Family. Minimum living standards. Defence of society.

A SOCIO-TECHNICAL APPROACH

by William Westley

Modern industrial society is characterised by rapid technological change, an explosion in knowledge and an increasing interdependence of processes and institutions. This has created what
Eric Trist called "a turbulent environment", meaning that rapid
change along with increasing interdependence makes every part of the
environment changing and unstable. This makes it difficult to establish predictable long-term relationships between or within parts of
the social system, or to establish a controlled environment in which
administrative decisions can have predictable results. To meet this
we need new forms of organisations which can encompass uncertainty
and be continuously adaptable to a moving system. The government,
like other parts of the larger social system needs to develop organisational forms which both transcend established bureaucratic sectors
and can be changed rapidly to meet the changes constantly arising
within each sector and within society as a whole.

The problem of interdependence, in this case the inter-
connectedness of social sectors, is of course, not restricted to the
government. Other institutions within the society have been grap-
pling with similar problems for some time. Within the health,
economic and educational sectors, planners have been struggling to
control interdependence and turbulence. Their ideas are represented
in the emerging policy analysis sciences and the use of open systems
theory in dealing with intra-sectoral problems.

Generally, technological and economic interdependence means that
the various public sectors penetrate each other and become organi-
cally related, making larger social systems. These growing system
relationships mean that the decisions taken within one sector are
increasingly likely to have consequences in other sectors (to some
extent they always did have consequences and the systems perspective
merely brings them to attention). It is apparent that there is a
kind of chain of actions in which a goal in one sector is a means in
another, e.g., the skills inculcated in schools are the means for
goal achievement in other sectors. However, this aspect of inter-
sectoral relationships has long been recognised and is not the reason
for the present emphasis on inter-sectoral planning. The reason is

that some of the goals of one sector can only be achieved within another sector, which means that different sectors often share goals and that there are modes of action arising out of the inter-penetration of sectors in which they have to co-operate to act at all and which justify inter-sectoral planning.

Goals of One Sector Realised in Another

The realisation of goals within another sector can be illustrated by the relevance of job design for health. Health authorities cannot reduce the physical and psychological damage resulting from work without redesigning jobs and work organisation. Such redesign may represent the best investment in prophylaxis. Similarly, welfare officials seeking to reduce unemployment and increase the economic and psychological welfare of people are heavily dependent on ways in which organisations employ and release their workers, and on the models of engagement and disengagement these organisations use. Thus, if work organisations decide to retrain and keep, rather than retire their older employees, this will have consequences for the funds and programmes the Welfare Department has to find for the aged. Furthermore, it is possible that the way to solve the problem of retirement is not to try to adjust people to it, but to eliminate it. This solution would require that the welfare and work sectors engage in some mutual planning. Perhaps what is needed is the investment of some welfare funds in enabling organisations to retrain their older employees and to keep them employed on a reduced and flexible work load.

Shared Goals

Full employment would be an example of a goal shared by many different sectors: health, welfare, labour, etc. In fact, there is doubt that this goal could ever be achieved, except under conditions of exceptional economic growth, without the co-operation of the sectors. It would require a very intensive study of the need for and ways of using all kinds of people. Substantial parts of our labour force remain unemployed but are paid in the form of unemployment insurance, welfare benefits, or pensions. Thus, increasingly, the unemployed are PAID unemployed and represent an unused resource. This suggests that the problem is to create new, economically non-competitive, and socially useful jobs. Any serious consideration of the essential services needed by modern communities would reveal an enormous number not being adequately staffed. If these services which might result in the humanisation of experience for the young, the very old, the chronically ill, for example, were adequately staffed, the new jobs could use up a substantial portion of the presently unemployed.

Similarly, the goal of human growth and development is one
shared by many sectors: education, work, government, health, welfare,
etc., all favour this development for different reasons. Education
needs it because it is a fundamental part of its stated function.
Work and government, because increasing interdependence, technological change, and the dependence or knowledge for their operations
require flexible, retrainable, and autonomous workers. Of course,
such workers can exist only under conditions which maximise their
growth and development. Also, such growth and development are certainly relevant to psychological if not physical health, and finally,
such successful workers help reduce the welfare load ordinarily produced by structural unemployment.

Both work and education are nodes of activity formed in the
inter-penetration of sectors. One deals here with symbolic rather
than a concrete node. It is in the nature and meaning of work, the
morality and technology of jobs, that all sectors join. The economy
is not the abode of work, nor is work strictly related to the functional sub-system termed the economy. Thus, when the quality of
working life, and the moral definition of work become of concern,
it is clear that we are faced with a goal, or a problem which appears
at the intersections of functional sub-systems and formal structures.

Co-operation by Necessity

The inter-relatedness of social sectors and the problems of
inter-sectoral planning are illustrated in the relationships between
education and work. Between the two there have been, of course,
many traditional linkages such as the movement of students from
school to work. Because of this, industry makes demands on the educational world for skills and standards, while schools through their
control of skill acquisition can affect the quality of the labour
force and the development of the work sector. In recent years this
has become complicated by: (a) recurrent education (in itself really
only a problem in co-ordination, though one of great magnitude) and
(b) the re-conceptualisation of work as education and of education
as work both of which have inter-related these two previously dis-
parate social sectors. We will deal with this in more detail later
as we deal with meta problems.

Work and education are curious sectors for each is a continuing
part of human experience. If we define work as any socially valued
activity (non-valued activity being defined as waste or play) then
it is clear that it is an intrinsic part of all sectors of society:
the religious, the educational, the health, as well as the economic
sectors. Thus, if we have a problem in the transformation of work
arising out of demands for the redesign of jobs to provide human
challenge and growth, then this is a problem for every sector of

141

society. It becomes an additional goal for each of these sectors
and to the degree that it is taken seriously it will force a change
in the organisations of the institutions necessary to the sector's
functions. We have a great deal to learn about work, about the
conditions which make it a socially valuable activity, about the
ways in which it is changing in response to social turbulence, about
the kinds of new skills which are coming to be needed, and about the
kinds of training which will be in demand for the acquisition of
these skills. However, one thing is clear. That the design of jobs
meeting these human goals will probably vary with the personnel
involved, the technology being used, and the environment in which
the organisation is functioning. This means that in order to rev-
olutionise the design of jobs, it will require the co-operation of
many sectors of society, but particularly of the educational sector.
It cannot be left to the department of labour, or the economic institutions of the society.

Education has somewhat the same properties. While people may
not be taught in every sector of society (though it would be surprising if they were not) presumably they do learn. The concepts
of growth and maturation both include the idea of constant learning.
As we have pointed out, this seems to be an essential property of the
modern job; it must have a learning and growth component. One
student of the job redesign sees work organisations as learning
organisations, structured to facilitate learning. We would argue in
fact that the educational sector lies at the intersection of many
sectors: the economic, the welfare, the political, and the health
sectors. Education is a key part of these sectors since it seems
necessary for the adaptation to change, as an intrinsic human experience, and as a selector and motivator. This suggests that the
monopoly of education by the educational sector has done serious
disservice to the society as a whole. It is an inefficient way of
handling the need for learning. We do not mean to suggest that this
sector should be eliminated but that its internal goals should be
reassessed and that it should give a large part of its skills and
energies to functioning as a resource for other sectors.

Work must have an educational component because the technology
of work changes so rapidly and because it has been found that unless
people find that they can learn and grow in their jobs they have an
increased tendency to physical and mental damage, decreased longevity,
and industrial accidents. There is evidence that work satisfaction
is related to health and life expectancy and that satisfaction is in
turn a derivative of the challenge, learning, and competence con-
firmation of work. With modifications for differences in technology,
this seems to mean we will have to redesign jobs to permit workers
to learn throughout their work careers and to experience personal

growth and advancement in the work world. This redesign must include in work or jobs something close to direct education in the skills of the job, in the theory of the work being done, in the comprehensions of the organisational environment in which the work takes place, and in the inter-personal skills necessary for working in and co-ordinating work groups. It is obvious that to the extent that these goals are met, some of the training now being offered by schools must and will take place within factories. On the other hand, it is also true that kinds of training never given to people in factories and more effectively offered in schools will be needed by workers and will have to be supplied by the educational system. The design of this inter-related training system meant to transform work into a learning environment must be common to both of these sectors. It should also be recognised, however, that two other sectors will necessarily be involved in this planning, and they are health and welfare.

People living in modern industrial societies, characterised by their turbulence, need to be able to develop special <u>capacities to work</u>. These are capacities to appreciate the context of the work they do and the decisions they make, to co-ordinate their own work with that of others in reaching collective decisions, and to work autonomously and learn what is necessary to adapt themselves to a changing work world. What they need are not simple skills but a broad range of capacities to function as autonomous individuals. This is what Warren Ziegler has called "civic literacy" or what Elliott Jacques has called "learning for uncertainty". The transformations of the work world calling for these new skills require transformations in the schools, in the structures of the organisations in which students learn, and in the goals of learning. In other words, the restructuring of the work world will require the restructuring of the educational world. But this will not take place without inter-sectoral planning for the development of these new abilities; for these two sectors must be interrelated in the life experience of people, so that they come to understand the connectiveness and develop the necessary skills.

A New Lifetime Model

A serious problem arising from rapid social change is the destruction of cultural models of how to live a good life. The only period of life which seems to be endowed with purpose is the period when people are working, for then they are directly involved in socially valued activities. The remaining parts of life, mainly before we begin work and after we leave it have become, for many, increasingly empty. These periods of youth and old age are almost pastimes between birth and work, and between work and death;

pastimes which are often empty, meaningless and thus destructive. Clearly both these periods have to be given purpose and reintegrated with the mainstream of social life. This may be a major human problem of industrialised societies and one calling for careful intersectoral planning.

One suggested model is that of frequent and fluid movement between work, education, and leisure, the latter to be a free creative or spiritual time. This model contains the suggestion of mid-life career changes, of opportunities for people constantly to adjust their lives and selves, giving them a chance to do a psycho-socio-technical analysis and transformation of their life space. Thus it has been seriously suggested that all workers should be given some form of sabbatical leave and indeed some unions are now considering bargaining for paid educational leaves. This suggestion is designed to reduce unemployment and increase national productivity by making semi-skilled workers mobile and thus creating a flexible labour force and through their mobility creating vacancies for unskilled workers who are now unemployed. To achieve this, both schools and factories will have to redesign for greater flexibility. Universities, for example, will have to find ways of admitting, guiding, and stimulating mature students; and work organisations will have to use people more constructively and fluidly.

This suggested lifetime model also includes the idea of changing the meaning of schooling by making it more optional and permitting earlier entry into the labour force, for example, entry to both the arts and sciences and into the professional programmes could be predicated on previous work experience. Thus, secondary school students would have to go to work (that term being broadly defined) before being accepted into post-secondary training of any kind. Thus, pre-medical training might require a few years of public service in some para-medical capacity such as medical orderly or nurse. The service would be chosen in some undesirable area like the care of the aged or the care of stroke patients, the reward of entry into medical school and thus, access to socially interesting and relevant work, high status, and high pay would be a major motivator for staffing presently understaffed areas of the health sector. If schools were changed in this way, it would mean that people would expect to return to school a few years after being at work and that work organisations would have to arrange themselves so that people would be allowed to return to school without penalty.

This reconstruction would involve a transformation of the present kindergarten through twelfth grade lock-step system of schooling, beginning with a recognition of individual differences and aims and interests, and by creating learning environments in which very young people can use educational resources to shape themselves, as in the English informal classroom system. Thus, initially we have to create flexible, intimate systems.

If education were blended with socially valuable activities, it would provide young people with roles in the community. These roles should be consonant with their abilities and interests and an initial problem would be to study the abilities and interests of young people and the needs of communities. They might work as social and medical aides, assistant policemen, firemen, etc. These young people with a base in the school should be working everywhere in the community and thus integrating with the life of the community.

As they mature and as they become interested, they should be encouraged to find their own balance between education and work with some working full-time, others being in school full-time and others choosing different proportions. In this system there would be no grades or certification and the using agencies would be encouraged to test prospective employees in ways relevant to the kind of work. In fact, the test of education would be its utility to the student.

No student would be permitted to go directly from secondary to post-secondary education, a prerequisite for entry into post-secondary education being a period of work and entry itself being based on a diagnostic test or study period which would place the student at the proper level in the parts of his preferred programme.

The focus of this "Lifetime Model" is not, however, the design of education. Rather it is the transformation of the pre-life period so that young people become involved in socially valuable activities. We happen to call all such activities work and our puritan conception of life equates useful life with work. It is very important, however, to keep in mind a broad conception of work which includes all socially useful activities from learning, creation, nurturing, caring, and producing.

This pre-life period contains people who are already supported by the economy but who are denied useful involvement. The futility and the unreality of schooling arises to a considerable extent from its separation from socially defined useful activity, mainly work. The "Lifetime Model" would encourage these young people to work. It would involve the design of socially useful work rules and provide training and allocation systems for them.

Similarly, on the other end of the life spectrum, where we worry about adjusting people to retirement, we might solve the problem by including everyone in the active part of society and thinking instead of late life career changes. Thus, just as we are already thinking of mid-life career changes which adjust a man to the transformation from early to mid-maturity, it would be profitable to think of late life career changes in which a man is trained to move into occupations capitalising on his life-time knowledge and adjusted to his diminished perhaps physical and emotional energies. Thus, perhaps no one should be licensed as a psychological therapist until he has passed sixty-five and thus gained sufficient wisdom and equanimity to help others unravel and enrich their lives. This idea could easily be widened to include a wide range of jobs which function to humanise the impersonality of our society, for example in the hospitals, the schools, the factories, the urban environment. Certainly, we already have money available in the social security and retirement funds which could be used to pay people doing these jobs. It is obscene to pay people to do nothing, to pay them to stop living and keep out of other people's way. These late life careers must be humanised and adjusted to the physical and psychological needs of the people performing them with short and flexible hours and long holidays and buddy systems which would permit them to be easily replaced.

It should be possible to identify areas of social life where people need social and emotional support and to devise a set of jobs which would meet these needs. It should be possible to develop programmes for training people to fulfil these jobs and to recruit people about to retire and to develop pension supplementary pay schemes. Presumably different interest groups within the society would be interested in different sets of jobs. For example, the industrial world would have different humanisation needs from the medical world which in turn would be different for the law enforcement world or the world of community relations. Urban communities would differ from the rural. In each case, our objective would be to draw upon the human experience of pain, of joy, of anger, of loneliness gained by these older people through their lifetimes and to train them to reach those parts of themselves and their experience, and to make it available to others in specialised circumstances. To train them in these late career changes would take time and special facilities but to a considerable extent they have the time and at the same time they could support themselves and might do a great deal of training for themselves collaboratively.

Most of our people over sixty-five are cut off from active participation in society and lead isolated and deprived lives. Yet these people are probably still useful and willing and may be badly needed. To the extent that this is true, they constitute a large pool of able, paid, and free citizens. To the extent that they are not used, they remain an inflationary and dissatisfied part of the population, and one which because of its dissatisfaction may become ill and a burden on welfare.

The argument for the utility of these seasoned citizens rests on a number of unproven but, we think, plausible assumptions. First,

we assume that it is possible to conceive of a later maturity phase
of employment in which jobs are designed to have interchangeable
occupants, and for a reduced work day. This would meet the arguments
that people past sixty-five cannot do a full day's work and would
lower the efficiency of organisations. In fact, there may be
reason to believe that retirement is not necessary in many areas of
work and that it is being used as a way of getting rid of physically
fragile and skill-obsolescent people. Since new forms of work organisation such as work modules, already permit reduced work loads, the
problem of fragility can be met, while the obsolescence of older
people is no more serious than that of the middle aged and can be met
through late life career training and change.

Secondly, we assume that it is possible to create new jobs vital
to the improvement of the quality of life which would add substantially to the effective functioning of modern industrial societies.
Some of these jobs are already being done by volunteers, jobs like
teachers and nurses aides, but they do these jobs without adequate
training and without much status and pay. We assume that if a careful study were made of the psycho-social needs of modern organisations and communities there would be a multitude of jobs for people
with skills in counselling and consolation, areas in which the older
people are already equipped and probably interested because of a
long life experience.

Thirdly, we assume that if one took late life career training
seriously, as seriously as early life career training for example
(social work or psychiatric training can take as long as four years),
these mature people could be provided with skills permitting them
to make an immense contribution to the community.

Fourthly, we believe that one of the serious failings of modern
industrial societies arises from the human costs incurred by rapid
change, rationalisation, and technological complexity and interdependence. As these increase, so does the need for a flexible
labour force, for new skills of civic literacy.

Obviously, we are already engaged in vast and expensive efforts
to cure urban blight, to work with people on welfare and with delin-
quent gangs, to rehabilitate people damaged by loneliness and impersonality, to introduce improvements in the quality of working life
through job redesign, to provide emotional and social support for
children, adults and the aged in different kinds of institutions.

We cannot afford to supply enough skilled people to man these
positions to meet these needs.

Our idea is that since all industrial societies are changing
rapidly, they have destroyed traditional sources of prestige for,
and utilisation of their seasoned citizens. At the same time they
have created two major needs or demands which indirectly bear on

these people. First, they need highly mobile labour forces able to move into areas of new skills; this need has begun to influence the educational sector to provide mid-career training, and the work world to provide both blue collar and executive sabbaticals. This is also reflected in skill-obsolescence which presses people into increasingly earlier retirement. To what extent and with what degree of success are retirement age people kept in the labour force through retraining or because they already have needed skills? Secondly, the rapid change and growth have swept away the psycho-social anchors and eroded older ways of meeting affective needs. Education, work, medical institutionalisation, urban residency, all tend to become depersonalised and leave people lonely and often alienated. This is a de-humanisation of experience. Traditionally, it has been the old people who were thought to possess these skills most, to be equipped by their experience for counsel and consolation.

The reintegration of both the young and the old into society essentially without cost, since they are obviously already supported, would contribute substantially to the quality of life and perhaps even to productivity. Certainly, the involuntarily retired, that is the unemployed, would under this lifetime model be automatically expected to go into career change training and perhaps in workers' universities and at least be employed in some humanising or integrating capacity. However, in most cases, we do not propose to add to the labour force in the traditional sense, but to create new jobs helping to reintegrate and humanise our society. In those cases where students do enter the traditional labour force, that is to work for a required period before going on to post-secondary training, they would surely be replacing others who had left the labour force to go back to school, so the labour force would remain constant.

For inter-sectoral planning the "lifetime" model would require substantial task force collaboration among the educational, the welfare and the employment sectors, with a careful integration of plans. Within this it is clear that key plans would be those of the educational sector.

The preceding discussion and illustrations indicate that a concrete approach to inter-sectoral planning might be through the attack on problems of the kind we have suggested. The attack on these problems would utilise the kinds of skills now being developed in large organisations to meet with the needs of flexibility and change. One model is, of course, that of the organic organisation in which multiple task forces attack specific problems and continue to exist for the period of the problem. Within the task forces, the members, though differing in skill and pay and attachment to larger organisations, function in a role of quality, doing the necessary jobs and adapting themselves to the interior requirements of the task force itself and its larger problems.

Solution: A Socio-Technical Analysis

The preceding discussion has developed the themes of social turbulence, the emerging recognition of the multi-goal character of modern organisations, and the consequent interrelated problems of modern society. It has, however, suggested no solutions. We propose to do this through a crude form of socio-technical analysis of parts of the educational sector. However, to make this analysis comprehensible we must first draw attention to some of the organisational forms giving rise to the problem.

We take for granted that in order to engage in complex co-operative activity we must develop ways of assuring predictability to the actions of every member of the organisation. Thus, activity is rationalised and the organisation which ensues has been called bureaucracy, which despite its dyslogistic connotation is nothing more or less than a rational and predictable set of social roles linked to some goals. The more complex the society, and the more people are interdependent, the greater our need for such rational forms of organisation. But these organisations develop problems, because they tend toward rigidity and the rules developed for goal achievement become the goals in themselves and the people in the organisations find their security in simple rule observance. In other words, these become rigid, self-sealing organisations.

It is important, however, not to lose track of the need for rational organisation because we become aware of the kinds of problems these organisations develop. Rational organisations need not be rigid or self-sealing. Modern organisational theorists stress the need to have the form or organisation appropriate to its goals, materials, technology, and environment. Among the more effective criteria for distinguishing the appropriate forms of organisations is that concerning the degree of stability and possible routinisation in the material, technology, and environment. Evidence presently available to scholars of this field suggests that where these three elements are stable and can be dealt with in a routine fashion, a highly centralised, formalised form of organisation (the classical bureaucracy) is appropriate and effective. Where this is not the case, where the materials are variable (as is the case with human beings) where the technology or knowledge is not established, and where the environment is turbulent, these centralised, formalised organisations are neither effective nor efficient. What is then required is a more decentralised, loosely structured organisation in which the members and their constituent groups function more autonomously.

Clearly the great public bureaucracies representing the different sectors of society have developed on the assumption that these three elements of organisation life are stable and can be routinised.

Whether they were ever justified in making this assumption (everybody did) is now beside the point. Today it is clear that substantial portions of their work involves them in instabilities, and where it does these systems (epitomised incidentally in the concept of civil service) become both inefficient and ineffective. The secretariat papers DAS/EID/73.40 and ED/73.27 make it clear that modern governments like the modern multinational corporations, are struggling to transcend old boundaries and adopt new forms. This suggests that there is a need for a careful social analysis of the operating conditions of these bureaucracies along the lines of a socio-technical analysis, at least minimally in terms of the rather elementary criteria which we have already suggested. We propose to illustrate such an analysis in terms of two parts of the educational sector: the school, and the university. First, however, we must describe the action of social technical analysis.

Socio-technical analysis has evolved through three general stages. The first stage was that in which F.E. Emery and Eric Trist of the Tavistock Institute in London developed the concept of socio-technical systems to describe their research finding that work on deep seam coal mining could be done with two different types of work organisation: the conventional, which combines a complex formal structure with simple work roles; and the composite, which combines a simple formal structure with complex work roles. They then found that the composite system consistently showed a superiority over the conventional in terms of production and costs. The superiority arose from the fact that given the technology of coal mining, which involved many unexpected contingencies, the composite system, in which each worker felt a responsibility for the whole task, adjusted more quickly and effectively. Subsequently this early finding was supported by the work of a number of investigators such as Burns and Stalker, Joan Woodward, and Charles Perrow, who provided detailed evidence of the need for using the form of work organisation which was appropriate to the technology.

The second stage in socio-technical analysis arose with the recognition that certain kinds of work organisation, mainly the composite, were superior in meeting the needs of workers for work satisfaction, sociability, and person 1 growth. This led to a search for ways of changing the technology to permit the use of composite work groups. These ideas arose principally in the work of E. Thorsrud and F. Emery at the Work Research Institute in Oslo. It resulted in demonstration projects such as the Norsk-Hydro Fertilizer Plant in Norway, and the General Foods Pet Food Plant in Topeka, Kansas, United States. In these cases, the plant was constructed in such a way that the technology permitted the use of a sophisticated composite group work organisation. Much of the work in the area of job enrichment or redesign now in fashion in the

150

United States and Europe is a low key version of this stage of socio-technical analysis.

The third stage of socio-technical analysis as now evolving represents the application of open systems theory to socio-technical analysis. Emery and Trist are largely responsible for this conceptualisation and they argue that given the turbulent nature of modern industrial society, socio-technical systems themselves had to adjust to changes in the character of the materials, the markets or the political economy. To do this they have developed the idea of social ecologies to describe these larger units of planning and analysis.

For the planner, the idea of open socio-technical systems simply means that in order to arrive at the optimum socio-technical design he has to include within his plan the transactions of his system with the changing environment. For educational planners this necessitates collaboration with colleagues from other sectors such as health, welfare and labour. The planner using socio-technical analysis will find that it generates a series of questions concerning the fit between social technical systems and the characteristics of the people, the tasks and the environments. For designing or adapting schools and educational systems to a changing society he could begin by asking:

1. What is the character of the social system of the school?
2. How is this system fitted to the evolving educational technology?

Using these questions he might note that if the school has a clear division of labour, a system of authority and decision-making, and a high degree of formalisation and centralisation, it approximates the model of the classical formal organisation which is highly stratified (between principals or directors, specialists, teachers, and students) and centralised (with decisions about curriculum texts, time-tabling, school rules and the spatial temporal conditions of work), and formalised in development of rules binding on all the role players. He might also find that like the worker in the traditional factory the student is without a voice even in those decisions which most affect his fate (being considered incompetent like the worker) and that his only means of retaliation is to slow down, disrupt, or leave the system.

Going further he might find that the educational technology which seems to be evolving in response to the heterogeneity of students and their goals; technology such as individualised instruction, computer assisted instruction, modular curriculum, team teaching, etc., is often resisted by traditional schools for it seems to require a different kind of social system in which the participants have more autonomy and more composite responsibilities. This may be the reason why some very ingenious ideas fail, and pass like fads. They suffer the fate of techniques in an inhospitable social system.

Addressing these first two questions to a school suggests answers indicating a bad fit between emerging educational technologies and traditional educational organisations. We have, however, only raised these questions from the perspective of the technologies rather than the participants in these systems. When we ask whether the organisation of the educational system satisfies and motivates its participants, whether it permits them to work under conditions in which they feel they can exercise competence and be effective, the answer seems to be that they cannot. Teachers have been complaining, organising, and striking, and their grievances increasingly centre on working conditions. These reactions suggest that whatever the viability of traditional forms of school organisation in the past, they are not presently suitable to the expressed needs and aspirations of the teachers, to say nothing of the students.

These questions seem to raise doubts about the adequacy of the present forms of educational organisation and to suggest that changes must be made in the direction of increased autonomy for teachers (thus providing the flexibility necessary to the optimal use of the new technologies and the psycho-structural resources for meeting teachers' demands), and an increased voice in decision-making by teachers and students.

The preceding suggestion should be seen as illustrative rather than prescriptive for the exact form of the socio-technical system must await research. Even so, we know that the restriction of our inquiry to questions about the social organisation and the technology blinds us to the even more critical effects of materials, tasks, futures, and environments. We have, in the past, considered education as a closed system. Since this is increasingly untenable in a modern changing and turbulent world, the socio-technical analyst must enlarge the spatial temporal boundaries of his inquiry. This inevitably leads him to problems of inter-sectoral co-ordination. This should become clear as we raise other questions which the educational planner can address to his schools and systems.

Our third question is:

3. What are the characteristics of the students and what effect will differences among them have on the kinds of socio-technical systems effective in educating them?

Presumably the student becomes educated when he finds that the skills and knowledge provided by the school are transmitted to him in a social system which he finds rewarding and in terms of a technology adapted to his interests. Students with different interests, moral and cognitive vocabularies, and prospective life tracks will experience a particular socio-technical system differently. Thus, we know that boys and girls respond to school differently, as do working class and middle class, or black and white children. Each will interpret the social environment of the school, and its technology (consisting of techniques coupled with skills and knowledge) differently. Many industrialised countries have found that working class boys seem to dislike school, to resist education, and to do poorly. There is reason to believe that this is because the social environment of the school punishes rather than rewards them (since it is geared to middle-class morality) and because they find what is offered by the school is irrelevant to their present and prospective lives, since both the form and content of skills and knowledge are geared to essentially white collar careers.

To the extent that the students are heterogeneous in ways significant for education, and that they respond differently to school, the planner may have to consider designing socio-technical systems that are adaptable to these differences, or to establishing a choice of alternative socio-technical systems within communities.

When the educational planner seeks socio-technical systems adequate to the education of these diverse students, he may find his search passing beyond the boundaries of the educational sector. Thus students who come from emotionally and economically aberrant backgrounds may require simultaneous action by economic, health, welfare and educational authorities if they are to be educated in the skills necessary to life in a complex industrial society. Both they and their parents may require secure incomes derived from both jobs and welfare, the student may require dietary, physical and psychiatric care, and he may have to be educated in a special school appropriate to his needs and development. The success of this effort is vital to the health and welfare officials, and perhaps the labour department, since the same student falls within their jurisdiction and they may find that his successful education is necessary to the successful accomplishment of their tasks.

Educational planners asking this question may want to explore the variety of socio-technical systems available to them, and to co-ordinate the education of their students with the efforts by colleagues in other sectors to improve their health, provide them with support, and to find them jobs. This emphasis on students with broad range deficiencies or problems is only illustrative of the way in which the task of the educational planner would involve him with socio-technical and inter-sectoral considerations. Obviously, students vary in many other ways including the kinds of demands they and their parents are making on the educational system and the community. Recognising their individuality and their existence as whole persons as any consideration of education must do, will involve co-ordinated or inter-sectoral planning on a fairly regular basis. We would, expect, however, that the range of differences and problems would be limited and that as they occur a rapidly adjusting, self-renewing society would encourage people at the level of the problem to form appropriate committees to co-ordinate community efforts on behalf of the groups or persons, and in the interest of task effectiveness in each of the sectors. Naturally, this would require legislative and financial support and facilitations. We will say more of this later.

This analysis has stressed only one of the ways in which an open socio-technical systems approach to educational planning involves relating the school to the environment. It is meant to be illustrative rather than exhaustive. The planner might also consider whether the actual role of the school is appropriate to the changing needs of the community, possibly phasing it out in favour of other modes of education (such as education at work), the degree to which instabilities in knowledge have changed the kind of training useful for students in their careers, and the implication of these changes for the socio-technical organisation of the school, etc.

Turning from the school to the university, we run into a series of special problems. One of these is the failure of the university to develop any kind of self-guidance system adapting the university to change in the environment. While the criteria of student homogeneity-heterogeneity and the technology remain important, it is the university's failure to recognise very substantial changes in the society which is bringing it some of its most serious problems. Apart from a few professions like law and medicine there seems to be decreasing assurance that the "education" the student receives in the university can be or is used by him in his post-university life. The fact is that the modern industrial community has become a powerful teaching institution in its own right, is actively involved in research, and heavily dependent on the production and use of knowledge. Higher degrees abound in the government bureaucracies and in the great corporations, and people with their higher degrees are engaged in research and (informal) teaching just as the university professors are. Because of this it is becoming increasingly clear that the classical insulation of the university from the community is becoming a barrier to its own progressive development. There must be a linkage between these advanced learning and research activities in the university and the community. These professionals in the community should become part of the university. Both students and faculty would profit from it. The success of the universities without walls in the United States demonstrate this. But the problem goes deeper. The obsolescence of knowledge means that more and more adults will be returning to school for career change and retraining, and to the extent that the society is highly educated this will mean returning to the university. However, as presently organised there is no place for these people in the university, which is designed to process age grades through a choice of relatively homogeneous experiences. Not only is there no place, but the separation of the university from the community means a sharp break in life spheres for those who need to return. If the university were more integrated with the community this would not be necessary.

We are suggesting that a socio-technical analysis of higher education would reveal that the universities blind themselves to changes in the environment and that their organisations prevent them from adapting to social changes even if they were to become aware of them.

Such an analysis if carried further, would reveal that within the universities there is a heterogeneity in the technologies of schools, faculties and departments, but that this is not reflected in the ways in which they are organised (though some informal arrangements are, of course, set up). Thus, in the sciences, where what is to be learned by undergraduates is fairly stable and can be routinised, the classical bureaucratic form of organisation of faculties, departments and courses accompanied by deans, chairmen, and professors is appropriate. In the social sciences, on the other hand, the knowledge taught to undergraduates is highly unstable and changes almost from year to year. These technological conditions demand flexibility and autonomy. Yet, the same organisation and formalisation is applied to both.

We have suggested throughout this paper that the turbulence of modern industrial societies gives rise to uncertainty in many areas, to new transcending problems, and to the inter-penetration of previously discrete governmental sectors. All these are good arguments for inter-sectoral planning. We have further suggested that socio-technical analysis is a useful tool for finding the general guidelines within which such planning can take place, and illustrated this by using some minimal assumptions for such an analysis on two areas of the educational sector.

THE FRAMEWORK FOR SOCIO-TECHNICAL STUDY OF EDUCATION
by the Secretariat

Socio-technical analysis of production may be interpreted as an assessment of the social system which organises the working participants in terms of the (i) goals, (ii) raw materials, (iii) available technology and (iv) environment of the enterprise. This kind of study aims to open avenues to the redesign and redevelopment of this whole system of relationships, based upon any considered set of values, including the possibility that the expressed needs of the participants could provide a fundamental purpose for reorganisation. One question posed by the guiding Secretariat paper is whether this approach could provide part of a useful framework for planning involving education (and by extension, other public services).

Westley has addressed this question in the paper; this commentary will attempt to develop such a framework further.

I.   A COMMENTARY ON THE WESTLEY ARGUMENT

The Westley argument can be structured as follows:

Modern society has undergone a momentous social change in which a dominant feature is that work, education and leisure have become the business of specialised organisations and institutions. This means that these elements which are basic to human life have become artificially compartmentalised, seriously draining meaning from people's lives and destroying many values upon which their activities would be sustained. It is not surprising that many developments have appeared to counteract tendencies of profound social disorientation.

The remedy in general terms is obvious: a reintegration of work, education and leisure. This implies a new "life model" as the pattern for people's typical lifelong personal and productive careers, in which their work lives at an early age would be interwoven with their education, and their education would be a well-defined part of their work. In turn, leisure would be structurally integrated as part of the necessary restorative processes in daily work and educational life and timed according to individual life patterns.

156

This life model would imply a fundamental change in the functioning of society's basic institutions. For example, in the case of education, involvement in the community's work would become a part of education and the barriers between educational institutions and those of work, culture and government would become blurred. In work organisations the educational function reflecting needs of the people engaged in the work would become important elements in the content and manner of these work organisations and their product. These rearrangements should particularly bring the young and the old back into active and appropriate participation in production. However, the major effect on social and productive institutions would be to break their specialisation and require their inter-relationship so that they might better fulfil multiple human needs.

This is the historical perspective and diagnostic which Westley sets out as a necessary basis for dealing with changes in the major institutions of society in terms of the techniques of planning and the technique of operation in such institutions. Socio-technical analysis and inter-sectoral study are such proposed changes in planning, while organic organisation is such a change in operations.

As stated above, if social and economic institutions are to integrate work, education and leisure, there would have to be a change in the content and manner of their functioning. One general model for such a change is termed organic organisation. This is an organisational reorientation which is being experimented with in a significant number of large organisations in the world today. It is the organisation form which defines "tasks" for which teams are brought together on the basis of the needs to solve problems which the tasks seem to present. The organic team will contain people from various parts of the organisation with various statuses, skills and relationships, but while this group lasts they perform any work necessary in order to complete the task. There is much more to this notion, of course, but Westley devotes only a paragraph to it, apparently assuming that this is not the subject of this paper. The important point here is likely to be that any such new operational mode must be particularly based on a recognition and an analysis of the nature of the organisation and its tasks, and the purpose of Westley's paper is to begin to deal with the problem of this kind of analysis. Since inter-sectoral planning and action by its nature will require some forms of horizontal relationships and relationships across the usual hierarchical boundaries, it can be seen that the kind of analysis required for an organic organisation of activity is pertinent. This leads to inquiry into the approach of socio-technical analysis.

Socio-technical analysis applied to education

Westley's specific application of the idea of socio-technical analysis is meant to be illustrative. It is an essay projecting some of the main conclusions that could be expected to arise from this kind of inquiry if applied to schools and to universities in many of the OECD countries. Westley begins with certain implications of socio-technical study for organisations generally in modern society. One aspect of this general form of inquiry delineates the character of the social organisation of work (including informal as well as formal structures) appropriate to the socio-technical factors:

   i) goals,

  ii) raw materials,

 iii) technology, and

  iv) environment of the enterprise.

Thus, if these factors are very stable, which is the assumption underlying traditional organisations, a hierarchical social organisation of the work force can be workable and productive. However, it is obvious that an increasing number of modern institutions, and particularly education, are "turbulent" systems in that their goals, raw materials (the students in education), technologies and environment are all in a major state of flux. Formalised, centralised organisations, the great private and public bureaucracies, which were based on assumptions that these socio-technical factors could be stabilized and routinised, have already become inefficient and ineffective. Modern governments and other organisations are struggling to transcend old boundaries and develop new forms. In the field of education new forms of administrative control, pedagogical practice and structures are emerging, as are closer relationships with other sectors such as health, welfare and labour services.

Three guiding questions are suggested by Westley to explore the possible redesign of the social system of schools and universities from this socio-technical standpoint:

1) What is the character of the social system of the school?

2) How is this system fitted to the available technology?

3) What are the characteristics of the students, and what effect will differences among them have on the kinds of socio-technical systems effective in educating them?

Inquiry into the first two questions would lead to a characterisation of schools as largely classical, formal organisations: ".... highly stratified (between principals or directors, specialists, teachers, students) and centralised (with decisions about curriculum, texts, time-tabling, school rules and spatial and temporal conditions of work) and formalised in the development of rules binding on all the role players". Socio-technical study would be expected to show in detail how this organisation form: 1) fails to provide

for the social relationships conducive to the kind of motivation
and participation required for effective education; and 2) stifles
innovative development and the use of technologies. Furthermore,
study of the diverse characteristics and needs of the students would
reveal that the socio-technical systems required to educate them
effectively would have to reach beyond the boundaries of the schools
to other public and private sectors. Thus, exploration of these
three questions could be expected to yield specific information for
a redesign of the socio-technical system for schools, involving
altogether greater autonomy, technological flexibility, participation and inter-sectoral relationships.

Turning to the special case of the universities, socio-technical
analysis would detail such incongruities as the heterogeneity of
the tasks and technologies of university schools, faculties and
departments which are, nevertheless, forced into a uniform bureaucratic organisation of courses, deans, chairmen, professorships,
etc. Perhaps the most important diagnostic reading from this study,
however, would reveal that "the universities blind themselves to
change in the environment and that their organisations prevent them
from adapting to social changes even if they became aware of them".
Three tendencies would be observed which would point to the need
to integrate and co-mingle many of the activities of the university
and the wider community:

1. a decreasing assurance of the social usefulness of what
   the student learns;
2. increased teaching and research in society's work organisations, now largely led by an educated elite; and
3. the demand for late-in-life career change and retraining
   services.

The role of fundamental assumptions

It can be seen that the conclusions, which Westley suggests
would emerge from a socio-technical study of schools in modern
societies, are congruent with his general historical perspective -
summarised in the previous section. His inquiry would also rest
upon a hypothesis - less fully developed in this draft - as to the
nature of the process by which education takes place. Thus, he
looks for a school organisation which "satisfies and motivates its
participants...under conditions in which they feel they can exercise
competence..." Without directly stating the underlying hypothesis,
the kind of educational process assumed here is apparent from a
critique of its organisation:

"...whatever the viability of traditional forms of school
organisation in the past, they are not presently suitable to
the expressed needs and aspirations of the teachers, to say
nothing of the students...

Presumably the student becomes educated when he finds that the skills and knowledge provided by the school are transmitted to him in a social system which he finds rewarding in terms of a technology adapted to his interests".

Thus, Westley's contribution illustrates that 1) some such general perspective is necessary in order to connect an analysis of the organisation to its external environment and, also, that 2) a hypothesis concerning the nature of the "productive" process within the organisation is the starting point for evaluating its social system. A socio-technical analysis, like any scientific study of social organisation, will only yield results in terms of such underlying hypotheses and perspectives.

Without subscribing precisely to Westley's formulations of such underlying themes for education, they are recognisably quite in line with viewpoints of much of the current OECD work in this field. It seems possible then to try to take the lead provided by his essay a few steps further.

II.   FURTHER DEVELOPMENT OF FRAMEWORK QUESTIONS FOR
        SOCIO-TECHNICAL STUDY APPLIED TO EDUCATION

From this exposition Westley shows not so much that new conclusions would be reached in a socio-technical analysis of education, although surprises could later be in store for us. Rather, the value in such analysis would perhaps lie in the way in which these conclusions would be substantiated - in the data collected and the manner of analysis leading to these conclusions - which would suggest diagnostic directions for the redesign of educational institutions. Can such an exposition be carried any further at this point?

Westley has briefly described three stages in the research and conceptual development of the idea of socio-technical analysis. In the first stage the notion substantiated was that it is possible to design the social organisation of work so that maximum advantage could be gained from the technology involved in the work. The second stage reversed this order and looked for opportunities to redesign the technology to better meet the social and psychological needs of the workers. The third phase recognises that any organisation so analysed is part of an "open" system of relationships in its total environment and, therefore, this analysis must be done in the context of the study of the society's "social ecology".

A blend of all of these socio-technical approaches must be applied in the study of education. Furthermore, the socio-technical factors considered for educational organisations - goals, raw materials (i.e. population to be educated), technology and environment - can only be defined within the context of social relationships.

This means, for example, that such study could not rest with a simple assessment of the social system of schools as it functions with respect to pedagogical technologies, students' characteristics or other socio-technical factors. Of course the basic aim of the socio-technical study of any educational organisation is to assess its social system (Westley's first question). However, this would in fact be accomplished by means of study which reveals aspects of the social system within each of the socio-technical factors. Such inquiry could be expected to reveal possibilities for change in many elements of the social and technical structure.

The following framework is aimed at such a change-oriented inquiry as part of an inter-sectoral approach to educational planning. (The questions which form the major items of this framework are numbered for convenient identification.)

The socio-technical factors

A) Goals

The goals for education are not only determined by the organisations directly concerned but by a complex social process involving the entire society. A changing society means, of course, that these goals are not fixed. The crude analogy of education seen as a production process is momentarily useful only to emphasize that its labour force (teachers) and "raw material" (students) have immediate effect on the actual goals pursued. The goals of education in operation are at least as numerous as the units of "raw material" input - the individuals being educated. Consideration of individual goals in education is only the first problem. If the goal for the education of young people is - naively stated, some would say - to produce educated young people, the definition of the content of this education is still open to the complex interplay of the influence and power of the various groups involved - the educators, the social and cultural leaders, the parents and the students themselves.

Perhaps for educational institutions it would be necessary at some point to deal in some detail with a "technical" delineation of manifest goals: such as goals of individuals and other minorities as against the goals of larger policies; or goals appropriate to future circumstances compared to those of today; or finally, goals which are clearly not "educational", like baby-sitting, social selection, keeping the young out of the labour market, etc.

Finally, however, rearrangement of the social organisation of educational institutions involves the question: whose goals? Thus, socio-technical analysis of education cannot avoid an attempt to delineate the goals that are related to and even fostered by its particular social organisation. Ultimately then, socio-technical study of education must become part of a larger effort to facilitate a bargaining process - perhaps in this era leading to a distinctly new bargain - concerning the goals of educational organisations. Furthermore, such inquiry must contribute more than a registering of the manifest capacity of individuals or groups to articulate their goals. It must include consideration of goals which may be revealed in small increments of experience and action by the people least prepared to state their goals in any other way. This particularly would be the style of the developing child, if his goals are to be entered into consideration. A goal inherent in the idea of education as human development would be to foster the capacity of the young to articulate their goals. This developmental goal need not be limited to the pupils and students, but could be accepted as a goal for teachers and all the other people involved in the educational enterprise, and could include the idea of opening up the goal formulation process to new knowledge.

These considerations underlie the most general assessment called for in socio-technical study: <u>Does the social system of an educational establishment fit and facilitate its goals</u>? This is the basic diagnostic question which is only to be answered in terms of further study of other socio-technical factors. However, this would be a simplistic question if it were interpreted as an exercise to "find" the educational organisation's goals in order to prescribe the "best" social system for meeting them. The goals for educational institutions in fact arise from the wider society and the "mission" of such institutions is to be found in the nature of their response to these goals, which must be reformulated by each organisation for itself.

<u>Therefore, the first operational questions for socio-technical study of educational establishments would be</u>:
1) <u>How does the social system of an educational establishment operate for the development of its goals</u>?
2) <u>What aspects of the social system govern the character of participation in the development of goals</u>?

B) <u>Participants</u>

1. <u>Their characteristics and the social system</u>

Education is of course not a production process: the socio-technical factor, "raw material", is largely irrelevant, and any other analogy drawn from production is seriously misleading. However, socio-technical study must deal with at least the main elements of a process, and therefore its application to education would rest on a notion of what this process in education is and/or could be. Obviously, then, a socio-technical study of education rests on the

162

assumption that despite its great complexity, the educational process is sufficiently knowable to provide a basis for such study. One of the virtues of socio-technical inquiry would be this demand that it would exert a greater understanding of the educational process.

This framework for a socio-technical inquiry is not based on an effort to state any such understanding of the process of education in detail. Rather, it is based upon a characterisation of this process, identifying its one main element, namely, the participants in education. Education, whether more or less, necessarily rests on some measure and quality of participation on the part of learners, not to mention the teachers and others engaged in this enterprise. Furthermore, "participants" is a designation which requires definition in context - who particiates in what and how. Study of the participants involves selective description of the enormous complexity and variety of their characteristics, which assume some coherence mainly in relation to their function in the social structure of education.

Groups of participants can be delineated, for example, according to social origin and membership, sex, family status, age, state of development, the history and tradition they carry with them, previous training, attitudes, concepts of what happens or should happen in education, self-image and role-image. Such characteristics may delineate groups of students, teachers, administrators, etc. in the light of their interrelationships and should help to illuminate the extent to which the school's social system differentially serves their needs and interests.

However, it is our judgement that the objective of such study should not be to establish a Draconian planning system in education which embraces all the complexities in its formal and informal social relationships but, rather, to raise the level of consciousness of these relationships. These considerations give rise to the following operational questions in a socio-technical study of education:

3) <u>What groups are identifiable by characteristics which are significant for their participation in the social system of the educational establishment</u>?

4) <u>What features of the social system affect the extent and the kind of participation of these groups</u>?

2. <u>Participants and the technical system</u>

Because education is a social process it is difficult to define the <u>work</u> performed in educational institutions. There can be an agreement, for example, that this work would be recognised as a number of examinations "passed", papers written, skills demonstrated or simply the number of hours spent or the number of books or other materials consumed. But all of these are quite fragmentary and artificial indices of the "real" work being done. Of course, what is finally considered to be the work of a school is itself decided in its social processes. However, this work can be seen as a special application, intensification or focus of the general social process of the school. It is that part of the system of the school's social relationships in which the teachers and other responsible people make the most deliberate effort to control the direction and content of their relationships to the students and at least to affect their behaviours in the short term. In this special aspect of the school's social-psychological processes the participants engage in the school's technical system.

The technical system of schooling, beginning with inadequacies in the definition of work goals upon which it is based, notably fails to serve many pupils and students. Therefore, a socio-technical study would include inquiry to discover:

5) What characteristics among the identified groups of pupils and students are significant in terms of the functions of the technical system for their education?

6) What aspects of the technical system respond to these characteristics?

C) Technology

The technology applied to the teaching of pupils and students, like the technical system itself, arises from the general social system of education. Therefore, educational technologies are not linked directly to the needs of particular populations subject to schooling but, rather, to the school establishment's predominant goals and system of participation. New technologies must fit this social system; otherwise, in fact, they would be involved in a change of this system.

Thus the first kind of inquiry with respect to technology can be a conservative one:

7) Within the recognised social system of an educational establishment, what available educational technologies could be applied for the education of given populations?

However, the promise of technology is in the prospect of less limited change. Here it is necessary to note that educational technology itself is fundamentally organisational and social in its nature. The "technical" process of educating students involves pre-eminently their inter-personal relationships with teachers, other adults and peers. Any change in the technology of education centrally involves change in the form and content of these inter-personal relationships. Thus, even when educational technology involves much visible equipment and predesigned organisational arrangements, it remains an abstraction which has no substance separate from the specific social and psychological process in which it is applied

164

and adapted. When Westley notes that new educational technology, which has appeared in response to new needs and conditions of the student body, has often not been successfully applied and maintained, this describes a situation in which change in the people involved and their relationships, the change which should be the essence of such innovation, was not present.

In brief, most innovative technology, particularly in education, involves a change in social relationships.

Thus, a basic question for socio-technical analysis of education is:

8) What changes in the social system would allow or promote changes in the social and psychological relationships and processes which are involved in the development and use of improved educational technologies?

D) The environment

All of the above questions show that the socio-technical factors of educational establishments are closely interrelated with the larger environment. Thus the whole process of inquiry has to be alert to discern the main lines of these relationships, putting other data from socio-technical study into some useful perspective. For example, the extent to which schools serve as social selection mechanisms for the society will greatly bear upon possible forms of participation, technology and other aspects of the schools' socio-technical organisation. Or, another example, whether or not the status of teachers in, say, the lower schools serves as a transition to other social status, will affect possibilities for social organisation within the schools.

Such interpretations must be sought, for example, to show why the goals of the educational establishment appear "insensitive" to changes elsewhere or why education seems to reject some of the client population or why it fails to recognise useful developments relevant to its technology. Recognising that this effort requires - as said before - some hypothesis about, or some characterisation of, this larger environment, this aspect of socio-technical study involves a general question which can then be re-phrased to call attention to its more specific elements:

9) What main function does a given educational establishment actually perform in the larger society?

10) In examining the socio-technical factors (goals, participants, technology), how is the particular social system of an educational establishment shown to be related to the social systems of other public sectors and of the wider community?

<u>The environment and the technical system</u>. The technical system, involving the specific schooling function of educational establishments, can be the subject of particular attention in relation to the environment beyond schools. For example, the question could be asked:

11) <u>What are the implications for schools and universities of the alternative, competing or supplemental learning activities provided by the wider environment</u>?

Another aspect of the technical system is the "future environment" as perceived by the students on the basis of the existing environment, and which they will enter. The socio-technical categories could be used to explore:

12) <u>How does the social system of the educational establishment contribute to the students' perception of the larger environment and their preparation to enter it</u>?

III. THE PERSPECTIVE FOR FURTHER WORK

The above framework of questions represents an effort to foresee the extent to which the idea of socio-technical analysis could provide a useful "pedagogical" tool for the planning of education in an inter-sectoral context.

Of course the interpretive bias behind this framework - now widely held in OECD countries - is the need for rethinking the relationships between the school and the rest of society and the disutility of the kind of separation that has developed. Careful socio-technical study of education seems likely to substantiate the view that 1) within the schooling process the element of socially useful work is indispensable to promote the best personal development of young people, and 2) within productive work in society the educational element is essential to adult development. These considerations would call attention to the possibility that the most effective avenue to improving the quality of life might be to promote the development of people.

The socio-technical study of educational establishments would require detailed criticism and elaboration of the questions posed above. The search would be for inquiry illuminating diagnostic directions and possibilities for design of educational processes. However, the value way to test and develop a socio-technical approach to the study of education would be by means of a careful application to a number of educational establishments in different countries.

THE ROLE OF INSTITUTIONALISED "THINKING"

by Amitai Etzioni

The Problem

It is both a matter of co-ordination and of participation. No society, even the best organised and most open, has completely solved it. Maybe it cannot be solved, but various degrees of approximation to a solution can be achieved. The problem in question is that different societal services are carried out in different sectors and agencies, and that no wholly effective ways have been found to co-ordinate and "conservate" their services either for a given need, in this case education, or for the overall societal effort.

The problem, discussed here with regard to education, is multi-fold firstly, as not all the educational activities of the society are carried out by one agency or within one sector. In the United States, for instance, practically every government agency and armed service has an educational programme, some larger than those of the United States Office of Education. This will be referred to from here on as <u>inter-agency fragmentation</u>. Secondly, there is a multiplicity of levels of governments, each in the educational "business". Aside from the Federal Office of Education, each of the fifty United States has some kind of Department of Education;(1) in addition, there are various inter-State, regional education bodies, city, and other local government education governmental programmes. This will be referred to as the <u>inter-level fragmentation</u>. (The levels are not co-ordinated into a neat or even near-neat division of labour with a hierarchy of authority.) Finally, and most significant, there is <u>inter-sectoral fragmentation</u>, with part of the educational activities carried out by government agencies, part by the for-profit sector (e.g. Berlitz language schools),(2) and part by "third sector" (not-for-profit) school systems, such as parochial schools, major universities, etc. All this refers to fragmentation of education

---

1) For data on state school systems, see Clayton Hutchins and Richard Bar, <u>Statistics of State School Systems 1965-66</u>, (United States Department of Health, Education, and Welfare, 1968).

2) For a list of such companies, see Leonard S. Silk, <u>The Research Revolution</u> (New York: McGraw-Hill, 1960), p. 177.

itself.(1) While other societies may have less diversified systems, they often are quite fragmented along one or more of these dimensions.(2)

But all this is only in the way of introduction. The two foci of the problem of "inter-sectoral planning", as I understand it, lie in the separation, the lack of co-ordination, among all these dispersed educational activities and the similarly dispersed activities which aim at serving other societal needs (e.g. health, welfare, productivity), which have a significant corollary impact on educational activities (and which in turn are affected by educational activities). Second, there is the question of the participation of those affected by the activities, "the people", in the shaping or guiding of the educational system.

The first core problem is illustrated by the fact that planning to educate a group of disadvantaged children, for example, requires taking into account their health and health services, "success models" in their sub-culture, housing, stability of their families and several other activities, "owned" and managed by non-educational sectors.(3)

To stay with this example, the second core problem deals with the education of these youngsters and the interface between their education and other activities "conservated" by those to be affected, the community. Faulty inter-sectoral planning because the people have been ignored may well be a major reason why such a plan will be both mis-directed and not given to implementation; why it may be unresponsive to the real needs of the citizens and why it may meet severe resistance. Busing of children for purposes of racial integration is a case in point. Many black and white parents oppose it to such an extent that it is difficult to carry out.

The "Thinking" Solution

The problems depicted here are so common and pervasive that few who have written about the government of domestic services have not touched upon them in one way or another. Numerous solutions have been suggested. This is not the place to attempt to review them, let alone to assess their relative merits. Instead, one specific approach, relatively rarely explored, will be outlined.

1) For more on the "knowledge industry", see Fritz Machlup, The Production and Distribution of Knowledge in the United States (Princeton University Press, 1962).

2) For example, see A. Girard, "Selection for Secondary Education in France", in A.H. Hasley, et al., (eds.), Education, Economy, and Society, New York: The Free Press, 1961, pp. 183-194.

3) Much has been written on education for disadvantaged children. The classic study in this area is, of course, the Coleman Report. James S. Coleman, et al., Equality of Educational Opportunity, Washington, D.C.: United States Government Printing Office, 1966.

The approach is based on the assumption that fragmentation may be reduced but never eliminated.(1) This holds for the educational system as well as others, like health for example. Despite whatever other steps will be undertaken to improve inter-sectoral planning, steps which may well be very worthwhile (maybe even more effective in results achieved than the one discussed here), the steps indicated will still be necessary because the other measures may reduce, but will not eliminate the problem. The deeper reason for this is that even assuming an all-powerful czar for domestic services, or, more narrowly, for educational services, these activities will still have to be carried out in a multiplicity of departments and levels, each with a measure of division of labour; hence, there will remain divergent perspectives, and interests, and therefore they will not be easily or completely compatible with the others. Even if such harmonious supra-co-ordination would be miraculously achieved, the need to plan for the future (and not just to co-ordinate the present efforts), which inevitably affects different segments in different fashions, would necessitate the following mechanism.(2) It basically assumes that a higher level of inter-sectorality can be achieved on the thought or analytic level rather than on the administrative ones.(3) We explore this matter first from the viewpoint of co-ordination, then of participation.

A co-ordinating think tank

A significant contribution to the multifold problem depicted above might be made if the appropriate think tank were set up in the field of education.(4) A think tank, or policy research centre,

1) This contradicts a more "rationalistic" model of decision-making and planning which is a widely held conception.

2) Others believe that the future cannot be planned in such a way at all. They believe in incrementalism because of the limited cognitive capacities of decision-makers and the requisite scope and cost of information collection and computation. For a greater elaboration of this point of view, see Charles E. Lindblom, "The Science of 'Muddling Through'", Public Administration Review, Vol. 19 (1959), pp. 79-99; Robert A. Dahl and Charles E. Lindblom, Politics, Economics and Welfare, New York: Harper and Brothers, 1953; David Braybrooke and Charles E. Lindblom, A Strategy of Decision, New York: Free Press, 1963; Charles E. Lindblom, The Intelligence of Democracy, New York: Free Press, 1965.

3) For a more general presentation of the author's views on this subject, see Amitai Etzioni, "Mixed Scanning: A Third Approach to Decision-Making", Public Administration Review 27, December 1967, pp. 385-392.

4) Much has been written on think tanks. For more on think tanking in the social sciences, see: "International Inventory of Organisations and Individuals Doing Research in the Sociology of the Social Sciences", Sociology of the Social Sciences 11 (1), pp. 83-97; Amitai Etzioni, "The R & D Processing of Domestic Programmes", Science 171 (26th March, 1971). For a journalistic account of the problems of think tanks, see David A. Loehwing, "Heyday for Think Tanks", Barron's, 12th February, 1973.

is simply a group of persons who specialise in collecting and analysing data relevant to a broad need area from the viewpoint of its
handling that area rather than "basic" knowledge (i.e. sheer better
understanding).(1) Policy research is concerned with mapping alternative approaches and with specifying potential differences in
the intention, effect, and cost of various programmes.(2) It differs
from applied research in much the same way that strategy differs
from tactics; it is more encompassing, longer-run in its perspectives,
and more concerned with the goals of the unit for which it is undertaken; that is, it is more critical.

Policy research differs from basic research as strategy differs
from theory. It is much less abstract, much more closely tied to
particular actions to be undertaken or avoided. While basic research
aims chiefly to uncover truth, policy research seeks to aid in the
solution of fundamental problems and in the advancement of major
programmes.

There is a distinction as vital to the policy researcher and
policy maker as it is irrelevant to the basic researcher, namely the
degree to which a variable is "moveable", that is, the degree to
which the phenomenon it characterises is malleable. Thus, sociolo-
gists regularly break down social data into categories of sex, education, income, class, and race since from a basic research viewpoint
they all have a similar (or "independent") status. From a policy
viewpoint, however, some of these variables are "given" or extremely
difficult to change (sex), while others are relatively more change-
able (income).

The ranking of factors in terms of their malleability is, of
course, important in itself. Malleability is not of less status
for basic research or general theory than, say, the distinctions
signalled by Parson's pattern-variables.(3) However, while for
general theory malleability is but one of many fruitful bases for

---

1) For a more lengthy and thorough review of the author's work on
   policy research, see Amitai Etzioni, "Policy Research", American
   Sociologist 6 (June 1971), pp. 8-12.

2) Hendrik D. Gideonse has developed a framework particularly for
   policy research in education. See his "Policy Framework for
   Educational Research", Science 170 (4th December, 1970),
   pp. 1054-1059. Also, see Robert C. Andringo, "Why Won't
   Educators Help Congress Write Education Laws?" The Chronicle
   of Higher Education, 30th July, 1973. This latter article
   focuses on a proposal for a national centre for post-secondary
   education policy research.

3) See, for example, Talcott Parsons "Family Structure and the
   Socialisation of the Child" in Talcott Parsons and R.F. Bales,
   et al., (eds.), Family, Socialisation, and Interaction Process
   (New York: The Free Press, 1955), pp. 50ff.

theory building and research, it is central to policy sciences. Policy science as a conceptual discipline must alert the researcher and the policy maker to differences in malleability; it must focus its attention and research efforts on the more moveable variables and on the conditions under which the less moveable ones can become open to modification.

From a consideration of differential malleability, the next step is to consider who can move what. On the macrosocietal level, I have found it fruitful to apply a conceptual scheme called societal guidance. I distinguish between controlled and uncontrolled processes, and I specify the attributes of the controlling agents in terms of their knowledge, commitments, decision-making strategies, and amounts and kinds of power; I also explore the capacities of those controlled and the conditions under which they are mobilised to support, as against oppose, the controlling units.(1)

Policy research also differs from basic research in its central methodological considerations, considerations that apply to a lesser extent to applied research. For the basic researcher, science is an open-ended enterprise. There are no intrinsic reasons for the completion of a study at any particular deadline, and the dictum "until proven otherwise" is always at least implied. For the policy maker, there are specific times when fundamental decisions will be made and the decisions made then will become the base for more detailed decisions. The policy researcher must schedule his research so as to produce conclusions by that point (unless, of course, he can delay the decision until better data and analyses are available). For the basic researcher to conclude that the data at hand are too thin to warrant conclusions is both fully legitimate and in line with self-interest (he protects himself from any backlash from conclusions based on insufficient data and increases his chances for obtaining additional funds for his work). For the policy researcher to reach such a conclusion, unless the data are extremely poor, is an abrogation of his responsibility; the policy maker is likely to make a decision anyhow, and he probably will make it less well if the policy researcher has not shared whatever data and analyses are available, highlighting their limitations, of course.(2)

For a policy research centre to be effective, the following attributes are required:

1) See Amitai Etzioni, The Active Society, New York: The Free Press, 1968, pp. 488ff.

2) For a further discussion of a policy research, see Amitai Etzioni, "Policy Research", op. cit. Also, see: James Fennessey, "Some Problems and Possibilities in Policy-Related Social Research", Social Science Research 1 (1972), pp. 359-383; Yehezkel Dror, "Approaches to Policy Sciences", Science 166 (10th October, 1969), pp. 272-273.

1. <u>Continuity</u>. A task force composed for a short panel usually
   cannot do the job, because it requires deep familiarity with
   problem areas, with solutions previously tried, and with the
   relevant data.
2. <u>Interdisciplinary representation</u>. As the problems which
   are under study by policy researchers have educational,
   health, economic, psychological, sociological and other dimensions, it is necessary that these disciplines be represented during the research effort.(1)
3. <u>Committed staff</u> willing to conduct policy research and analysis is needed, rather than individuals who will try to
   "Robin Hood" funds or data for basic research (or partisan,
   political) work.(2)
4. Staff willing to look at the world from an <u>interdisciplinary
   focus</u>(3) which means - as each researcher is an active member of one, at most two, disciplines - they must learn to
   understand the basic assumptions and concepts of the others,
   sufficiently to be able to follow their points.(4)
5. <u>A division of labour</u>. Some persons committed to data collection and analysis; some to strategic thinking and concepts; some to communication with policy makers and publics.
6. <u>Sufficient economic and political autonomy</u> from the educational agencies to be free to explore new alternatives;
   sufficient access - to be able to understand the constraints
   and to avoid "utopia writing".

Such a centre would be of service to any one government agency,
level, or sector.(5) Actually, many of those centres which exist

1) For a review of the importance, scope, and process of inter-
   disciplinary research, particularly involving the social sciences,
   see "Interdisciplinary Research - An Exploration of Public Policy
   Issues". A Study Prepared for the Sub-Committee on Science,
   Research, and Development, United States House of Representatives.
   Washington, D.C., United States Government Printing Office.

2) See Amitai Etzioni, "Redirecting Research Dollars", <u>Washington
   Post</u>, 11th June, 1972 for a further elaboration of "Robin Hooding".

3) For a critique of departmental boundaries, see Dael Wolfle, "The
   Supernatural Department", Science 173 (9th July, 1971).

4) For more on this particular subject, see "Toward Developing
   Experimental Social Research that Constructively Criticises
   Public Policies and Programmes", by Leonard Goodwin of the
   Brookings Institution. The paper was presented at the August
   1972 annual meeting of the American Sociological Association in
   New Orleans.

5) For a discussion of the relationship between the federal government and scientists which pays particular attention to education,
   see Philip Hardlee, "The Federal Government and the Scientific
   Community", <u>Science</u> 171 (15th January, 1971), pp. 144-151. Also,
   see Henry W. Riecken, "The Federal Government and Social Science
   Policy", <u>The Annals of the American Academy of Political and
   Social Science</u>, 394 (March 1971), pp. 100-113.

are monocratic from this viewpoint. For example, the United States
Air Force was thus served by RAND.(1) Soon the United States Army
and Navy set up their own "think tanks" while the Department of
Defence relied more on the Institute for Defence Analysis for its
think tank back-up. The United States Office of Education has five
centres of its own (although a far cry from the suggested model);
the Office of Economic Opportunity - the Institute for the Study of
Poverty, at the University of Wisconsin (Madison).(2)

These centres are of only indirect interest here. A centre to
help ease the problem of lack of co-ordination in education would
have to bridge at least two elements, possibly all three - that is,
inter-agency, inter-level, and inter-sectoral fragmentation. Thus,
an inter-agency centre for educational activities would deal with
this source of fragmentation; it could add on persons for other
levels of government, and for other sectors. Most important, it
may have to encompass those who concern themselves with non-
educational activities as well as educational ones, if this is the
bridge which is being sought.

If the centre mixes researchers, strategic thinkers, and administrators on loan from the relevant agencies, levels and sectors, it
will - and should - experience within its confines the relevant
tensions: the researchers and thinkers may well be more dedicated
to the overall purposes but they may also be inclined to lack
reality-testing; the persons from various administrative backgrounds
may be more in tune with difficulties of implementation and other
problems more relevant to their particular segment of the world.
The tug of ideas and positions which would be worked out in the
centres, to the extent possible, is "what it is all about", so to
speak. Exempt from direct agency, level, or sector representation,
freed from making specific binding decisions (in contrast to, say,
inter-agency committees), on leave from the respective administrative
bodies, the development of a shared perspective, notion of reciprocal
links and effects, and commitment to overall educational purposes
is more likely (I chose my words carefully) to prevail and be worked
out.

Thus, here one might, with relatively greater ease, ask: how
can efforts in education, nutrition, guidance, housing, etc. be
articulated so they support rather than ignore, if not undermine,
each other? In the policy research centre, specific cross-sectoral

---

1) RAND has reportedly been changing its focus since the Ellsberg
   case. For an account, see Richard Saltus, "Rand Corporation
   Alters Research Direction", Washington Post, 29th July, 1973.

2) For descriptions and comparison of such government-connected
   "think tanks", see Think Tanks, by Paul Dickson, New York:
   Atheneum, 1971.

plans could be worked out and explained. These in turn, could then be carried to the various implementation bodies where, with proper rotation, they may be promoted by the administrators who were previously at the centre, shared in their development and shared in the joint perspective developed. This is, of course, in part optimistic. The shared perspective is easy to lose; departmental loyalties - quick to re-establish, but it may be relatively more effective than any other procedure.

To clarify further what such a policy research centre is and what it attempts to do, it is perhaps useful to specify what it is not. It is not a continuing education seminar where a selected group of policy makers are invited to listen to one or a number of learned professors lecture in their areas of expertise. The object is not to bring a group of people to the feet of a master who has the answers in his pocket and the charisma to put them over. Rather, the aim is to make possible a dialogue among a group of equals who each have different but overlapping areas of competence and experience. Nor is the policy research centre to be a kind of planning agency. Whereas planners typically begin de novo without any personal grounding in what has gone before or in implementation, the purpose of the policy research centre is to engage the participation of those who are going to carry out the policy and those whose past experience has acquainted them with the important reality constraints. The chief advantage here is that if those who are to carry out a policy participate extensively in formulating it the plan is more likely to be a workable one and they will more likely remain committed to it than if the plan is totally the product of outsiders no matter what their professional qualifications. By the same token, it is important to differentiate the policy research from an inter-agency committee. In order to draw people out of their accustomed roles and their habitual ways of thinking, it is necessary to bring them together as individuals and not as representatives of their respective agencies. Yet in contrast to places like the Centre for Advanced Studies, where people go as individuals to do their own work and need have little or no contact with one another, a major purpose of the policy research centre would be to spark communication between administrators on problems common to them in their respective agency experience.

Perhaps the closest analogue to the policy research centre is the President's Council of Economic Advisors. It has a permanent senior staff of three, who, when the President comes to them with a particular question - such as what could be expected to happen if we pursue this or that anti-inflationary policy - pull together a group of people from various departments and agencies who have the relevant knowledge and experience and conduct an inter-sectoral

study. Along these lines, then, one would imagine the policy research centre as staffed by a small group of senior researchers as
well as a larger group of permanent, in-house research assistants,
while the bulk of the participants would be rotating groups of administrators chosen according to the particular inter-sectoral mission at hand.

Communication with policy makers

Under the arrangement just outlined, or through other schemes,
policy researchers still must communicate their "products" to the
policy makers, whether they are the President and his staff, the
Iowa Department of Education, or a local chapter of the League of
Women Voters. While this may seem obvious, it is in fact not fully
understood, and the need for communication is often overlooked.

The typical and traditional way research findings are communicated is through publication. Papers read at professional conferences,
articles, books, and even stencilled reports are the most widely
used modes of communication. Experience suggests, however, that
while these may be the most effective channels for communicating
basic and applied research, they do not serve policy research nearly
as well.

Policy researchers must expect some resistance to their conclusions, resistance on the part of the policy maker that is emotional (due to commitments to other policies), cognitive (due to
lack of information and training), and self-interested (the recommended policies may serve some groups less well than the obsolete
ones do).(1) Formal means of communications, such as those listed
above, are particularly ineffective in overcoming such resistance.
Frequently repeated, face-to-face exchanges seem very necessary.
Pre-socialisation (preparing for the report) and follow-up (after
it is handed in) are essential. The report itself is often not
really necessary; it serves more to fulfil contractual obligations
and to provide an opportunity for and legitimisation of interaction
with the policy maker than to communicate with him.(2)

---

1) Further insights into the problem of resistance to accepting or
   using the social scientist's conclusions are presented in Alvin
   Gouldner, "Explorations in Applied Social Science" in Alvin
   Gouldner and S.M. Miller (eds.), Applied Sociology, New York:
   The Free Press, 1965, pp. 5-22. An earlier but not less insight-
   ful statement of the problems confronting the application of
   social science is given in Louis Wirth, "Responsibility of Social
   Science", The Annals 249 (January), pp. 143-151.

2) Or perhaps with his aide. For more on this, see Robert Sherrill,
   "Who Runs Congress?" The New York Times Magazine, 22nd November,
   1970.

If the rotational scheme just discussed were adopted, problems in the area of communication would likely be less severe. Yet the communication needs of policy research require skilled individuals, and administrators on loan from the various agencies or departments involved would not solve this problem. Policy researchers, unlike basic researchers, must be willing to invest a significant amount of their time and energy in communicating. They must learn how the world looks to the policy makers, how best the policy makers will absorb the new ideas, which means of documentation and presentation will be most successful, and in what sequences the findings should be offered.(1) The co-ordination of perspectives possible by "borrowing" administrators for periods of time from the various federal, state, and local agencies concerned with education would help to make this task somewhat easier.

Perhaps an example from another sphere will illustrate other forms of communication which are required for a policy research centre to be effective. Thus, one of the secrets of RAND's success is the hundreds of briefings RAND sets up for people in the Air Force, Department of Defence, Congress, the press, and groups of citizens.(2)

A successful policy researcher seems to require a psychic profile quite different from that of a basic researcher. Basic researchers can be "loners", people who get along best with libraries, computers, test tubes, and research associates. A policy researcher must be able to interact effectively with politicians, bureaucrats, housewives, and minority leaders.

It may be argued that the task of communicating might be delegated to go-betweens, leaving the researchers in their cubicles, but this is inefficient. Direct contact with policy makers, with the questions they raise, is useful and necessary to the policy researcher; it clarifies in his mind the constraints policy makers face and must live with and must be shown how to overcome. Frequently the policy researcher alone has the authority and knowledge to deal with the policy-maker's questions.(3)

1) For a discussion of this issue with particular regard to school systems, see Roderick F. McPhee, "Planning and Effecting Needed Changes in Local School Systems", in Designing Education for the Future, Vol. 3, Edgar L. Morpet and Charles O. Ryan (eds.). New York: Citation Press, 1967, p. 185.

2) Bruce L.R. Smith, "Strategic Expertise and National Security Policy: A Case Study," in Public Policy, Vol. 13, pp. 69-106. Bruce L.R. Smith, The RAND Corporation, Cambridge, Mass.: Harvard University Press, 1966, Chapter 6. Nick A. Komons, Science and the Air Force: A History of the Air Force Office of Scientific Research. Arlington, Va.: Office of Aerospace Research, 1966.

3) Yehezkel Dror, "Public Administration: Four Cases from Israel and the Netherlands", in The Uses of Sociology, Paul Lazarsfeld, W.H. Sewell, and H.L. Wilensky (eds.), New York: Basic Books, 1967, pp. 418-426.

Probably the least useful tool for communication between policy researcher and policy maker is the one most commonly used - the hundred-odd page stencilled report packed with statistics, footnotes, and technical terms. The shortcomings of this mode of communication are more than stylistic and cannot be overcome simply by providing an abstract or a "rewrite" in idiomatic English, sans tables and references.

A major difficulty is the level of abstraction (or analysis) at which the problem is conceptualised.(1) The more abstract the conceptualisation, the more difficult it is to provide concrete recommendations. Social science disciplines differ considerably in the extent to which they are abstract (or analytic). History and much of social anthropology are relatively concrete in the concepts most widely used. Parsonian sociology is extremely analytic. Institutional economics is much less analytic than econometrics.

The more analytic sciences use an esoteric language that must be translated before it has any meaning for policy makers, and the technical terms often contain assumptions that are typically not specified when such translation takes place. This is the case because the assumptions are universal and hence not more relevant to one report than to another and because they are numerous and hence to recite them in a report dealing with a specific question would make the communication ponderous. Many policy researchers are not even conscious that they subscribe to these assumptions (for example, the assumption that man is not rational), but without sharing these assumptions their recommendations are not fully intelligible to the policy maker. Even if the assumptions were spelled out with greater regularity most policy makers would not have the long training necessary to take them into account systematically in evaluating the reports.(2)

Policy science, on the other hand, furnishes non-abstract concepts that are understandable to the policy maker; it furnishes practical knowledge that has no analytic foundation but is useful for moderating or complementing analytic knowledge, and it is, in general, not far removed from the observed world and that experienced by the policy maker. It thus reduces the need for transition and translation. For example, the person who attempts to run a school

---

1) For a further discussion of this problem from the point of view of the social statistics researcher, see Albert D. Biderman, "Information, Intelligence, Enlightened Public Policy: Functions and Organisation of Societal Feedback", Policy Sciences 1 (1970), pp. 217-230.

2) For further analysis of this issue from the point of view of planning, see Donald N. Michael "On Coping With Complexity: Planning and Politics", Daedalus 97 (Fall, 1968), pp. 1179-1193.

system on the basis of a psychological or sociological theory will soon find that practical experience is a needed element. One who seeks to run an after-school programme on the basis of an analytic science will soon find it necessary to know the bureaucratic and legal constraints and the cultural habits of the recipients.

Participation

The problem we have addressed so far is that of preparing a cross-sectoral map, perspective, approach, which could serve as the intellectual basis for inter-agency, inter-level, and inter-sector endeavours. It is time to add a key segment, the people.(1)

Planning which occurs in most think tanks is disassociated from the political reality. This is probably the most common reason why plans fail and policy makers distrust planners. By far the best way to secure realistic plans, and a greater acceptance of plans, is to have a participation, or representation, of those to be affected by the plan.(2)

There are many different ways this can be achieved. One approach, tried by the Institute of Society, Ethics, and Life Sciences, is simply to invite people to participate in the deliberations on an equal footing. In the case at hand, a discussion of physicians, medical researchers, ethicists, and lawyers, about the treatment of Down's syndrome, was expanded to include two couples who have children afflicted with mongolism. The underlying assumption here is that any one person - a welfare mother, a school teacher - can reflect what the category of individuals he or she is part of would say, without a more formal representative procedure or sample being required.

A variation of the same approach suggests inclusion of "known" leaders of the particular community or communities that would be affected by the plan.(3) For instance, if a decentralisation of schools is planned for a black community, black leaders in that community would be invited to participate in the inter-sectoral planning.

Another mechanism that could be used is formal representation of the interests to be affected. One example of where this has been tried is in the French planning committees. When these

1) For a review of the literature on political participation, see Lester Milbrath, Political Participation, Chicago: Rand McNally & Co., 1965.

2) This point is often made in the literature. For example see Patricia Cayo Sexton, The American School, Engelwood Cliffs: Prentice-Hall, Inc., 1967, especially Chapter 5.

3) For an early study of decision-making with regard to public schools, see Robert A. Dahl, Who Governs?, New Haven: Yale University Press, 1961, pp. 141-159.

committees concern themselves with production, business and labour leaders are invited to participate (but, oddly, no consumer representatives are invited to attend). When higher education is concerned, university administrators and professors (but not students) participate.

Public hearings by various commissions is still another format. For example, in recent years commissions have included the Kerner Commission on Civil Disorders, the Eisenhower Commission on the Causes and Prevention of Violence, and the National Commissions on Marijuana and Drug Abuse, Obscenity and Pornography, and Population Growth. Various congressional committees also have public hearings where "the people" are allowed (sometimes encouraged) to contribute.

The communication between policy makers and the communities also can go in the other direction. For example, the training of persons to carry the planners' message to the community, often a community unaware of its needs, at least as perceived by the planners, has been tried by the Institute of Policy Studies in Washington, D.C.

The degrees and modes of participation of community members affect the work of the policy research centre. They enhance its degree of reality; they reduce its utopianism; they put more premium on political symbols, strategy, consensus building, coalition formation, and mobilisation than on model building, data processing, and analytic focus.[1]

Obviously, each centre will have to balance its co-ordinating and its participatory components according to its specific missions. A greater emphasis on co-ordination will surely be found in a government-controlled and oriented centre than in one set up by a left-wing radical social movement. And, additional experience will have to be drawn upon as it is best to combine the two functions into one centre, two or more sub-centres, or phases on the work of one centre, beginning with a more participatory agenda setting, moving to a more analytic phase, broadening and focusing the agency's work.

1) For an overview of community participation in education, see "Community Participation", Harvard Educational Review 38 (Winter, 1968) pp. 160-175.

Part II

<u>THE POLITICS OF INTER-SECTORAL PLANNING</u>

<u>AND OECD COUNTRIES' EXPERIENCE</u>

POVERTY, EDUCATION AND
INTER-SECTORAL PLANNING
by Herbert J. Gans

INTRODUCTION

This paper attempts to present a planning model, a scenario for
a social process, which concerns itself both with education and the
achievement of greater economic equality, and thus has implications
for inter-sectoral planning. More specifically, the planning model
is oriented toward the achievement of two social goals:

1. the economic intergration of the poor, i.e. underemployed
   and unemployed and unemployable - and their children - into
   the "mainstream" economy; and
2. the dynamic use of education by this population.

By economic integration, I mean here the ability of the poor, particularly the urban poor, to leave the "secondary labour market" of
underpaid, unstable, and dead-end jobs and the insecurity and dependence of being on public welfare for the "primary labour market" of
well-paid permanent jobs with potentials for upward occupational
mobility.(1) In this paper, I define greater economic equality in
occupational rather than income terms; I am less concerned with questions of income and wealth redistribution than with "occupational redistribution", although an effective programme for occupational redistribution would also require some redistribution of income and
wealth.(2)

By dynamic use of education, I mean the ability of people to
obtain and use education for purposes of individual and/or social
growth in vocational and non-vocational ways, for self-improvement
and/or upward social mobility. This may be contrasted with a
static use of education, i.e. to learn only as much as is necessary
to remain in one's present socio-economic position. Needless to
say, a dynamic use of education implies more than mere school
attendance, for as the paper itself will make clear, I think

1) For a good discussion of theories of primary and secondary labour
   markets, see D. Gordon, Theories of Poverty and Unemployment,
   Heath, 1972.
2) H. Gans, More Equality, Pantheon, 1973.

that little is to be gained by having poor children attend schools
if they are unable or unwilling to learn - even if school attendance
keeps them out of the labour force or off the streets.

The aim of the paper is to describe a planning model by which
these two goals might be achieved. A planning model, as I use the
term here, is a description of a deliberately initiated social process which is designed for the achievement of stated goals; it
differs from a planning strategy in that it only suggests what should
be done, rather than how it should be done and implemented. Since
the model presented here must overcome both economic and political
obstacles before it can be implemented, it is less a proposal for
action than the statement of an ideal situation; as such, it may,
however be relevant for use as a model for inter-sectoral planning.

My competence to deal with the issues raised in this paper being
limited to the United States, the paper will be concerned only with
my own country. Even so, many of its observations and the planning
model itself apply to other countries which are beset with the same
kind of poverty that is found in the United States; the presence
of a rural population which has been pushed into the secondary labour
markets of the cities, or into unemployment and welfare dependency.
As such, the paper may be relevant to a number of European countries still undergoing urbanisation of its rural population, and to
others which are currently receiving immigrant workers - on other
than a "guest" basis - from rural areas of other countries.

I. THE ROLE OF EDUCATION IN ECONOMIC INTEGRATION

For over a century, urban-industrial America has been in the
process of absorbing rural immigrants and attempting to integrate
them into its economy, first, European emigrants during the 19th and
20th centuries, and then black and Spanish emigrants from the rural
areas of the United States, the Caribbean and Mexico since about
1920. As might be expected from a society the dominant elements of
which are committed to laissez-faire, little deliberate planning for
economic integration has taken place during the last 100 years.
Governmental anti-poverty efforts began only during the 1930s, and
even then, W.P.A. and public welfare programmes were aimed almost
entirely at those made temporarily poor by the Great Depression.
The more permanently poor did not become clients for governmental
programmes until the 1960s, and even then the programmes were small
and under-funded, and not really aimed at economic integration. In
terms of monetary expenditures, the most significant anti-poverty
programme - which was not even deliberately planned - was the expansion and liberalisation of welfare, which raised the incomes of many

poor people but only cemented them further into an already existing underclass, inferior to, separate from, and dependent on the rest of American society.(1)

Instead, the main thrust of deliberate planning has been educational, and the planning model has centred on the dynamic use of education, the argument being that if poor Americans could obtain the same education as middle class Americans, they would grow individually and socially and would thus be integrated into the economy like the middle class. Whether the major goal of this model - and the governmental efforts to implement it - was the economic integration of the poor is itself open to doubt; more likely the goal of education was social control: to reduce crime, pathology and "deviant" political and social behaviour on the part of the poor, although it was also believed that if schooling could alter the social and cultural behaviour of the poor, they would then be more easily integrated into the economy.

In order to understand properly the relevance of the educational planning model, it must be broken down into two separate elements, the supply of education and the use of education, although this distinction has not often been made by educational planners. Until the 1960s, at least, they tended to argue that if the poor could be supplied with the same amount and quality of education as everyone else, they would also make the same use of it as everyone else, and if they failed to do so, then the fault was theirs, and the planners' responsibility was ended.

Reviewing the historical and contemporary patterns in both the supply and use of education indicates that the poor have neither been supplied with what I call dynamic education, nor have they been able to use it for that purpose. (Indeed it is even possible to doubt that the majority of the middle class uses education for dynamic purposes.) The findings of Jencks and his associates suggest that education has played a much smaller role than heretofore thought in the economic integration and upward mobility of the children of middle class parents;(2) and it may be that educators and academics, who used education for upward mobility themselves, were simply translating their own life histories into a planning model for the entire society.

There is considerable evidence that the poor have always been undersupplied with education. During the 19th century, as Greer

1) F. Piven and R. Cloward, Regulating the Poor, Pantheon, 1971.
2) C. Jencks et al, Inequality, Basic Books, 1972. See also I. Berg, Education and Jobs: The Great Training Robbery, Praeger, 1970, and B. Harrison, Education, Training and the Urban Ghetto, Johns Hopkins University Press, 1972.

and others have shown, the poor had only minimal access to the schools, and were often labelled as retarded or uneducable and then pushed out of the schools at an early age.(1) Even for most of the 20th century, schools in poor neighbourhoods were physically and otherwise different from those in affluent neighbourhoods; they were housed in older buildings, had fewer teachers and larger classes, and received less money, per capita, then the schools in affluent urban and suburban neighbourhoods. These differences still exist in many cities, although the Coleman Report of 1966, which compared educational supply between blacks and whites (and indirectly between the poor and the rest of society) found that these differences were no longer significant.(2) The findings of the Coleman Report are still being debated, and since they did not compare schools on the basis of family or neighbourhood income, but on the basis of race, they undoubtedly understated the supply differences between the schools serving the poor and the non-poor.

Moreover, and perhaps more important, case studies of slum schools and studies of teacher behaviour and teacher expectations suggest that on those indicators of supply which are crucial to the use of schools and proper school performance, the schools of the poor are still grossly inadequate. The most important finding to my mind, at least, is that teachers have lower expectations for the educability of the poor, and apply these expectations in their instruction, so that through a self-fulfilling prophecy, the poor receive inferior teaching even when and where school facilities and teacher quality (as measured by their education and amount of experience) are equal to those in schools in middle class neighbourhoods.(3) It would be wrong, however, to blame this phenomenon purely on the teachers, for teacher attitudes toward their students only reflect more general middle class attitudes toward the poor Moreover these attitudes themselves have an important latent function; they serve to persuade the poor that they are inferior, that they do not deserve to be upwardly mobile, and that they ought to prepare themselves for adult life in the underclass. In fact, a number of writers have suggested that one major function of the public school is to sort children by class, and to supply whatever education is required to adapt them to the class to which they belong as children.(4) This argument holds that the school is basically a

1) C. Greer, The Great School Legend, Basic Books, 1970.

2) J. Coleman et al.,Equality of Educational Opportunity, United States Government Printing Office, 1966.

3) See e.g. R. Rosenthal and L. Jacobson, Pygmalion in the Classroom Holt, Rinehart and Winston, 1968.

4) Greer op. cit.; see also S. Bowles, "Getting Nowhere: Programmed Class Stagnation", Society, June 1972 pp. 42-49.

conservative institution which supports and continues the existing class hierarchy, and for this purpose, provides what I have called static education to most poor children. Children who are especially interested in the kind of teaching provided by the school may be assisted in upward mobility, and supplied with dynamic education, but the proportion of such children is small, probably even in the middle class, and it is minuscule for the poor. Although most teachers would reject the notion that they are deliberately trying to hold back poor children, nevertheless they make little or no effort to assist them toward a life of upward mobility. The conservative stratification function of the school is latent, but even if it were made manifest, it would not disappear.

In addition, inequities in the use of education continue to exist although there is still no agreement as to the causes of that in- equity, and no final explanation as to why poor children perform less well in school than others. I shall not review here the current dispute over this issue, which includes such explanatory variables as genetic inferiority on the part of poor blacks, malnutrition of both parents and children which leads to intellectual inferiority, family instability and matriarchy, the culture of poverty, and others. My own inclination is to explain the user-factors in the inability of many poor children to perform adequately in school in three ways.

First, despite all the educational reforms and other changes which have taken place in recent years, the school is still a middle class institution, at least in the sense that it approaches poor children with expectations that they are middle class, not to men- tion a curriculum, a vocabulary, and a cultural milieu that is based on the dominant middle class (or more correctly, lower middle class culture) of American society. Many poor children, however, come to school with a different culture, which is both a result of poverty and of what Rainwater calls "lower class culture";(1) also their upbringing prior to school does not include the anticipatory socialisation for going to school that many middle class children (and all upper middle class children) receive, notably the emphasis on verbal and cognitive performance, and familiarity with books and other printed cultural materials through which the school provides much of its education. Whether this lack of anticipatory socialisa- tion is called cultural difference or cultural deprivation does not make much difference in terms of the final outcome, even though the latter term has important political-symbolic connotations; the fact remains that when poor children come to school they are defined as inferior from the start.

1) L. Rainwater, <u>Behind Ghetto Walls</u>, Aldine, 1971. See also D.P. Moynihan, ed. <u>On Understanding Poverty</u>, Basic Books 1968.

Second, although poor parents want their children to succeed in school and often place great emphasis on education as a means to economic integration and social mobility, particularly in the black community, many parents cannot provide sufficient cultural and other support to their children once they are in school. Since such support is not provided by the teachers either, and since peer groups in poor neighbourhoods often discourage children from becoming emotionally and intellectually involved in the schools, the initial absence of anticipatory socialisation is compounded throughout the poor child's school career.

Third, and most important, poor children grow up in a society and culture which demonstrates to them that education is not a very effective means of economic integration and upward mobility for them, and that unless they are unusually brilliant and conform completely to school regulations, education is not likely to have a significant pay-off. Not only do poor children learn early that a high school education is not a guarantee of employment, but they also see that most of the adults who achieve economic success in their neighbourhoods - and those who are most visible to them - have become affluent without education. This is not unique to the poor; lower class culture is in many ways similar to working class culture, and until recently, even the children of working class parents have not received much evidence that going to school pays off; they saw instead that physical strength, manual dexterity, having the right contacts in the factory and/or the union were sufficient to obtain a secure and well-paying blue-collar job, and education was only of minor importance. The message that education is not likely to have a significant pay-off for poor youngsters is transmitted particularly by the peer group, and through it and the gangs that are so important in slum neighbourhoods, younger children learn from older ones that it makes little sense to do well in school. Given the lack of anticipatory socialisation and of continued parental support, as well as peer hostility, poor children soon decide that the demands the school makes on them are not worth the lack of eventual benefit, and since facing a culturally strange school, unsympathetic teachers, and a curriculum of dubious relevance is hard and alienating work, many poor children begin to drop out emotionally at an early age, and by junior high school they either stop paying attention or begin to rebel. From there it is only a short step until they become defined as disciplinary problems or underachievers, and while most stay physically in school until graduation, they have left it emotionally long before they get their diplomas. Their ability to perceive that education offers them little opportunity is of course mirrored by the findings of Jencks and his associates on the lack of association between education and mobility,

and is reflected by the decline in reading scores among poor children
as they reach the age where they begin to understand the depressing
future which society has in store for them.

The rediscovery of poverty in America during the 1960s has led
to some alteration in the basic educational planning model, for
many educational planners began to realise that the supply and use
of education were interrelated, and that in order to improve the
use of education among the poor for dynamic purposes, changes would
have to be made in the supply as well. Although some planners and
many teachers still believe that failure to use the school properly
rests solely on the shoulders of the poor, others have proposed a
variety of educational policies to affect the supply of education
so that dynamic use would be encouraged. One set of policies has
been sociometric; mixing poor students with middle class ones in
the hope that the contact between social classes would encourage the
poor to make more dynamic use of education - and also to give them
access to schools in middle class areas. The major policies have
been racial integration, and more recently, busing, and where such
policies have been permitted by the local school districts, and by
white parents, they seem to have had some success; some poor children have improved their educational performance, as measured by
the school, although there is as yet no evidence whether these same
children have achieved upward mobility in adult life. The Coleman
Report had already indicated that where poor black children were
able to go to school with middle class whites their educational
performance improved, but Coleman's data could not determine whether
this improvement was due to racial integration alone or also to self-
selection, that is, whether the children who benefited from integration came from homes which encouraged them effectively to seek
upward mobility. My own hypothesis is that self-selection played
as large a role as integration, particularly since in many cases,
black children who were sent to predominantly white schools remained
in a quasi-segregated position inside their new school. Undoubtedly
integration per se helped some students as well, but I suspect that
the major effect of integration has been what anti-poverty researchers have called "creaming"; providing the possibility for
the dynamic use of education to the ablest and most predisposed of
the poor. Although "creaming" is sometimes opposed because it
offers the most help to those who need it least, it should not be
forgotten that even these children might not have improved their
school performance without such help, and the major disadvantage
of creaming is that it is misinterpreted, giving the appearance that
a policy has been successful for all intended clients when it has
only helped some.

The second educational policy to affect the supply of education in order to improve its use has been compensatory education,

enriching the curriculum, teacher-training, and other aspects of
school supply. Most of the evidence regarding the effectiveness of
compensatory education has been negative or inconclusive, however,
and educational planners have not yet developed an educational
supply programme that would encourage large numbers of poor children
to become dynamic users of education. My own feeling is that the
search for such a programme may be fruitless; until poor children
realise that education can have an adult pay-off for them, neither
integration, compensatory education, nor any other programme is
likely to be very successful.

Education and Economic Integration: An Historical Analysis

The failure of the educational model to achieve the economic
integration and upward mobility of the poor is not a recent phenomenon, and Colin Greer has in fact argued that this model, which he
calls "the Great School Legend" has never worked.(1) Although
historical data are still scarce, it seems likely that much the
same pattern of unequal supply and use of education existed in
earlier periods of American history, e.g. among the European immigrants who came to America between 1850 and 1920. These immigrants
can be divided into two groups, those from peasant and farm-labourer
backgrounds, such as the Irish, Italians, Poles, Greeks, etc.; and
those from urban backgrounds, notably the Jews. Some Jews did use
education for upward mobility to a considerable extent, and they
have served as a model and illustration of the effectiveness of
education as a device for escaping from poverty. Unfortunately, the
educators and other policy-makers who then and now emphasized the
importance of education in occupational mobility drew much of their
"proof" from the Jews, and failed to notice that the peasant immigrant groups had a very different experience. They also faced an
educational system which could not teach them and did not want to
teach them, at least not in other than accepted ways, and they also
rejected education in much the same way as many of today's poor.
For these immigrants, however, education was not as important as
it is for today's young people, partly because they could find
unskilled jobs in larger number, partly because their families and
ethnic groups often had the proper social connections and the
numerical dominance within certain occupations to assure their
children access to jobs, and partly because the immigrants' work
expectations were much lower; they seem to have been more resigned
to underpaid and unstable jobs. Not only did the children of the
immigrants receive little encouragement from their parents to stay
in school, the parents wanting them to go to work and add to the

---

1) Greer, op. cit.

family income, but they themselves wanted to go to work quickly, and dropped out of school at an early age. Indeed, they dropped out in much larger numbers than today's students.

The peasant immigrants escaped from poverty much more slowly than is commonly thought, arriving in the middle class in large numbers only with the 3rd (second native-born) and 4th (third native-born) "generations". More important, they made their escape largely through occupational mobility and without much help from education. Even after children were no longer allowed to work, the peasant immigrant groups and their descendants did not show much interest in education, the feeling being that their children could obtain the same kinds of jobs as their parents, and that education, at least that provided in the schools, was neither necessary nor relevant for such jobs. Such attitudes can still be found among working class groups today, at least among those who hold the best-paying, most secure and most satisfying blue-collar jobs, but among most others attitudes toward education have changed in the last 20 years. They still think of the school as a middle class institution which does not have their interests at heart, but they now want their children to go to school, and even to college, not because they necessarily believe in education as an end in itself, but because they realise that further occupational mobility i.e. a secure white-collar job, cannot be achieved without education, and that even blue-collar work is no longer so easily obtained without a high school diploma. As automation and the decline of economic growth result in a decrease in blue-collar jobs, even non-mobile parents now accept the fact that their children must graduate from high school to find a niche in the primary labour market.

The history of the peasant immigrants and their descendants suggests a hypothesis about the role of education in economic integration and upward mobility which is just the reverse of the traditional educational model. For the poor, education is not a cause of or a mechanism for integration and mobility, but an effect, and children are neither supplied with nor use education for a dynamic purpose until after their parents have achieved a threshold of economic security in the primary labour market. Only when parents have found a secure place in the economy are they able and willing to provide the anticipatory socialisation and other support to enable their children to become dynamic users of education, and only when children realise that their parents have become full members of the economy and of society and that they themselves have a good chance for similar membership do they begin to realise that education may have a pay-off for them, and to perceive that they can use education as a means of achieving mobility. In other words, economic success leads to educational success, not the other way around; the historical experience seems to indicate that education is not a very

190

effective mechanism for the escape from poverty, becoming useful
only later, in the move from working class to middle class status.(1)
Moreover, only when parents have achieved economic security can
they pay some attention to their children's schooling; perhaps
equally important, only then do they have the political influence
to make sure, at least to some extent, that the supply of education
is adequate to their children's needs. To be sure, even after
parents have obtained economic security, many children do little
more than sit through the school experience, and only a minority
make dynamic use of education, but at least the opportunity for such
education now exists and can be made use of effectively by children
who are seeking further mobility; and even the children who only
sit through the school experience seem to receive sufficient social
credit and certification to be ready to enter the primary labour
market as long as they have done their sitting in a non-slum school.

The American economy and American society have changed considerably since the European immigrants began their slow march up
the socio-economic ladder, but the immigrant experience is still
relevant today, particularly because many of today's poor are also
from peasant and farm-labourer backgrounds, from the American South,
Puerto Rico and Mexico. Most of today's poor have higher occupational aspirations for their children than their European pre-
decessors, and they also realise much more clearly the importance
of education in an economy where unskilled jobs are rapidly dis-
appearing, but their ability to obtain access to a dynamic education
is still limited, as it was in the past, and the children are not
willing or able to participate in the educational process which is
available to them. Indeed, many would prefer to work rather than
to go to school if the laws permitted it, and I suggest that one of
their problems is that neither the economy nor the society enable
them to follow the immigrant pattern of beginning with occupational
mobility, and resorting to education only when enough mobility has
been achieved to assure a modicum of economic security and integration in the primary labour market.

Finally, there is one other difference between the immigrant
poor and today's poor: race - for the former were white and many
of the latter are either black or brown, and thus subject to racial
discrimination and segregation. Undoubtedly, racial antagonism slows
up the opportunity to escape from poverty, and in fact, even during
the 19th century, urban blacks were often kept in the lowest status
jobs, and those who had bettered themselves were often pushed down
again when white immigrants arrived. Even so, it must also be noted
that many of the immigrants, particularly those from Eastern and
Southern Europe were perceived as members of "inferior races" when

1) Greer, op. cit., p. 85.

they arrived, including the Jews, and were also subject to racial discrimination, although of lesser intensity than the blacks. However, once the immigrants had begun to move out of poverty, their alleged, or rather perceived, racial difference disappeared, and eventually they were treated like other whites. This would suggest that racial antagonism is strongly intertwined with class antagonism, and that the perception of racial difference declines with the prosperity of the alleged or real racial group. Consequently, I suspect that if greater occupational opportunities were extended to today's "non-white" poor, white perception of their racial difference would then also change, as indeed it already has, in limited amount, in the last 25 years. However, the present American economy does not really need the poor, and it is therefore all too easy for white Americans to argue that occupational failure is racially caused, and that if blacks cannot obtain or hold jobs, they are not entitled to policies to improve their job opportunities. As a result, even under optimum conditions, blacks and perhaps even Puerto Ricans and Mexicans can never repeat the occupational mobility process of the European immigrants in exactly the same way, for the continued existence of racial discrimination and segregation will continue to slow down their mobility, at least in the foreseeable future.

II. IMPLICATIONS FOR POLICY: AN OCCUPATIONAL PLANNING MODEL

The major policy implication of this analysis, and the planning model which follows therefrom, is that education is unlikely to be a sufficient factor in bringing about the escape from poverty, and that educational policies, both for supply and use, will be most effective after the escape from poverty has been achieved. A planing model which aims to bring about both economic intergration and the dynamic use of education as defined above, would therefore require a staged plan, which begins with the provision of jobs, enabling poor people to obtain secure and well-paying employment. Once they are integrated into this labour market, and they and their children see that there is a pay-off for going to school, educational policies then become relevant to provide additional upward mobility. The nature of these educational policies is beyond the scope of this paper, although it may be noted that the people I called the descendants of peasant immigrants appear to have achieved upward mobility into the middle class without special educational help; they have simply attended the schools available to them in their neighbourhood. It is of course possible that they would have moved up faster if they had had access to "better" schools, that is, schools deliberately planned to hasten their mobility, but such schools are not often available. In fact, most public schools do not seem to

concern themselves explicitly with student mobility, and only some
schools catering to an upper middle class population seem to stress
it at all explicitly, responding to parental pressure to "help get
their children into Harvard University".(1)

The planning model described briefly above assumes a linear
temporal relationship between economic integration and the dynamic
use of education; once the former is provided, the latter will
follow. However, whether a simple linear relationship exists and
how long it takes for its fruition is as yet an unanswered question.
The relative slowness of the peasant immigrants' movement into the
middle class - and at a time when opportunities for middle class
jobs were growing rapidly - suggests that the process may be slow
for everyone, and may in fact take more than a generation. Although
sufficient data to develop a "mobility-scenario" for these immigrants
are not available, it would appear that the typical pattern was for
peasant immigrants to remain unskilled labourers, who spent their
surplus income on obtaining property rather than investing it in the
education of their children.(2) The second generation moved into
the primary labour market by holding fairly secure semi-skilled and
skilled blue-collar jobs (or unskilled white-collar jobs), and only
the third generation, now coming into adulthood, is likely to be
moving firmly into the middle class. Even in this generation the
majority of young people do not go to college, however, and only a
small number obtain semi-professional or professional jobs, other
than public school teaching.

There are several reasons for the gradual nature of the mobility
process. One reason has been opportunity; until the last 10 years
opportunities for working children of working class homes to attend
college have been few. Although almost every State provided free
attendance at state universities, in many cases these universities
were located outside the major cities where the working class lives,
and children from working class homes could not afford to live away
from home. Another reason is lack of proper educational qualification; whatever the reasons, children attending public school in
working class neighbourhoods have not had the academic prerequisites
to make them eligible for college, and only when two-year community
colleges were set up (and "Open Enrolment" was established in
New York City to allow working class people with average grades in
high school to go to a four-year college) did the third generation
descendants of the peasant immigrants begin to stream into college
in large numbers.

---

1) For one illustration, see H. Gans, The Levittowners, Pantheon,
   1967, Chapter 5.:
2) S. Thernstrom, Poverty and Progress, Harvard University Press,
   1964.

A third reason is cultural and familial; there appear to be limits on how great an inter-generational change families will tolerate. For a working class child, entering the middle class - or going to college - represents a potentially drastic change in family relationships, because this kind of upward mobility often requires a cultural and attitudinal transformation which increases the social distance between parents and child, and sometimes neither parents nor children want this to happen. Parents may fear that their child will no longer have anything in common with them, or will look down on them as unschooled and inferior, and they will therefore discourage excessive upward mobility, or will try to persuade the child not to undergo cultural and attitudinal change even while taking advantage of college for occupational reasons. Children may feel less impelled to be loyal to parental culture and attitudes, but even so, upward mobility puts them under cross-pressures, from parents to remain in the parental culture and from college peers to adapt to the campus culture, and such cross-pressures are not easy to live with. Children can, of course, make a virtual break with their families, and they sometimes do so when the opportunities for upward mobility are very tempting, but even so I suspect that such a break takes place only among a minority.

There is yet another unanswered question: what kind of economic integration is required before favourable conditions for an "educational take-off" are created. I have heretofore implied that such a take-off will occur once parents have achieved economic security above the poverty line within the primary labour market; that is, when they have obtained a steady and permanent job with long-term promises for economic security, but reality is undoubtedly far more complex. In fact, I do not know whether my assumption is tenable, for even among second generation descendants of the European immigrants, wages were not high, and jobs were not secure. Consequently, it is possible that I have overstated the requirements for economic integration, and it may be that readiness for the dynamic use of education can occur once parents have escaped from poverty. It is even possible that the escape from poverty is not a prerequisite; it may be that parents are ready to encourage their children to achieve upward mobility through the schools if they have a relatively secure income below the official poverty line, for example, if they obtain welfare payments but know that these are likely to continue. Of course, in most cases, being a welfare client also means permanent insecurity, for the rules of eligibility for welfare change frequently, and few welfare recipients can ever be sure that the payments they receive one year will still be given to them the next year.

Finally, whether or not a significant number of children will make dynamic use of education depends also on the relevance of education to occupational success. From what I can read between the lines of the existing studies of mobility, most people are not particularly ambitious, or to put it another way, they are unwilling to pay the social and other costs of mobility which outweigh benefits, and most seem content for their children to improve their own status by only a small amount. Moreover, as long as education is not needed for a small amount of mobility, it will not be used for this purpose; as I noted earlier, working class Americans did not encourage their children to do well in school as long as they believed that their children could obtain well-paying and secure blue-collar jobs. Today, however, educational achievement, or at least educational credentials, seem to be required for almost all jobs in the primary labour market, so that the macrosociological conditions for the dynamic use of education are favourable.

The previous discussion suggests that the exact nature of the major variables in my planning model is still unknown. Consequently, I can only hypothesise that if the present generation of poor people with young children could be assured an income above the poverty line, preferably through secure and dignified employment, some parents would be ready to assist their children to make dynamic use of education, although in many cases this use of education would only take place among their grandchildren, that is, with two generations of economic integration.

The most effective anti-poverty policy, therefore, is not one that begins with education but with the provision of jobs, enabling poor people to obtain a yet unknown level of income, occupational status, and economic security, with the intent that once they perceive themselves to be free of poverty and its insecurity, they will be able not only to obtain access to a qualitatively and quantitatively better supply of education but they and their children will perceive that there is a pay-off for going to school. Thus I would argue that the prime thrust of inter-sectoral planning for educating the poor must be occupational, and that even if the planning goal is educational, that is, to encourage children to make dynamic use of the schools, the planning for this goal must begin in those agencies of government which function in the occupational sphere and in the labour market.

In the United States my planning model would require a policy of full employment, which may entail some job-creation, either by government directly or through governmental subsidy of private firms and community development corporations, both in manufacturing and in the now rapidly growing service industries, to provide jobs for the unemployed. The model would also require a policy of wage subsidies and job-enrichment for the now underemployed, the so-called

working poor, who work at full-time jobs for wages below the poverty
line. Their number is far larger than the unemployed poor; in 1972
about one-fourth of all poor people held full-time jobs, whereas
only about 5 per cent reported that they were unable to find jobs.(1)
The working poor need wage supplements to bring their incomes above
the poverty line, and improvements in working conditions; above all,
the provision of job security and the opportunity for advancement.
Such improvement is probably best achieved by further job-creation,
so that the present working poor can move up to better jobs.

Perhaps the primary need for job-creation is to be found among
poor young people who have dropped out of school, for unemployment
rates for this age group are much larger than the overall rate,
rising to as much as 50 per cent in some urban ghettos. Some of
these young people are school drop-outs and lack the skills needed
by today's labour market. Some economists have argued that adjustments should be made in the minimum wage law so that they can be
hired at sub-minimal wages, but while this may bring them jobs, it
is also possible that they would replace adults, who must be paid
a minimum wage, thus only shifting unemployment to a higher age-
group. The job needs of the young will have to be met by job-
creation, but here the policy problem is particularly complex, since
they need jobs which provide some opportunity for advancement, perhaps with a chance to return to school later, even though many of
them lack skills.

Incidentally, I would also be inclined to argue for job-
creation for even younger people, those who are truant from school,
or who have dropped out emotionally, and would be in the labour
market if compulsory school attendance were not required. Until
child-labour laws were passed, these youngsters often went to work
at an early age, and if it were possible to develop a job-creation
programme that provided them jobs with some educational potential,
a chance to return to school later, and freedom from exploitation
by employers, allowing them to work would be more desirable than
forcing them to stay in school.

Job-related policies have one major limitation; they are irrelevant to people who are unable to work either because of disability
or family responsibilities. Many of the American poor fall into this
category, although not entirely by their own choice, for many poor
mothers who are family heads would prefer work to welfare, provided
they could obtain better-paying jobs and could find day-care facilities for their children.(2) While one can argue that such women

1) United States Bureau of the Census, "The Characteristics of the
   Low Income Population", 1972, Current Population Reports, Series
   P-60, No. 91, December 1973, Table D, p. 5.

2) See L. Goodwin, Do the Poor Want to Work? Brookings Institution,
   1972, and L. Kriesberg, Mothers in Poverty, Aldine 1970.

should be allowed to remain home to care for their children, it can also be argued that if they want to work, and can find help in caring for their children, they should be allowed to do so, on the assumption that their income and morale would be higher, and they might move closer to economic integration, and thus persuade their children of the possibilities for a more hopeful future. If jobs cannot be provided, however, such women, and other unemployable poor people need income grants in lieu of work, which can provide them a decent and secure standard of living, the assumption being that if economic security is provided the children's willingness to perform in the schools would be enhanced. Even when there are no job holders in the home I suspect that the provision of income and income security would reduce family despair and depression, and give at least some children the feeling that they are not inevitably condemned to underclass status.

Implications for Educational Policy

If the preceding analysis is correct, education plays a subsidiary role in economic integration and upward mobility; by itself, it can do little to achieve either, at least for the mass of poor people. From a policy perspective, however, the more important point is that education is an intrinsic part of both the economy and society - an old idea to be sure, but one that has often been ignored by educational planners who see the school as somehow standing outside of society and altering it. Planners are not alone in this view of the place of education; in most American communities the school and the board of education are viewed as outside the political process, "above politics", so to speak, although in reality they are very much part of that process, even if the symbolic imagery is non-political. For this paper, the school's relationship to the economy is most important, but that relationship is largely passive and powerless: the school can train students to prepare themselves for the available jobs in the economy, but it cannot itself affect that economy, for being a local institution, "above politics", and without direct economic functions, it cannot even use its taxing power, its capital investment or its payroll to intervene in the economy. Teachers' unions often have more national and local power than school boards. Presumably, if an entire school system went on strike, it would have some power arising from a threat to the social order, but while a garbage collectors' strike can force concessions because of an imminent danger to the public health, the schools would have to be closed for a long time before equivalent dangers would appear or be perceived. Even then, the primary source of danger would not be the disappearance of education but the fact of having many thousands of bored youngsters running loose in the community. Educational dangers would, however, be minimal; even if a city were without schools for a year it is doubtful if permanent ill effects would result. Some children would not learn basic verbal, mathematical and graphic skills for a year, but they would learn them the subsequent year, and most everything else they could probably learn from television, other mass media and from library books - and as far as marketable skills were concerned, these would be provided quickly by expanded job-training on the part of industry.

These observations are not meant to suggest that the school is superfluous, but only to indicate its limited political and economic influence. But if the school does not have any leverage over the economy how can it be expected to help the poor escape poverty? One could visualise a hypothetical situation in which such leverage could be exerted; in a community faced with labour scarcity and with industries unable or unwilling to provide job-training the school could play a decisive role in supplying trained workers, and it could then use its role and the resulting leverage to require industry to hire poor graduates. The example is only hypothetical, but it does suggest a useful policy perspective, to ask:

1. under what conditions can the school play a role in the economy? and
2. when it cannot play such a role, how can it isolate itself from the leverage that the larger society has over it, and free itself to do other than prepare poor children for adulthood in the underclass?

These questions yield several policy possibilities.

First, impressionistic evidence suggests that when schools are directly tied to economic activities and jobs they seem to function much more effectively than when they are separate from the economy, if only because students discover at an early age that there is an educational pay-off in the form of jobs. In American small towns the schools often functioned as job-trainers for major local industries; and while this also resulted in the expenditure of public funds for subsidising private enterprise, and narrowing of choice for the students involved, it would be useful to discover whether such schools were - and still are - more effective in teaching poor children than urban schools. Another kind of evidence comes from independent sub-cultures which are able to close the gap between their economic institutions and educational ones in ways that the larger society is unable to do; for example, the Black Muslims appear to have developed effective schooling to train their young people for Muslim enterprises, as have other self-sufficient groups with their own micro-economies, such as the Amish and the

Bruderhof.(1) Unfortunately, the experience of such groups cannot
be relevant to urban economies and schools, at least in America,
and it is hopelessly utopian to suggest that such schools should
develop their own economic organisations - or tie into ongoing
community development corporations - to provide jobs for their
graduates.

A second possibility is one which is implicit in the occupational planning model; to institute schooling in connection with a
job. The job-training experiments of the 1960s have shown that
such training schemes worked educationally when jobs were guaranteed
to trainees prior to training, because the trainees could see that
participation in the training scheme would have a pay-off. This
would suggest again the first policy possibility mentioned above -
developing a school which is explicitly organised for training for
a guaranteed job. Since it is impossible to offer job guarantees
to young children such a policy can only be applied later, when
poor young people are looking for work, and particularly when they
must work because they have familial responsibilities. I suspect
that if ways could be found to send poor people to school in their
late teens and early twenties, to schools which combine job training
and other forms of education, they would learn more quickly and
effectively than in the present schools. After all, middle class
young people function on much the same schedule; many only begin to
study hard in their senior years in college or in graduate school,
when the need to prepare for work becomes urgent.

Of course, by the late teens and early twenties, poor people
take on bread-winning responsibilities which make it impossible for
them to take the time and the income loss to go to school, but it
might be possible to develop schools and scholarship programmes for
young adults which would enable them to go to school and also pay
them an income so that they can support their families. Probably
the easiest way to institutionalise such a school would be as part
of a job-training scheme, with the relevant government agencies subsidising employers or prospective employers to expand and lengthen
the job-training programme so that it will provide the basic education the trainees did not receive in childhood.

A variant of this approach would be to send people to school
while they are already working, a kind of expanded job-training which
has long been used by American industries who send some of their
workers back to school. Of course, they usually provide such educational opportunities only to their higher-ranking workers, and then
frequently through in-house "schools", but some "para-professionals"
who are working for public agencies are being sent to community

---

1) B. Zablocki, The Joyful Community, Penguin Books, 1971.

colleges to catch up on their education while also receiving further job-training. The military services already approach this kind of model in their own educational activities, for they take adolescents and young adults and support them while training them, either for their own economic organisations within the military, or for post-military careers; the Israeli army seems to have been especially effective in teaching poor young people before they go back into civilian life. Military organisations are, for a variety of reasons, often more efficient than civilian ones, but while I would certainly not suggest that education of the poor be given over to the military, it would be worth analysing military programmes to discover if civilian equivalents could be established.

If the schools cannot exert leverage on the economy, or coordinate their activities with that economy, another approach is to look for conditions under which they can escape the leverage exerted on them by the larger economy and society. The first policy possibility here takes off from the findings that among poor children, school performance declines as they become older; consequently, one might argue that the most effective role for the school is when poor children are very young, too young to have learned either what society has in store for them, or what is taught by the street culture of the slums. The primary example of education for very young poor children is Headstart, and it has sometimes been surprisingly effective, although its impact disappeared quickly as its graduates were thrown back into slum neighbourhoods and schools. In some instances experimental schools have sprung up in American ghettos which were able to isolate children from the outside economy and society by employing a curriculum geared to the children's own experience and by employing teachers who did not approach their students with low expectations. Even so, a school geared to the culture of the poor has its own limitations, for it cannot easily prepare children to face a world in which there are few jobs for them, again because such schools are not connected to economic organisations that could hire their graduates. Ghetto culture is relevant to the ghetto, but not to the society outside which provides the majority of jobs.

A second policy possibility for shaking off at least some of the leverage of the larger society is to attempt to reorganise the school to eliminate the structure imposed on it by the larger society, insofar as that structure impedes dynamic use of education. What I have in mind here is a kind of community control, the community being parents while children are young, and the children themselves as they get older. A school in which the students themselves have some control over school organisation, curriculum, regulations and even over teaching might inspire more interest in participating in the school on the part of students, and might even evoke better

school performance.(1) Of course, it might be difficult to recruit
teachers for such a school, and there is the danger on the one hand,
that the educational benefits would accrue mainly to the brighter
students, or on the other hand that students with little interest in
education would dominate it and turn it into a community centre or
even an anarchic playground. Moreover, even if such a school were
successful, it could not solve the post-school problem, for while
public and private agencies might quickly hire the most able student
leaders, the other students would still have to be content with the
existing labour markets. In a sense, such a school would provide
only a temporary and essentially escapist interlude - although in
that case it would duplicate one of the functions of the liberal
arts colleges.(2)

A third policy approach is to copy those educational approaches
which already seem to be effective for poor people, even if they take
place outside the school. Probably the most effective educational
agency for young people is the peer group and gang, although its
"curriculum" is very narrow, highly pragmatic, and developed for
very short-range learning needs. Another such agency is television,
for the poor are often heavy users of television and some other mass
media. Television has only rarely been geared to education, however,
except through the use of television in the schools, where it becomes
subsidiary to the conventional pedagogical methods. "Sesame Street"
has been shown to be a useful educational programme for poor children,
however, and I suspect that if more programmes like "Sesame Street"
could be provided, and if special entertainment programmes could be
developed for poor children which provide education as part of the
kind of entertainment they seem to prefer, even the ordinary TV
adventure and cartoon programmes, they would provide much better
education than most schools.(3) To be sure, much of television's
success is a function of its unique curriculum, and if entertainment
were ever transformed explicitly into education, its attractiveness
would decline quickly - as it does with educational programming
today. Moreover, it is difficult to institutionalise the teaching
and learning situation of television, because part of its appeal is
the voluntary nature of its usage, but even so I would suspect that
teachers who know how to use the popular culture of television for
didactic purposes would be able to provide a superior form of education, at least in some subjects.

None of the policy possibilities I have suggested are very
likely to be tried out on a large scale, and for the foreseeable

1) Gans, More Equality, op. cit., pp. 219-226.
2) Needless to say, other kinds of educational community control
   efforts are also relevant here, as well as parent-control schemes
   such as the proposed voucher experiments.
3) H. Gans, "The Mass Media as an Educational Institution",
   Urban Review, February 1967, pp. 5-14.

future most poor children will continue to go to conventional schools and some to schools in which various kinds of reforms are being tested. Although I am sceptical that any major change in their school performance will take place until there is a change in their post-school future, and until they have some assurance that there is a proper place for them in their economy and society, it is nevertheless worth continuing the search for schools, or classes within schools, where poor children are being taught to use education dynamically, to study the "success stories" and to apply them on a larger scale. Some useful lessons might be learned through more cross-cultural analyses of how other societies educate their poor children, and why they are successful, although the experiences of other nations and cultures cannot often be imported, because social structures and stratification systems differ even between industrial societies. For example, it would be difficult to apply the educational successes achieved by the Cubans and Chinese among their own poor to the American situation, since in both countries the educational system is tied to a revolution which was waged on behalf of the poor and which resulted in a considerable improvement in the fortunes of the poor.

The Occupational and Educational Model and Planning Strategy

In essence, this paper has suggested that the best way to help the poor escape poverty and obtain the opportunity to use education dynamically is through the provision of jobs, and that continued reliance on and hope in the schools as an anti-poverty mechanism is illusory. The adoption of the occupational model and the rejection of the educational model for which I have argued can be defended as long as the analysis is limited to what I earlier called a planning model; it is not a planning strategy, however. Consequently, my analysis can be questioned simply on the basis that it is utopian:

1. that there is little chance of an occupational model being implemented; and
2. that possibilities for change are more likely in the educational system than in the labour market and in the economy.

To be sure, a full employment, job-creation and job-enrichment policy is difficult to implement, for it is expensive in public funds and requires structural economic change as well. The American economy is, like most other economies today, mainly capital-intensive; management aims to replace workers with machines wherever possible in manufacturing, whereas a job-creation policy can only be effective when the economy is on a labour-intensive course. The services industry is, however, still largely labour-intensive, and in most cases, will remain so. Consequently, this is the sector of the

202

economy in which job-creation policies would be most relevant. In the private sector of the service industry, however, jobs are often poorly paid and thus not very attractive to young people today, particularly since their job expectations are often high. The public sector holds better promise here, except that in the United States, at least, it is heavily financed by State and local taxes, and thus under State and local control. States and localities have never been very enthusiastic about programmes for the poor, however, since the poor are only a small part of their constituencies, and the tax-payers are unwilling to divert funds to the poor. As a result, the outlook for occupational policies in the public services sector is not optimistic, at least in the short-run. In the long run, as automation and international competition further deplete the jobs in manufacturing, the Federal government may be forced to become an employer of last resort, but even if this seems likely, there is no guarantee that the government's employment policies will be comprehensive enough to embrace the poor; it is quite possible that, as in the Great Depression, the majority of the poor would once again be left out.

Nevertheless, the possibilities for educational reform do not look any brighter. Of course, far larger amounts of public money are being poured into education than into job-creation and job-enrichment schemes, and it will probably always be easier to persuade American taxpayers and politicians to appropriate money to educate the poor than to employ them. However, most of that money does not go to the users of education, but to the suppliers, and it may well be that the funds will continue to flow only as long as these suppliers continue to act, intentionally or not, to prepare the poor for underclass status. Public education in America has almost always been a conservative institution, despite its egalitarian rhetoric, and because it is so extensively controlled by local power-structures, even when the funds come from Washington, it is utopian to expect that the schools will ever be very different than they have been. In fact, the schools may be conservative in part because they are the only major institution which has responsibility for and continued contact with the poor - except for welfare agencies, but they increasingly function as transmitters of transfer payments, and their case-work and counselling activities are being reduced all the time. The school, or rather the urban school, thus becomes a major agency of social control of the poor; it has the primary responsibility of preparing the poor for underclass status, and thus cannot easily take on another and very different function, at least not until another social control agency is invented in its place. As I noted earlier, the school is not conscious either of its social control or stratification function - except when students in large numbers become disorderly and rebellious; but the combination of local political

control, of the kinds of people who are recruited to staff the
schools and of the authority they are given, and the curriculum they
are asked to or choose to teach, have the result of making schools
into agencies of social control. It would be difficult to imagine
that any slum school or set of slum schools which prepared its students for militant political activities would be allowed to stay
open, but it is equally unlikely that they would be allowed to stay
open if they could suddenly train their students to fill good jobs
in the primary labour market, sending a group of poor adolescents
with high expectations into a saturated labour market. Until the
non-poor society needs the poor to fill jobs - and other functions -
not now existing, the schools cannot undertake the educational activities which they incorporate into their rhetoric.(1)

    At the level of planning strategy, the occupational model is no
more and no less utopian than the educational model; in the final
analysis, they are both planning models which have little chance of
being implemented. Among planning models, I must continue to argue
for the occupational model, because it is in the end more rational,
at least in the sense that it is a better means to both the anti-
poverty and educational ends with which I began this paper.

III. IMPLICATIONS FOR INTER-SECTORAL PLANNING

    The main purpose of this paper has been to present a hypothesis
for the elimination of poverty and for the dynamic use of education,
and before it is possible to develop implications for inter-sectoral
planning it would be necessary to conduct some cross-country and
cross-cultural research in a variety of countries, particularly those
which have undertaken or are undertaking extensive anti-poverty programmes. Essentially, such studies would need to test the hypothesis
presented here, and to compare the impact of both the occupational
and educational models on the reduction of poverty.

    Since a number of European countries were able to absorb their
rural labour surplus in past decades, and never developed the kind
of poverty that exists in America, one research approach would be
historical: to discover how the rural migrants into the city were
absorbed, and what roles were played in this absorption both by the
private and governmental labour market and by the educational system.
If such countries put the rural migrants to work first and then
enabled them and their descendants to make dynamic use of the schools,
then my hypothesis would receive some verification; if these countries began by enabling the migrants to be properly educated, and if

_____

1) H. Gans, "The Positive Functions of Poverty", American Journal
   of Sociology, September 1972, pp. 275-289.

the migrants began their upward mobility in the schools, then the educational model would be applicable instead.

Another research approach would be contemporaneous: to study the absorption of current rural migrants, particularly foreign ones. Since some European countries are now permitting so-called guest workers to become permanent residents, it would be possible to launch studies to see whether and how they escape the low socio-economic status which they presently hold in these countries, and particularly what happens to their children who are being raised in the cities. In some respects, these migrants are "replaying" the 19th and 20th century European emigration to America; in other respects, they are in the same position as blacks and Puerto Ricans and Mexicans in America today, although the economies in which they work differ somewhat from the United States, and government roles in that economy differ even more widely. Consequently, useful research could be conducted into the economic and education roles and problems of rural migrants in different European economies and politics, and to determine what factors encourage the most rapid escape from poverty. At the same time it would also be useful to set up policies and programmes to assist the migrants, to develop - and then evaluate - policies and programmes, occupational as well as educational, to assist the migrants to achieve upward mobility.

If my hypothesis and my occupational model can be validated the implications for inter-sectoral planning are almost self-evident. Presumably, governmental agencies concerned with the economy and the labour market (and with income and welfare policies and services) would do most of the planning, but if my hypothesis that education will be used only when an occupational pay-off is perceived is accurate, the main thrust of inter-sectoral planning would be between economic welfare and educational agencies, so as to create a closer relationship between the economy and the school. If economic agencies can provide and guarantee jobs after school-leaving, the schools can attempt to make education more relevant to the occupational future, and even provide a combination of job-training and other education to young adults already in the labour market. Conversely, education agencies can co-ordinate planning with economic agencies so that jobs can be made available to young people who are not doing well in school, with the idea that they might return to school later.

Another type of inter-sectoral planning should take place between the educational agency and other agencies and institutions which provide education formally or informally, explicitly or implicitly. In countries where the military services provide education, more co-ordination should perhaps be set up between them and the educational agency; and in all countries which provide television programming to their citizens some co-operative relationship

should take place between the educational agency and the television
programmers so that educationally relevant television programming
can be created.

Finally, and in some ways most important, the concept of inter-
sectoral planning must also be introduced within the educational
agency itself, so that those sectors of the agencies concerned with
the vocational aspects of education can interact with the sectors
concerned with non-vocational education. If poor children are to
be educated more adequately than they have been in the past, considerable educational reform is needed to make the structure and
culture of the school, the staff, and the curriculum more relevant
to the needs of poor children. For example, while non-vocational
education is as important for poor children as for non-poor ones,
it is doubtful that, in America, at least, the traditional liberal
arts perspective, which suffuses both the high school and the
colleges, has much meaning. Of course, the poor need liberal arts,
but as long as they are poor they need liberal arts quite different
from those originally invented to produce an enlightened cultural
elite.

Some Possible Dysfunctions of Inter-sectoral Planning

In closing, I must call attention to possible dangers, or at
least dysfunctions, in inter-sectoral planning that seeks greater
co-ordination between the economy and the school. As I noted earlier,
the school can then become a publicly-funded agency which subsidises
profit-seeking enterprises by doing much of their job-training for
them; in addition, the occupational choices of the students are
narrowed, and sometimes the school could virtually force them to
become employees of the firms for which the school is doing training.
A closer tie between school and economy also has conservative political consequences, for increasing the interdependence between them
also increases the dependence of the school on the economy, and
reduces the possibility that the school can encourage economic and
political change.

Although I am fully aware of these and other dangers, in the
end, I believe, the benefits outweigh the costs. If the price of an
escape from poverty is that schools must subsidise profit-seeking
enterprises, I think the price is worth paying. As for the danger
of narrowed occupational choice, this would be a problem only in
communities dominated by one or two major industries; in most cities,
however, the economy is diverse enough to make it difficult for the
schools to become a recruiter for specific firms. Besides, the
occupational choices of the poor are already narrow, and ultimately
narrowness of choice that guarantees a secure job is preferable to
the present situation, narrowness of choice without job security,
or even a job.

The political consequences of increasing the dependence of the school on the economy cannot be ignored, but at the same time, it must also be noted that this dependence exists already, and that except at the level of rhetoric the schools are not agents of economic and political change. If there were a possibility that politically militant schools could be created to encourage the poor to alter their lot through political means, it might be reasonable to argue against greater interdependence between school and economy, but I do not believe that such schools can be created, and even if they could be, I do not think they could do much to encourage the poor to become politically militant. Poor people are too concerned with basic survival needs and, as a result, too dependent on existing economic and political institutions to risk political activity, and this is particularly true in the United States, where they are a small and powerless minority. Indeed, there is now enough evidence to suggest that major economic and political change is not instituted by the poor, but by "higher" social strata, so that it is even reasonable to suggest that if the poor could be enabled to escape from poverty, they would thus move up into strata in which they can become politically active and effective.

THE EVALUATION OF A PERSPECTIVE PLAN
IN AN INTER-SECTORAL CONTEXT: NORWAY
by Olav Magnussen

This paper attempts to evaluate one specific perspective plan
in an inter-sectoral context. The emphasis therefore is not on discussion of the total public sector and relationships between each of
its sub-sectors. It is rather on the analysis of how the educational
sector attempts to cope with the many sometimes bewildering demands
made on it by the rest of the public sector and society as a whole.

To evaluate a perspective plan, a theoretical framework is
needed. Without a set of concepts and a set of relationships between
them, no evaluation or analysis of consequence and impact is possible.

This paper consists of three parts. The first is a preliminary
analysis of what would constitute inter-sectoral planning in general
and more specifically inter-sectoral planning for education. The
second part is an attempt to apply these concepts and considerations
to one specific planning exercise, the Long-Term Plan for Norway
1974-1977. In this plan, perspective analysis and plans for some
sectors are included. The third part is an evaluation of the benefits from utilising perspective plans to cope with problems of inter-
sectoral planning and policy-guidance.

I.   A PRELIMINARY ANALYSIS OF INTER-SECTORAL PLANNING AND
                ITS RELATION TO EDUCATION

A number of concepts are important in analysing inter-sectoral
aspects of government planning. They are static consistency, dynamic
consistency, decentralisation and centralisation of decision-making
power, process and product. We shall first need an analysis with
respect to the time horizon, i.e. planning in its static and dynamic
contexts and its relation to decentralisation and centralisation of
decision-making power.

It is my impression that static consistency with emphasis on
centrally conceived objectives is the dominant theme in inter-
sectoral planning. It is assumed, explicitly or implicitly that
the government sector as a whole has a precisely formulated set of

208

over-arching goals to which each sub-sector such as education, health and transportation etc. contributes. The outcome or product of each sub-sector influences processes and products within each of the other sectors simultaneously. A situation of static consistency prevails if at a certain point the organisation of each sector reflects this collective influence on the various goals as well as the interrelationships between sub-sectors. If this is not so, i.e. that plans and administrative routine in one sector do not reflect these perceived interrelationships, a change towards static consistency is regarded as desirable. In other words the whole concept is tied to the problem of how to ensure that sectors act together in a "rational" way.

The difficulties with such an approach to government policy are evident. First, it requires in general a centralised decision-making structure. Decentralisation is not ruled out, but is only applicable in the extreme situation when all important groups have the same preferences. Secondly, only outcomes or measures of product are regarded as important in the various sectors. For education these are income-effects, the influence on certain behavioural variables such as political participation, socialisation, the ability to function in a complex society, etc. Thirdly, even if we can conceive of a flexible centralised decision-making structure, the time lag in information between sectors is very large, so that inter-sectoral planning within this framework will be extremely rigid. Last, but not least, beyond a certain point inter-sectoral planning may become increasingly expensive. In organisations where other objectives than inter-sectoral planning are important, diminishing returns will set in fairly early. As a general rule, for an imperfect society to perform reasonably well it is never wise to let one sub-sector perform perfectly well or one objective to be pursued "en outrance".

This type of analysis can also be applied to dynamic consistency of centrally given objectives. The requirement that all decisions and plans be consistent as the system evolves will gradually petrify it, undermining the ability to adapt and transform. In fact, a requirement of consistency between plans and decisions in systems developing slowly in an uncertain world and often with unknown objectives, or at most only hazily-conceived objectives, seems to me to be a contradiction in terms. The need for a clear expression of conflict and diverging preferences among sub-groups becomes increasingly important.

These arguments against inter-sectoral planning as representing only a framework for consistency between sector plans are particularly important in the case of education. It was emphasized above that this particular definition of inter-sectoral planning will stress outcome or product as the most important variables in the

preference function for the various sectors. This may have large
negative effects on the organisation of the educational sector.
Monitoring progress towards or regress from certain goals in terms
of inputs to other sectors will tend to neglect the value of the
process itself. The negligible importance of the educational process
within this planning system will have the result that only those processes will tend to be chosen which have the largest possible positive impact on the product variables. However, many will argue that
the process itself is more important than perhaps most product variables, and that the process only can be evaluated by the individuals
experiencing it. Stressing consistency in terms of products or outcomes only on the central level not only neglects perhaps the main
aspect of education but also deprives the individual from expressing
any preferences about his educational situation. Processes resulting
in large products and strong impacts on the development of other sectors may in fact be a bad experience for many individuals.

But if the educational process is itself important, and I cannot
see how anyone can argue otherwise, as most individuals today spend
12 years or more of their most intense years in the educational system, then a requirement of consistency with plans and goals in other
sectors cannot be fulfilled in any strict way. For as we have
pointed out, processes do not necessarily relate strictly to any end
product. Implications of processes will only be seen in the future,
thus the consequence today is very uncertain. Bringing this aspect
of education into the analysis of inter-sectoral educational planning
leads to the conclusion that this kind of planning in education to
some extent must be pursued by other means than consistency with
other sector plans at any point in time or over time. If it is
accepted that different groups have different preferences and that
the educational process itself is important, it is not an optimal
planning procedure to maximise the interrelatedness between the educational sector and any other government sector.

Inter-sectoral planning of education may now be defined differently. Inter-sectoral educational planning may simply mean a
planning procedure which allows individuals and groups to express
their own main preferences in the educational situation rather than
objectives given centrally. Different social and political groups
have different notions about education and society. An educational
system reflecting the interrelatedness of social decisions would
therefore allow any group a reasonable ability to function on the
basis of own preferences. Preferences of smaller groups are certainly not one-dimensional with regard to education. They will
attempt to create an educational situation which reflects their view
of society and the place of education in that society.

The role of central planning in this structure is to create the conditions under which participation of different groups is meaningful for themselves and where they become involved, through the educational process, in important societal problems. Planners should be on the look-out for structural long-term changes in society which ought to lead to the reorganisation of the educational system, a reorganisation which would allow the system to adapt to social changes and if possible, transform them.

In addition planners must be concerned with creating incentive systems which would induce people to participate and suggest the set of factors to be determined by local groups. The organisation of the incentive system must satisfy the need for participation in important decisions and at the same time lead to results for all groups which taken together satisfy certain overall constraints on their behaviour.

Different participation schemes and various sets of factors to be determined by local groups lead in general to different incentive schemes. Incentive schemes will, of course, also vary with the structure of preferences. Some incentive schemes may only be feasible given some preference scales. If, for example, equality is not important while decentralisation and consumer sovereignty are, any voucher scheme would be feasible. This scheme would be less feasible if equality were important. A discussion of incentives would therefore be closely linked to any discussion of preferences, participation and decentralisation procedures. Otherwise, there will be an air of unreality about the plan. Most of us are only able to assess the consequences of different plans if we have a notion of how they will be carried out in practice.

Compared to an educational system consistently programmed to fit into the development of other sectors, this educational system may perhaps look like a negation of the former. Its main characteristic would be diversity and variety of solutions, but these solutions would be consistent with the preferences of at least one group. A variety of solutions may be more costly than the solution presented by central decision-makers, but only seen from the latter's point of view. Whether a central solution is better than the decentralised variety can be answered only with references to the preferences of the group in question.

To put the problem of educational planning somewhat differently, how can large systems like education or for that matter society, which are necessary for control over important factors determining human welfare, at the same time satisfy people's need for both participation and individual decisions? Or, how can the individual be an effective decision-maker within a smaller group and at the same time influence constraints which must control the behaviour of such smaller groups?

II. THE NORWEGIAN PERSPECTIVE PLAN AND INTER-SECTORAL
GOVERNMENT PLANNING

A few inferences from the preceding discussion will help in
evaluating an educational perspective plan or analysis and its consequences for inter-sectoral governmental planning. If inter-
sectoral planning is defined as a mechanism which co-ordinates otherwise independent activities centrally, we might find that the relative importance of such planning would depend on whether education
operates as a decentralised process, or whether it is organised so
as to provide a centrally determined output to be delivered to other
sectors and to influence general welfare. In this perspective I
shall attempt an analysis of interrelationships between inter-
sectoral planning and perspective analysis based on the Norwegian
Long-Term Plan 1974-1977.

This long-term plan is a four-year plan for the whole government sector. Some policy issues have longer timetables. These are
published under separate headings entitled Special Analysis. The
part devoted to education has seven chapters apart from the
introduction:

1. Size of the educational sector.
2. Long-term quantitative development of the educational
   sector.
3. Social indicators in education.
4. The decision-making process in education.
5. Possible development of the decision-making process in
   education.
6. Objectives and the decision-making process.
7. Possibility of choice for the individual.

The characteristics of this perspective analysis can now be
evaluated on the basis of the framework drawn up in Part I. That
framework is only partly formalised, and there is no accepted fashion
in which to evaluate plans. Thus, the discussion will necessarily
depend on my preferences.

The empirical material is very limited. It consists of the
plan document and a few working papers. Very little was available
about the process of planning itself, it had to be inferred when
possible from the documents available. The comments following must
be read in the light of these problems.

The main part of the planning document is devoted to chapters
3-7 and is a good illustration of the contention that planning concerned with education as a process would not emphasize education as
a delivering sector, but stress decentralisation and the problems of
organising an educational system where the important aspects are
determined by the participants themselves.

To what extent then is the emphasis on processes and decentralisation relevant in the context of Norwegian society? There are three main reasons why policy perspectives of participatory democracy are particularly relevant just now. The public administration of education is, despite some minor reforms, excessively centralised, and this creates a massive burden on the rather scarce manpower resources in the central administration. More important, however, is the long tradition of local self-government which is slowly but surely building up competence and manifesting itself more powerfully in some areas, among them education. The periphery is slowly being strengthened relative to the centre. The new district colleges are an example of this development. A more basic factor is the structural change which is taking place in the Norwegian labour market, away from the traditional authoritarian organisation of production on the factory floor, towards a wider participation of workers in the decision-making units of firms and enterprises. Pilot experiments have been undertaken for some years already with self-controlled groups, and these experiments are yielding encouraging results. A law providing the legal basis for participatory democracy in industry has been passed by the Parliament. Educational planning without any consideration for these clear signs of change in the power-structure of Norwegian society could hardly be politically relevant.

The philosophy of this plan is that the educational system can be regarded as a preparatory testing ground for participatory democracy in all important fields of public life. Instead of concentrating on education as a product influencing the development of other sectors as well as over-arching goals through a centrally determined process, this perspective analysis argues that any contribution of education to over-arching social problems is best handled by training people to undertake a variety of tasks in a largely self-controlled way.

Political issues of this sort are, of course, eminently suited for a perspective plan. For such a plan is first and foremost a mechanism for learning about the physical, institutional, and political constraints on the development of the public sector and society. As such, the perspective plan is a framework for exchange of information and co-ordination of otherwise independent activities.

An important part of the plan is an analysis of the constraints needed on a self-controlled process, and the conditions under which a process can be defined as self-controlled. In my view the discussion of the latter problem is the weakest point in the analysis. There is a tendency here to be exceedingly general in utilising an approach which has been baptised the Nirvana approach. An example will suffice to illustrate this: "Real self-government is conditioned upon participation in the decision-making process by all those in the self-governed unit." This is a definition of self-government which can never be fulfilled in practice, and which is therefore without political value. The more basic, but far more difficult problem which must be solved in a real situation is: "How can a system of self-government be organised and developed in a world where different participants have different notions about the importance of various decisions even within the same group?"

A related problem is the set of instruments required to ensure a reasonable degree of self-government for an individual or smaller group. And which variables are local groups allowed to control? The discussion of these issues i.e. the question of implementing mechanisms is strong and wide-ranging. The discussion does not contain blueprints for action, but a low key presentation of various approaches to participation. As we have pointed out already, discussion of plans in terms of implementing mechanisms does tend to reveal conflicts and inconsistencies between objectives pursued by the system which very often are not perceived when only stating the problem. We only become aware of our preferences through a learning process which reveals the consequences of different preference structures. While most implementing mechanisms discussed in the analysis can only be introduced rather slowly and probably far into the future, one specific mechanism is already in the process of being organised. This is a system of subsidies to local governments which will allow the latter to control the distribution of resources on activities, while the central government determines the absolute level of resource use in each local community. This scheme thus combines equality in use of resources between local units with an allocation of resources reflecting local educational needs.

One implementation mechanism has been rejected a priori even though it is closely related to the problem discussed. I refer to the price mechanism which in Anglo-Saxon literature has been presented in the form of so-called educational vouchers. Such a system permits education to be sold and bought in something similar to a competitive market. As in the case of a competitive market, the voucher scheme permits a participant to reveal his preferences for different educational services by agreeing to buy or not. If the set of services supplied by a certain school is other than what he would demand at the going price, he can shift his demand to other schools supplying education more consistent with his preferences. Thus, such a system will provide a variety of educational experiences consistent with the preferences of each household. This is in perfect concordance with one of the basic premises of the perspective analysis which argues that: "The educational system can best be evaluated by those already in the system, and especially by those served by it, i.e. pupils and students."

The use of prices in the public sector to decentralise decision-making and provide information about preferences and real costs has been discussed for some time. The Long-Term Programme referred to above includes a discussion of the price mechanism. It does seem a little odd that a perspective analysis stressing decentralisation, the need for an educational structure based on the real preferences of participants does not discuss the most powerful mechanism invented to do just that, the price mechanism.

There is no reason to believe that some kind of price mechanism is unknown to the authors of the analysis. An a priori rejection of the use of prices may therefore have two explanations. Either there is a distaste for regulation of government activity via the market which does not seem to be consistent with the Long-Term Programme - the latter is hesitant on the issue but does not reject it outright - or it can be seen as a rejection of other implications of the market mechanism. Segregation may occur or be strengthened, richer people might demand more education than is supplied by the voucher and thereby create inequalities in the system. Perhaps the implication is that equality of opportunity and socialisation are the basic objectives of Norwegian educational activity, and that decentralisation and participation in decision-making are only allowed insofar as this does not conflict with the former objectives.

The reason for bringing in this discussion is not a desire to plead the case of a price mechanism. It is rather to show the effect of planning procedures which exclude powerful, if sometimes extreme, alternatives. The effect is as we have attempted to show, that the pedagogical value of the plan is considerably reduced. For it leaves open the basic question: "What are the relationships and conflicts between equality, socialisation and freedom of choice?" It is plausible that planners wanted to keep that discussion open by not taking sides, but that is not done by excluding cases which can highlight conflicts between objectives.

III. THE VALUE OF PERSPECTIVE PLANNING IN AN INTER-SECTORAL CONTEXT

Within an inter-sectoral framework the main objective of a perspective plan must be a pedagogical one, i.e. to bring forward for discussion all changes in society which may have relevance for the educational sector or new insight into the educational process with relevance for the rest of society. If this can be done, planning is successful. The plan must measure its effect on educational policy-making by its ability to open up the educational sector and make the latter more flexible by turning it into a self-controlled mechanism. The relationship between educational policy and perspective planning must not be one of trial and error and an endless stream of new solutions thrown into the sector from the central government. For educational reforms are only valid in relation to assumptions of what a given society will be like in 30 years, but on the other hand, it takes 30 years to perceive its results. Thus the basic premise for educational planning must be a largely self-controlled system flexible enough to adapt to and contribute to transformations of society.

THE PLACE OF EDUCATION IN INTER-SECTORAL PLANNING IN FRANCE
by Thierry Malan

The education system in France is by tradition highly centralised and it is also sufficiently autonomous to be impervious to
explicit pressures from other sectors. Moreover, the classical cultural tradition maintained in the schools as well as the university
tradition of independence tends to deflect attention from some of
the major aims of other sectors of modern French society.

Although inter-sectoral approaches are seldom explicitly used
within the educational administration, people within the system are
more and more aware of the need for such approaches. They feel that
the social efficiency of decisions taken in education is not maxi-
mised when interrelationships with other sectors are not sufficiently
taken into consideration. Consequently there is increasing feeling
that there exists a need for an integrated approach to planning.

In order to study the problem of education in its inter-sectoral
context and the subsequent problem of inter-sectoral planning for
education in France, the following points will be dealt with:

1. Some major inter-sectoral aspects of educational policy.
2. The need for integration in government policy planning.
3. The need for integration at regional and local levels.
4. Impact of status and role differences on inter-sectoralism.

For all these points, some of the main difficulties met in
dealing with inter-sectoral aspects of policies will be explored,
first for French society and the administrative system as a whole,
and then for the educational system.

Inter-sectoral planning may thus be seen as part of a broader
movement aimed at replacing traditional methods by new methods based
on "planning by objectives". The specific objectives of each political and administrative sector appear in turn as the means to
achieve even broader social and economic objectives.

Such planning tends to increase concern for the qualitative
aspects of education. The sectoral answers to social needs have
been a response to the need to satisfy obvious quantitative short
falls in education services. At present these demands are met
within certain minimal standards. However, when these standards
are widened to include effective service, qualitative requirements,

217

especially in education, cannot be assured by a single sector, which will always try to channel the social demands, so as to be able to answer them on its own traditional terms.

I. SOME MAJOR INTER-SECTORAL ASPECTS OF EDUCATIONAL POLICY

The decision as to which sectors should be co-ordinated in the overall framework of inter-sectoral planning is strongly influenced by developments in value systems; developments which will determine which different conceptions of the school services will be in conflict and those which will predominate. The evolution of the objectives of French secondary education has been studied by Mrs. V. Isambert-Jamati (in Crises de la société, crises de l'enseignement - Sociologie de l'enseignement secondaire français - P.U.F. 1970 - Paris): reviewing official speeches delivered during the period 1860-1968, she distinguishes several periods during which the emphasis was laid on different values: initially, teaching was primarily considered as the transmission of moral and esthetic values; a major consequence of France's defeat in the Franco-Prussian war in 1870 was that greater stress was placed on the acquisition of practical abilities. Transforming the world by education or withdrawal from it into an internal and gratuitous culture, cohesion and discipline or critical education, learning of fixed contents or learning of methods, general culture or acquisition of vocational skills, these forms subsequently provided a series of alternatives which were not always clearly defined. The consequences for the role of education as compared with that of other sectors as far as the families are concerned have been numerous and varied.

In the 1960s there was public pressure for a higher percentage of total public funds for education because of the fast growth of student numbers. The assumption was that education is one of a nation's most efficient and useful investments. In the 1970s, however, any increase in the relative expenditure on education will have to be justified more carefully. Numbers are no longer growing as quickly. Many studies indicate that education was perhaps not in itself an efficient policy tool for meeting certain social objectives. A major example was the role of education in the reduction of social inequalities. In this case it has become apparent that policy measures in other sectors are also relevant to this goal and may in fact be more important to it. Any planning for education must now justify more clearly additional expenditures in relation to broader social and economic objectives. This is a natural conjunction for inter-sectoral considerations.

It seems however that the ways in which the educational system interacts with its environment are not immediately apparent. The

contribution of the education system to the achievement of broader
economic and social objectives is a more complex problem than had
been thought and if this contribution is to be valid there must be
co-ordinated intervention from other sectors.

1. Some examples of interrelationships

a) Equality of educational opportunity

One of the major objectives of educational policy in recent
years - quality of educational opportunity, or more soberly, reduction of inequalities - is now seen more and more in relation to a
broader objective; equalisation of social opportunities. Indeed it
can no longer be assumed that a progressive equalisation of educational opportunities will automatically have a positive influence
on social mobility.(1)

Moreover this objective cannot be achieved by measures taken
within the educational system alone. Other influences such as the
family, housing, health have a major impact on educational achievement, and this objective, which may seem at first glance to be peculiar to the educational system, can only be achieved with the help
of other sectors.

It is clear that social segregation in towns gives rise to educational segregation. School populations tend to have either a majority of children from privileged families or a majority from under-
privileged families. In each case the cultural and social background of the children and their expectations, will be different and
will, in turn, influence the teachers' behaviour and expectations
and the possibilities of achievement offered to the children. In an
attempt to counter social segregation a recent regulation of the
housing department states that in every big new building programme
it will be compulsory to include a minimum number of houses with
lower rents. It is hoped that this will have a positive influence
on urban segregation, but it is as yet too early to estimate the
effects.

b) Education and tax policy

The French tax system encourages the wealthier families not
to let their children work until they are 25 - in other words to
continue their studies. The tax relief, which is called "quotient
familial", means that income is divided by a given number of parts
(a part for each adult, a half part for each child) and only one
part is taxed. This tax is then multiplied by the number of parts

---

1) Some studies seem to show that, on the contrary, it may be
   correlated with an increase in inequalities; see Boudon,
   L'inégalite des chances, Armand Colin, Paris 1973.

in order to calculate the total amount of tax to be paid; the tax
burden is thus reduced according to the number of children. It can
therefore be calculated that the reduction of income tax ranges
from Frs.9,325 per child for the highest incomes to Frs.152 per
child for the lowest. This system cannot be applied once the children are over 21, unless they go on studying, in which case it applies
until they are 25, so that the higher the income the higher the incentive to further studies.

c) Education and industrial development

The major economic objective of the VIth Plan (1971-1975) is
to accelerate the industrialisation of France. The greater number
of students choosing humanistic studies rather than scientific or
technical ones and the predominance of humanities and "pure sciences" in the scale of values of French society are considered as
obstacles to this objective. There is a general political and educational effort to promote technical studies at every level; secondary, university and recurrent education. This objective is reflected in the law of 16th July 1971 which also allows for greater participation of people from all walks of life in the decisions concerning education.

2. Adaptation to new goals affects all aspects of the existing educational system

a) Structural changes

The different methods of achieving new social and economic aims
are still being debated within the educational system. A reform of
the first cycle of secondary education in 1963 postponed vocational
studies to the end of this first cycle (which consolidates basic
intellectual skills) and gave vocational training, in the second
cycle, such broad characteristics as to enable the students to envisage a wider range of jobs. These broad characteristics were also
intended to enable them to switch more easily, if necessary. The
difficulties in designing the same first cycle for all, the weight
of tradition and conservatism in the conception of technical studies,
the pressures coming from the employment sector, accustomed to the
former degrees, have given rise to a change in the means to attain
this objective; children are now allowed to start an apprenticeship
or specialised technical studies before the end of the first cycle.

b) Curriculum changes

At the same time, some curriculum changes are being progressively implemented in the first cycle, especially in the fields of

mathematics, technology, introductory studies in economics and social affairs. This should enable more children to follow scientific or technical studies after the first cycle.

Traditional teaching in mathematics is highly selective and plays an important part in the orientation of children towards literary or scientific sections. It is thought that, in order to diversify, a greater distinction should be made between the training offered for the selection of highly qualified mathematicians and a teaching which would aim at giving as many people as possible a useful understanding of practical mathematics. Traditional teaching is much influenced by the idea of selecting a small elite of mathematicians, in order to prepare them for entry into the French "Grandes Ecoles", which give access to top positions in the civil service, and increasingly in public or private enterprises. The "Grandes Ecoles" take only a few hundred students a year and the entrance examination to the scientific ones lays considerable emphasis on a knowledge of mathematics. This example shows how different inter-sectoral approaches in the same field (relationships between employment and education policies) with conflicting values (quality or quantity?) (elitism or diffusion of culture and skills on a broader scale?) will have different consequences for the planning of new curricula within the school system. It also shows that the definition of "general culture" has a major influence on the capacity of the educational system to act in an inter-sectoral way, since the system is influenced by the prevailing conceptions of the relationships between "culture" and society as a whole.

For a long time the idea of "culture" was more or less associated with the idea of leisure. At the same time, it was thought that the future elites of society required as broad a general culture as possible; it was supposed at least to provide the overall views and ideas required for the management of complex systems.

The content of this "general culture" became less and less adapted to a clear understanding of modern society because of an increasing inability on the part of the majority of students to link the knowledge transmitted through the study of humanities and even sciences to the real situations with which they had to cope in their professional and daily life. This situation was aggravated by the growing awareness that these studies could no longer provide access to definite professions. There were two possible reactions to this situation:

i) to continue teaching an "unchanged" general culture while increasing specialisation elsewhere. This division was part of the "Fouchet reforms" of secondary and higher education;

ii) to try and redefine "general culture" in order to make it available to and useful for all. This was the basis for Edgar Faure's idea of the "three languages" - the mother tongue, mathematics, one foreign language.

The attempts to create a more specialised curriculum in order to adapt it to employment forecasts and to overcome the "irrelevance" of the traditional general culture have caused difficulties in defining what the new contents of this general culture should be. Differences of opinion have grown among those who think that there is no need to prove the relevance of traditional studies in the humanities - although there is evidence, in secondary and even in higher education, of a growing lack of interest - and those who think that, although not directly relevant, these studies will provide a better training than too narrow professional studies, and those who consider this "adaptation" problem as simply one of forecasting. The latter insist that given precise and accurate employment forecasts for the next five or ten years, they could make the necessary adjustments in the educational system, although they may not know the ways in which job structures will evolve or the various kinds of training and education in fact needed for different jobs.

c) Education and work

The idea that "on-the-job-training" is one of the best ways of educating young people conflicts with the idea of extending compulsory schooling. The way of dealing with this conflict has major consequences for the concept and contents of "general culture" and for the administrative organisation of the educational sector where its relationships with other sectors are concerned. The idea may justify and facilitate a development of training institutions outside the Ministry of Education (under the responsibility of the Labour Ministry for instance), and the beginning of apprenticeship in industry and trade at the age of 15 rather than at the end of compulsory schooling at the age of 16.

Another point in the discussion is the inclusion of social and vocational activities in the normal curricula of both secondary and higher education. The introduction of these activities will reflect the amount of influence exerted by the economy and by society upon the autonomy of the school system since they are intended to provide for a greater adaptation to the future tasks of the children and students and to furnish them with a greater capacity for further adaptation. The educational system will express its own autonomous values; it will try and show that such values may ensure a still greater efficiency in pursuing the objectives of the economy and society than the measures proposed by the representatives of these "sectors". The educational sector will assume, for instance, that a greater capacity for further adaptation is best granted by a development of general education, whereas the other sectors will require earlier specialisation for children and students.

d) School and the outside world

Other issues touching on the inter-sectoral aspects of social objectives are under discussion. The principal area here is education. School has long been considered as an isolated world, where a permanent culture is transmitted. Such autonomous activity no longer seems the best way to prepare young people for co-operation and self-development in social life. Many parents expect the school to assume more responsibility than before in the education of their children. They feel that schools should be not only teaching establishments but have more contacts with other social institutions; schools and children should be in touch with various social activities, which provide early contact with practical aspects of daily life, and allow them to assume progressively a greater role in community life. Such changes are seen by many teachers as a radical modification of the nature of their own activity, and they may well be unacceptable since more emphasis would be given to collective activities and practical skills than to intellectual subjects. The teachers feel that they have neither been prepared nor recruited for the type of activity which, in their opinion, should be the responsibility of the parents or of other institutions. Many parents are also liable to distrust such a development, sensing that it is likely to give the school and the teachers too much influence over the children.

The evolution reflects some facts concerning "sectors" other than education; more and more women are working outside the home and no longer have enough time to take care of their children; parents wish to devote more and more of their time to other activities and therefore expect schools to play a greater role in education. If the schools are to respond to these demands there will be important consequences for teacher training and for work schedules. Teachers would have to be on duty full-time in the schools, instead of spending only their compulsory teaching hours in the building. This in turn would necessitate architectural changes in schools, since extra rooms where teachers could meet together with their colleagues for team-work, or with the parents for advice and information would have to be provided. A number of guidance and counselling posts would have to be created and counsellors would have to be particularly concerned with finding places in other schools or enterprises for school-leavers. Such changes should lead to the multiplication of open schools, of community centres in which various

social services such as crèches, traditional schooling, recurrent
education, cultural activities, would be made available. Certain
sectoral regulations which govern the educational system and other
social services may present obstacles to this development. An
example would be the regulations concerning the responsibility of
school directors, which would of course be increased with the new
activities although there would not be a corresponding increase in
their powers of control. Other obstacles will come from the parents
who will feel suspicious of too much originality in the school and
too many divergencies from the norms of activity in other schools.
They may also have doubts about their children's success in examinations. Here there is a conflict between the organisational and pedagogical consequences of two different sets of values, both of which
are being given equal emphasis: the values of autonomy leading to
co-operation with other sectors on the one hand, and the values
underlying individual performance and success on the other

II.   THE NEED FOR INTEGRATION IN GOVERNMENT POLICY PLANNING

Before dealing with inter-sectoral approaches to the problems
in educational policy planning described in Section I, it is useful
to have an overall view of the general problem of integrating sectoral policies in the French political and administrative system.
This will be given in Part A, and in Part B some specific problems
of educational policy planning will be studied.

A)   <u>Approaches to inter-sectoral problems in government policy
planning</u>

The degree of centralisation which obtains in France leads
French administrations to aim at homogeneity in their relationships
with their environment and this makes adaptation to changing circumstances difficult. Faced with new problems that are becoming
increasingly inter-sectoral and that seem at first view hard to
routinise and to deal with in the normal framework of their activities, ministers and administrations hesitate among different
approaches:

- the creation of new administrative bodies;
- the use of new management techniques, without any change
    in the pattern of existing institutions.

These two methods are not incompatible and can be adopted
simultaneously, while the organisation of overall planning in France -
in the "Commissariat général du Plan" - may be considered as a third
and complementary method.

1. Creation of new administrations

This leads to increasing differentiation and fragmentation of administration as new problems arise. For example, agencies for scientific research, regional development, vocational training, road safety, development of computer use, improvement of labour conditions may be created.

As a result, there is an improvement in co-ordination (by focusing energies and activities on a major inter-sectoral problem), but also a greater need for further co-ordination as the traditional administrations still remain competent in these areas and try to develop their own actions. Most of these new agencies are inter-ministerial ones, because they have to deal with problems arising on the boundaries of two or more sectors. They are more than task forces, or project groups, because they have a tendency to perpetuate themselves rather than to disappear when the problems they had to solve are taken over in turn by the traditional structures.

In theory, these agencies, in charge of "horizontal" tasks, are supposed to be small, with a limited number of civil servants and people from sectors other than the civil service. Their role is to initiate the work and they should act through the channels of the traditional administrations. Civil servants should not spend more than a few years in these agencies; they should come from different sectors, in order to promote inter-disciplinary and inter-sectoral viewpoints; a few years in these agencies for civil servants should be a good means of promotion in other sectors. The limited amount of time which people spend in the agency is intended to prevent the constitution of a specialised corps, which would be interested in perpetuating its existence even after its initial mission had changed.

The financial resources of these agencies should not be large in comparison with those of the traditional administrations. Since they have no management responsibilities, or less than the traditional administrations, these resources can be used to promote and facilitate operations which will subsequently be supported and financed by the traditional administrations.

However, the increasing number of agencies and services which are more or less independent of the original ministries leads to other problems. There are many types of institutions and it is difficult to classify them and to control them administratively. The Court of Public Accounts in France issued a warning some years ago against a proliferation of agencies created for specific new political and administrative purposes, since their existence made the control of administrative activity and efficiency much more difficult. Indeed it was necessary to find new methods of control. These agencies provided special opportunities and salaries for the people working in them, who were for the most part civil servants, and this led to inequalities in working conditions between the agencies and the traditional bodies. They also led to a multiplicity in the distribution of competencies, to co-ordination problems, and to the duplication of many studies. They tended to survive their initial purposes instead of letting the ministries take over the full responsibility for the new activities they had developed.

There is also a major difficulty in that these agencies have to develop their own network of communication and information and sometimes their own services for implementation. Overlap and co-ordination problems on the national level are then increased rather than simplified on the local level, where the various sectoral, or inter-sectoral, policies have to be implemented.

2. Use of new management techniques

Another possible approach is to promote, within the existing bodies, those functions and services which are equipped to study the new inter-sectoral problems, and to propose co-ordination and improvements within the traditional service. In this case, the new functions and services must have an appropriate status within the organisation, in order to make sure that they will be able to make their views acceptable to the other services.

The introduction of new tasks of synthesis and co-ordination in a traditional administrative environment is sometimes accompanied by a regrouping of separate administrations or agencies within the framework of a new single administrative body. An example of this was the Ministry for Social Affairs which at the time grouped together the Ministry for Labour and National Insurance and the Ministry for Health and Population. Such a new organisation may be faced with new problems, arising out of its huge size: co-ordination advantages, obtained by centralisation of the various bodies concerned with newly emerging inter-sectoral problems, can then be lost because of greater co-ordination difficulties within the new organisation. A deconcentration is necessary at this point if the organisation is not to become unmanageable.

Besides a choice about the creation of new services or agencies, there is a choice for the administrations concerning the financing methods for their new tasks. The identification of a new problem may give rise to a special budget, or to a fund with just enough resources to incite traditional sectors to contribute more, or to a new item in the estimates of an existing ministry.

3. Planning

There are two methods employed in France to meet the increasing needs for decisions of a more inter-sectoral nature: to multiply the number of special agencies and funds or programmes; to work as much and as long as possible through the traditional sectoral channels, in the hope that they will adopt new sets of objectives and methods. In this case, they will transform progressively their traditional activities and this prevents the proliferation of separate public bodies with separate resources. When separate agencies do appear, they may provide arguments for the traditional sectors not to undertake these new activities. Many ministries have been involved in pluri-annual planning processes, but these have not been co-ordinated with the five-year plans done by the "Commissariat général du Plan" (CGP).

The organisation of overall planning by the CGP can be seen as a third method of dealing with inter-sectoral aspects of sectoral policies. Planning, as a distinct administrative function, began in France with the necessity to rebuild the economy at the end of the Second World War. The planning took place principally within a distinct small administration, the CGP which was directly responsible to the Prime Minister. Its first purpose was to ensure the best use of limited resources and an equal growth of all the key sectors in economic development. After this initial period, planning activity was extended to public equipment, and subsequently to the functioning of the various public services.

The VIth Plan (1971-1975) introduced two procedures, which are relevant for inter-sectoral purposes:

a) the "collective functions";
b) the "finalised programmes".

A "collective function" is designed to provide an overall view of all the actions which, regardless of administrative divisions, tend towards the achievement of a particular given objective. It should help the various administrations to discuss their views and to co-ordinate their policies so that there are no excessive overlaps and important issues are not neglected. Ten "collective functions" were defined and each of them was the responsibility of a commission. The commissions dealt not only with problems of equipment, but also with other relevant functional problems: education and training, social action, culture, sports and socio-educative activities, health, urban and rural development, transportation and research.

The commissions are composed of representatives of the different ministries concerned, of the unions and of other associations and agencies. They discuss their particular collective function and draw some general outlines for the next five years. They can therefore pave the way for interministerial co-operation and the further elaboration of interministerial programmes. Although the commissions have very little power, the unions and other associations agree to participate, principally because it gives them access to wider information.

Although the notion of a "collective function" can help to harmonize the actions of different ministries and agencies which serve the same end, and is an inter-sectoral approach in that it is interministerial, it does not of itself represent a step towards a broader inter-sectoral approach. Such an approach would imply the introduction of the education function into a social or economic objective, which goes beyond education as such. This could very well occur within the existing administrative structures: education may for example have an important part to play in a policy of rural development, which would include social measures, farming subsidies, housing and equipment improvement schemes, etc.; all of which are the responsibility of the Ministry of Agriculture.

Moreover, there is no direct connection between the forecasts of the Five Year Plan, prepared by the commissions and the CGP, and the budgeting decisions taken every year by the Treasury and the different ministries: the Plan gives them guidelines only, except in the limited case of the "finalised programmes" of the VIth Plan.

The "finalised programmes" are an inter-sectoral planning and financing procedure: they aim to achieve a set of objectives through the co-ordinated activity of various ministries and agencies. These programmes should co-ordinate measures and they include a moral commitment on the part of the various sectors concerned to provide the resources needed and to take the necessary decisions. They therefore represent an intersectoral approach, not only in planning, but also in programming and budgeting. However, in order not to multiply the budgeting channels for activities which should not necessarily outlive one or two plans, the financial resources of these finalised programmes go through the different sectoral channels concerned. This means that their implementation depends very much on the "goodwill" of these sectors and yet there are no incentives other than pressure from the "Commissariat général du Plan" and from the agencies responsible for the programmes. Six of them only have been adopted by the VIth Plan: road safety, new towns, improving the functioning of the labour market (these three programmes are under the responsibility of special agencies), pre- and post-natal care, keeping aged people at home (under the responsibility of the Ministry of Health), protection of the Mediterranean forest.

The VIth Plan should offer an occasion to widen this planning experience so that it may meet broader sets of objectives. The generalisation of this experience will have to be done with great care if the different sectors are to be prevented from considering these programmes as being principally a way to get additional resources, without having to re-orientate their more traditional activities and expenditures.

The administrations also develop their own internal planning methods and services. They attempt to meet the demands of the "Commissariat général du Plan" and, at the same time, to preserve their independence from its intervention. Since 1970, progress in administrative planning methods has been marked by the adoption, on an experimental basis, of techniques of management by objectives and output budgeting.

These methods may encourage each ministry to adopt its own set of objectives. This may be therefore a progression in internal co-ordination, but not necessarily in inter-sectoral co-ordination, since there is no overall authority strong enough to oblige the different administrations to adopt those sets of social and economic goals which necessitate co-operation among different sectors. One risk is that these methods may lead to a reinforcement of sectoral interest if the different ministries use them principally to back up the arguments they use when presenting their traditional sectoral estimates.

The detailed co-ordination necessary to fit all sectoral sets of objectives into an overall set of social and economic objectives cannot be provided by the "Commissariat du Plan" which does not have adequate powers for this. It is not an overall management body but rather a consultative and innovative organisation. Planning as a function may therefore become more administrative and less participatory. The characteristic of the traditional planning done by the "Commissariat général du Plan", is the organisation of a widespread co-ordination among sectors and a widespread consultation of the various groups concerned so that they may discuss all the issues relevant to the collective functions. Such planning, although it depends upon the goodwill of the administration to provide reliable information, is more participatory than the purely administrative planning, which is tied to the budgetary estimates and decisions. Unless traditional participatory planning is concentrated on major inter-sectoral issues which are not included in the planning framework of each separate ministry, it is likely that the co-ordination of these two kinds of planning will lead to a situation in which purely administrative planning will predominate.

B) Approaches to inter-sectoral problems in educational policy planning

The central administration of education has a tendency at times to narrow its responsibilities and at others to enlarge them. For example, in 1959 a section of the Ministry of Education became the Ministry of Cultural Affairs; in 1963 and 1966 a section of the Ministry of Education became the Ministry of Youth and Sports. It was considered less important to have an integrated approach to all problems of cultural and educational "development" than to maintain manageable administrative groupings in the absence of actual decentralisation.

On the other hand, the creation in 1970 of a new division responsible for recurrent education indicates a desire to see the public educational system acquire a large share in the new "recurrent education market" by unifying the dispersed efforts of the various services in this field and giving them new vigour.

At the same time, new agencies are being created, outside the ministry, in order to deal more effectively with the major problems of vocational training and adult education. Examples are: the Agency for Information on School and University Courses, Trades, Professions and Crafts; the Research Centre on Curriculum and Qualifications; the Agency for the Development of Adult Education; the Office for Modern Educational Technology. These agencies are a form of "technical decentralisation". They are under the control of the Ministry of Education, but other sectors have representatives on their boards. They enjoy more flexibility where decision-making and expenditures are concerned than the existing traditional services of the Ministry.

Changes have been introduced, on an experimental basis, in the central organisation of the Ministry of Education, which was reorganised in March 1970 in order to experiment with new methods of management by objectives and output budgeting. These methods included pluri-annual administrative planning and the drawing up of social indicators of education. In 1973 a new function of "project leader" was created in the Ministry of Education. The project leaders were to be given specific inter-sectoral tasks within the traditional structure of the Ministry: this innovation had little success, chiefly because of the difficulties of intergrating these posts into the traditional structure of the Ministry. The project leaders were to elaborate programmes, comprising a great variety of elements, each of them under the responsibility of different divisions in the Ministry. The hierarchical position of the project leaders within the traditional structure is not very clear and those people responsible for the different divisions feel more involved in their own hierarchy than in the aims of the project leaders. Moreover, the traditional hierarchy has its own objectives concerning the use of the means at its disposal.

Another reason for the lack of success of this innovation is the absence of specific incentives - supplementary funds, a guarantee of resources for a period of some years so that planning is possible, or more personnel - for the implementation of the programmes controlled by the project leaders.

Another reform of the central administrative structure of education took place in April 1974 when an autonomous Secretariat of State for the Universities was created. It is hoped that the Secretariat will be able to encourage greater involvement of the universities in joint projects with the outside world, and especially the business world. The Ministry of Education itself, which is responsible for primary, secondary, and recurrent education taking place outside the universities, was also restructured. The different cycles were separated into specific divisions of primary and pre-primary schools, first cycle schools, second cycle lycées and recurrent education. Each division was made responsible for the management of all the means required for its specific aims. An overall co-ordinating division was made responsible for pluri-annual planning and co-ordination between these independent divisions on the one hand and the Ministry of Education and the Secretariat of State for the Universities on the other.

The frequent changes in the central structure of the educational administration are indicative of the Administration's difficulties in keeping a clear view of the sufficient control over its social environment. The use of new techniques, like output budgeting, indicates the need for more clarity in projects and expenditure.

However, it does not seem likely that the new problems, emerging from the turbulence of the environment of the educational administration, and from the Administration's difficulties in routinising its reactions can be dealt with by reforms which concern principally the central level. To quote Michel Crozier:(1) "the theoretical freedom of action of the central administrations (insofar as redefining objectives is concerned) may at first glance seem to be a great advantage. In fact, it paralyses them because they can be effective only in maintaining the status quo; they are not capable of changing the equilibrium (or symbiosis) which exists between their local services and the social environment; this equilibrium has crystallised independently of them and against them". One could say as well that they are not capable of changing the balance of their relationships with each other. Insofar as more and more changes imply change, in a more inter-sectoral way, of the patterns of relationships between central administrations on the one hand and between these administrations and their environment on the other, it is likely that inter-sectoral planning will develop firstly as a means for the Ministry of Education to maintain control over its environment. Co-ordination with inter-sectoral approaches developed by other departments may prove to be difficult. An example of this is the attempt in 1969 and 1970 to make proposals for new curricula in the universities. New patterns of curricula were proposed in the

1) M. Crozier, La société bloquée, Le Seuil, 1972, p. 121.

different areas of higher education by commissions made up of university professors and representatives from the professions. Once the Ministry had agreed they were put to the universities.

This approach, although under the auspices of the Ministry of Education, was thought to be clearly inter-sectoral. The universities, however, made rather little use of it.

Planning: The ministerial framework perhaps makes it difficult to have an overall picture of the possibilities which exist within public services as a whole. For example, a policy or rural development - directed principally by the Ministry of Agriculture, and by specially created bodies like the commissioners for rural development - should have among its objectives a smoother transition of a part of the rural population to urban activities and an urban way of life. It should therefore be closely linked to urban development policies and, at the same time, include the changes in school programmes necessary to fit young people for life in a new urban environment.

The "collective functions" of the VIth Plan (see p. 227) attempt to provide an overall view of all the possibilities of action within the same "sector". The collective function "education and training", for example, groups together those actions concerning education and training which emanate from the Ministries of Education, Labour, Health, Agriculture, Defence, etc.

The Education Commission of the VIth Plan tended to be dominated by the Ministry of Education, and this reinforces the sectoral approach. At the same time, the Ministry was experimenting with output budgeting which, after one year, became pluri-annual and developed into an administrative planning (see p. 227) which goes far beyond the yearly budgeting process. Moreover, other procedures are being used, on the initiative of the Ministry of Education - but independently of the administration itself. They represent a type of participatory planning in areas more limited than those of the five-year plan. On the whole these procedures involve representatives of the groups which constitute the immediate social environment of the Ministry of Education and they tend rather to reinforce a sectoral view and to orientate the search for solutions towards quantitative requirements for the various groups involved. Procedures which would be an exception to this tendency would be those which create situations encouraging participants in the educational system to develop their own planning processes (see p. 237: the 10 per cent recommendation in secondary schools put forward by the "Commission Joxe sur la Fonction enseignante dans le second degré, 1972).

III. THE NEED TO INTEGRATE POLICIES AT REGIONAL AND AT LOCAL
     LEVELS. "DECONCENTRATION" AND DECENTRALISATION

Policies and planning at the national level must be integrated
if the central administrations are to keep a minimum of control over
their social environment. This integration cannot in itself ensure
that "clients'" needs are satisfied. The gap between central decisions and actual services remains too large and greater integration
is needed at the implementation level. This is particularly true
for all social services which deal directly with individuals. At
regional and local levels integration may take two different forms:

- "deconcentration", which means transferring powers of decision
  and co-ordination to the local representatives of the various
  administrations, who remain directly responsible to their
  superiors;
- decentralisation, which means transferring powers to bodies
  which are more or less independent juridically - local authorities, offices and agencies, universities, even directly to
  individuals in the case of a voucher system, etc.

Decentralisation and "deconcentration" can either be technical
or geographical. In the first case, power is delegated with no geographical limitations but within a limited sector of activity to an
agency, or to a public or even private body so that it may work more
freely. In the second case, the power is limited to a given geographical area, which may not be the same for all the sectors of
activity concerned. Examples of these attempts at a better integration of policies and the difficulties involved can be found both in
French administration as a whole (A) and in the educational system
(B).

A) Decentralisation and "deconcentration" in French administration

The movement towards a certain interministerial "horizontality"
on the national level has been followed by efforts to promote and reinforce this "horizontality" in the services of the local and regional
ministries. In 1964 all State services in the "départements" (the
basic French administrative circumscription) were put under the sole
authority of the Prefect (Préfet), who has a triple role. He is the
government's representative in the "département", the "département"
executive for all decisions legally attributed to the circumscription and the "département" representative to the State. All information and correspondence between the ministries and their local
services has to pass through the Prefect's office and he can thus
ensure such co-ordination measures as he deems appropriate. In the
same year the role of the regional circumscriptions was redefined

in order to give greater responsibility for planning and co-ordination to the "Préfet de Région" vis-á-vis his colleagues, the Prefects of the "départements". This seemed to provide a better administrative framework than that of the "département" alone for the planning of public equipment and regional economic development. The Préfet de Région is assisted in his new responsibilities by a small interdisciplinary team of civil servants. They have an overall view of the major economic and social issues concerning the regions and provide the Préfet de Région with inter-sectoral information and suggest any co-ordination measures which appear to be necessary. In fact, the part of their activity concerned with the planning and programming of public equipment tends to be predominant, and the various services of the ministries retain a wide range of autonomy, which varies from region to region, and direct relationships with their ministry. This situation is particularly important for the educational administrative services which are directed by the Rectors in the academies, since the academies are specific educational circumscriptions which do not always coincide with the general administrative region.

The significant development in the VIth Plan (1971-1975) of a regional approach to planning has allowed the planners to have an improved perception of the spatial and inter-sectoral aspects of development. The regional authorities have been led to formulate their investment priorities by functions, within overall financial estimates. However, since the government arbitrates financially in the first place among the various functions at the national level and the resources allocated to each function are subsequently distributed among the different regions, several regions have found that their priorities have not been respected. In some cases they received more resources than they hoped for in sectors which they did not consider to be top priority.

Moreover, the mechanisms for drawing up the State Budget and for its application to the regions do not allow for a satisfactory implementation of the Plan, even in cases where a national or regional inter-sectoral approach has been developed. The budget is prepared and voted, ministry by ministry, according to the demands of each one. The achievement of inter-sectoral objectives is therefore dependent upon each ministry agreeing to consider as priorities - from the point of view of its own sectoral policies - those actions which are considered to be priorities within the framework of inter-sectoral plans. These plans may be national, as the finalised programmes, or regional, and since they have no financial means of their own they cannot be implemented unless they go through the traditional sectoral channels.

It was therefore difficult for the regions to design and implement genuine regional inter-sectoral policies, and to utilise means from such diverse origins in a co-ordinated fashion, since they have no control over the allocation of those means. The improvement of the inter-sectoral approach is, in this case, closely linked to a reduction in concentration and centralisation and the attribution of greater powers to the regional and local levels.

All types of public equipment, for example, have been classified, since 1970, into three categories according to the appropriate administrative level of decision - national, regional or departmental. There is nevertheless a tendency for the ministries to interpret this classification in a restrictive way, in order to keep overall or even detailed control over investments which, according to the regulations, should be decided upon by the lower levels of responsibility. Another way for the ministries to keep their power over local decisions in their sector and make inter-sectoral decisions at the local level more difficult is to go on drawing up detailed regulations, adapted solely to their sectoral preoccupations, for the building, functioning and use of their sector's equipment, such as schools.

The social demand, especially for social equipment, is, in most cases, an inter-sectoral one in that it asks for a set of services and for the satisfaction of education, cultural and promotion needs. This more or less vague demand is interpreted by the various sectoral services as a precise demand for the type of equipment of service for which they are responsible and which they are accustomed to provide.

The precise definition of priorities as between the different sectors on the regional and local level is not always followed by the different ministries which have their own views of the priorities in their sectors for the regional distribution of resources. The result is that the local and regional services of the various ministries tend not to situate their own sectoral needs within the inter-sectoral regional framework, but rather to try and get a bigger budget directly from their ministry.

B)   Inter-sectoral policy and planning in the education system
     at implementation levels. Some problems of decentralisation.

Most ministries show little concern for the differences in local situations which should in theory lead to differentiated solutions to the same problems. This is particularly true for the Ministry of Education mainly because of its autonomous hierarchical organisation and its interpretation of the equality requirement, which is seen to mean equal treatment whatever the actual differences of the situation may be. Moreover, although the local

authorities and the population show a greater sensitivity to a
variety of issues concerning education, they tend to feel at the
same time that all these issues are chiefly the responsibility of
the central government.

There is thus a built-in contradiction in the approach to the
decentralisation problem: decentralisation is very much in demand,
and, at the same time, it is much distrusted for fear that it will
in fact result in more, or at least not less, power for the central
administration. As a result, when greater possibilities for autonomy
are provided, they are often very poorly used, and even when they
are taken up it is not always in the interest of promoting co-
operation with the other sectors.

National guidelines are often used by the various sectors concerned to protect themselves against the risks involved in co-
operation at the local level.

This difficulty will be illustrated by some examples:

a) "integrated equipment";
b) the "10 per cent recommendation" in the secondary schools;
c) "university autonomy" since the law of 1968;
d) recurrent education.

a) "Integrated equipment"

They have in most cases been designed for the "New Towns" or
for the new areas of older cities. They are part of urban operations which are, from the beginning, fundamentally horizontal and
inter-sectoral. The aim is to provide, in a very few years, buildings and equipment which would normally require generations. These
cases provide the optimal conditions for rational planning: an
overall management responsible for the planning, the organisation
of participation by the inhabitants, the building and promotion of
the town and its equipment; no planning and building constraints from
the past.

For these reasons, the difficulties encountered in creating new
inter-sectoral approaches to educational, social and cultural problems in these cases are particularly illustrative. Since the regulations governing the building, the running of it and the status of
the personnel are fixed within the different ministerial frameworks,
considerable difficulties arise when there is a question of using
these establishments to satisfy needs other than those originally
conceived; for example using a school for cultural or social activities for adults. Each ministry tends to develop its own specialised
equipment which is duplicated over and over again, and this tendency
is further aggravated by the standardization of equipment in the
form of standard plans which aim at time and cost-saving in instal-
lation. In cases - so far extremely rare and experimental - where

integration is sought at the initial stages of building and equipping ("integrated equipment") difficulties arise for the financing of the establishment, which does not conform to the different norms of the various ministries involved. The saving hoped for from the provision of several functions in one place (education, culture, social activities, etc.) with total utilisation of the equipment can be eaten up by the additional costs of the subsequent running expenses.

b) The "10 per cent recommendation" in the secondary schools (1972)

The possibility for each secondary school to allocate 10 per cent of the time-schedule to self-determined objectives should allow the school community:

- to take into consideration the different needs and attitudes of students;
- to design its own set of objectives, alongside the compulsory learning objectives set by ordinary time-schedules, and thus to set up a dialectical movement between these two parts of the curriculum;
- to communicate with the external social environment and in this way to create incentives for inter-sectoral attitudes and activities more easily than could be done by any precise national regulation.

The 10 per cent recommendation is an innovation in that it has created a framework within which local initiative - in the school - has to develop. Many schools will not take advantage of this possibility; others will provide a greater variety of experiences which can then be communicated.

Schools and teachers find themselves in a new situation in which they have to explore their own - albeit limited - sets of objectives, instead of simply complying with national regulations. Consequently, social relationships in the school are bound to change in a pluridisciplinary, inter-sectoral way.

The inconvenience of this formula is that there are no additional resources which could create supplementary incentives for such innovation and induce some kind of financial impetus to planning.

c) "University autonomy" since the law of 1968

Various measures which were intended to encourage inter-sectoral approaches in teaching were included in the 1968 reform of higher education:

- the very principles of the "loi d'orientation": autonomy,
  pluridisciplinarity, participation;
- the creation of experimental universities;
- the possibility for the universities to define their own
  curriculum and to grant their own degrees.

The possibilities offered by these measures have not been sufficiently exploited. When the major principles of the "loi d'orientation" were implemented, more attention was given to "constitutional"
problems and to relationships among the various groups within the
universities than to new contents of curricula and degrees. Moreover, the possibility of creating new degrees has been inhibited by
the fact that both professors and students preferred their degrees to
have "national validity". Innovations were therefore limited. Students and their families expect the degrees obtained at school or at
the university to have the same value for all, whatever the differences in content and methods may be. The "national validity" of degrees is an important factor in the French system since it implies
that all degrees of the same level give identical rights and opportunities to enter, for example, the civil service and to reach a given
salary level within it. The major trend is therefore to maintain
national degrees rather than "university" ones, because both professors and students fear that the university degrees may be too
restrictive and non-egalitarian; in other words not as useful in a
career as the national degrees, and too much influenced by short-
term or local considerations.

However, some original curricula have been created by the
universities, mostly as a complement to more traditional studies.
There are for example courses on urban planning, regional studies,
oceanology, etc., most of which use people and institutions outside
the university.

d) Recurrent education

The development of recurrent education courses in the universities following the Law of 17th July, 1971 should also provide
opportunities for creating new patterns of relationships between the
universities and the outside world, and consequently for encouraging
inter-sectoral approaches to teaching.

Whereas the preference of all universities for national degrees
rather than for university ones /see (c)7 tends to reduce competition among the universities, initiatives in the field of recurrent
education are likely to heighten competition. The universities will
be competing with other institutions and private educational firms
which are trying to obtain as large a share as possible of the funds
provided for "vocational and continuing education". There is a

special tax of 0.8 per cent of the wage bill for all enterprises employing more than ten people, and it will soon be 1.5 per cent. They will also be competing with each other in terms of reputation and image with a view to obtaining a larger share of these funds in the future.

The flexibility provided by this special financing of vocational recurrent education and the newness of the field is likely to have more of an impact on the reform of the traditional school and university system than reforms actually made within the traditional system. The latter do not create a sufficient challenge to the traditional view of specialised studies by sector corresponding to teachers' and professors' specialisations, and of science as the continual addition of small, even more specialised branches of knowledge.

IV. IMPACT OF STATUS AND ROLE DIFFERENCES ON INTER-SECTORALISM

Inter-sectoral approaches are determined, to a very great extent, by the strategies of the various administrative bodies or pressure groups which intervene in the different sectors. The civil service was initially created by the State in order to have a sufficient number of people regularly employed in key sectors of the administration. Each branch has therefore a sort of monopoly in a given type of job (for instance road and construction engineers, mining engineers, finance inspectors). They also try to extend the boundaries of their initial sector of activity and to create monopolies, or at least important positions, in the new sectors of activity which appear, as State involvement in economic and social spheres increases. These new sectors of activity (city planning, for instance) are more and more inter-sectoral. They resemble new sectors of science which appear at the intersections of two or more traditional sectors. The training given in the "Ecoles", which train candidates for the civil service, is sufficiently general and multidisciplinary to allow the students to enter these new sectors of activity. The student will probably spend only the first few years of his career in a basically traditional sector of activity.

One of the major aims in creating the National Civil Service School (ENA) in 1945 was precisely to try and break down these sectoral divisions between the various administrations. Many years ago this same objective was reflected in the creation of the so-called "Grands corps" such as the Finance inspectorate, the Councils of State and the Court for Public Accounts which were small elite public bodies, hierarchically set apart from the other administrations and with a higher status. They are responsible for auditing, inspecting and reforming the other administrations.

In the School the administrators were supposed to acquire interministerial, that is inter-sectoral, views and capacities and to avoid early specialisation by virtue of the same interdisciplinary studies. Status is uniform and there is a kind of compulsory "mobility" in the form of an obligation to spend at least two years, after the first four years in one administration, in another. This is a condition for further promotion. The inter-sectoral approach was further encouraged by the fact that this corps of administrators was under the authority of the Prime Minister's services, wherever they might work. In fact, differences periodically appear which tend to encourage sectoral rather than inter-sectoral activities and careers.

The new forms of organisation, the regroupings or differentiations of existing administrations or agencies and the definition of new planning areas will depend, to a great extent, on the strategies of the various categories competing for the control of these new spheres of activity. The resulting organisation may not be adequate to meet problems arising from those inter-sectoral preoccupations which are felt but rarely precisely expressed by public opinion. In the case of real inadequacy, co-ordination will have to be continuously improved and this will provide the different administrative corps with opportunities to extend their areas of responsibility. The strategies for defining the inter-sectoralism which is to prevail will be of considerable influence.(1) The strategies will be all the more important in a centralised country like France, since centralisation means that the different administrative corps themselves have a rather rigid national organisation; they are in competition with each other at the national level, where they permanently compare their professional and financial advantages.

In the educational system, a large number of new tasks are appearing. They require new definitions of roles and status for the people involved in them. In many cases the new status may be attractive to people already working in the system: they may try to obtain a major share of the jobs which the new roles create. More and more of these new roles are inter-sectoral ones, on the boundaries of the traditional educational system and the different sectors of its social environment; for example, information counsellors, acting as liaison officers between school and professions or crafts; school psychologists, between school and the families (many members of these two categories are recruited from among primary school teachers); public relations specialists, between the educational system and the mass-media; recurrent education delegates, between the educational system and the enterprises. These categories are created by the Ministry of Education, which both recruits and pays them. Many of

1) See: L'ère des technocrates, by J.C. Thoenig - Editions d'organisation, 1973, Paris.

these people come, in the beginning at least, from other areas within the educational sector. Similar inter-sectoral views lead other ministries to organise their own system for dealing with the problems which appear on the boundaries of their traditional sector: for example, the Ministry of Education will promote studies on employment opportunities, whereas the Ministry of Labour will promote studies of vocational curricula. The new tasks of the information and guidance counsellors (Ministry of Education) will often coincide with tasks of the employment agency counsellors (Ministry of Labour) and co-ordination between these two Ministries will have to be developed in order to define precisely the tasks on both sides. This co-ordination will in certain cases lead to the creation of inter-sectoral agencies under the auspices of both Ministries, and of certain other related ministries or agencies (the vocational training committee for example).

There is also co-ordination within each ministry to select those inter-sectoral aspects which are most relevant for the organisation. For instance, the educational system's ability to achieve its aims depends on two other factors at least: the family and social environment which should stimulate the child's desire to learn; the labour market, which has to provide jobs corresponding to school or university qualifications. Teachers and professors are often mediators between the family, the school or university and the working world. Some of them are better at this or do it more willingly than others. Their success depends upon their aims, experience, and specialisation and upon their conception of inter-sectoral responsibilities. The attitude of university professors towards participation in research outside the university, towards counselling students about entry into the professional world, or towards associate professors coming temporarily from the professional world, will have a major influence on the type of inter-sectoralism which will develop in the universities.

If teachers and professors are mainly concerned with communicating intellectual abilities and knowledge, so that their students may reach a higher level of knowledge - and this is a major aim of secondary education - they will probably pay less attention to the social environment of their establishment.

Since 1972 several hundred teachers in technical schools have been given the possibility of spending one year in business enterprise. Some categories of teachers in the technical schools can be recruited from among professionals with a minimum of five years' experience. These measures testify to a certain desire for enlarging the school activity, although they do not reflect a systematic and widespread policy. One reason for this is that such experimental co-operation between sectors is felt to be too costly for the initiating sector. Studies might possibly show that supplementary expenditures by the educational administration to organise these contacts with other sectors are compensated for by savings in other sectors or improvements of productivity in the educational sectors. However, since the relevant decisions are not taken simultaneously nor by the same people in the different sectors, studies showing these savings would not be likely to be taken seriously in sectoral decision making.

The problem of establishing contact with the social environment of the educational system will then be dealt with by other specialists such as the information and guidance counsellors; the definition of their tasks and of their training will depend very much on the inter-sectoral view which prevails for educational policy. If the family's role and the emotional life of the students are thought to be major factors in academic success, training for counsellors will put the emphasis on psychology; if employment prospects are thought to be more important, the emphasis will fall on economy and a knowledge of the labour market.

The counsellors are well aware of the ambiguities inherent in their tasks. On the one hand it is a question of helping the students to obtain a training best suited to their aptitudes and, on the other, of orientating them according to a fixed notion of the economic needs of society, or according to the number of places available for a given subject. The counsellors themselves have little power to solve these contradictions. In order to avoid becoming too specialised themselves, counsellors will consider that they are responsible for the more inter-sectoral aspects of the students' life which are not dealt with by traditional institutions and roles. Some consider themselves to be educational generalists, a one-man-band, able to deal with problems arising from the family environment, and with problems of curriculum and work as well. A too narrow specialisation is likely to be considered as detrimental to the development of the counselling service but the counsellors will nevertheless continue to specialise. There was in 1970 a project for a unified body of school psychologists and guidance counsellors, to be recruited from among primary school teachers. There were two possible areas of study for the students during their training - psychology and economy. Subsequently it was decided that there should be two separate bodies. This example shows that creation of a new group, whose role is never precisely defined - as in the counsellors' case - does not necessarily lead to an inter-sectoral approach; too many tasks - connecting educational institutions to the economy, to health services, to the family, etc. - become the responsibility of one person, whose task becomes impossible. However, the role of the counsellors reflects some of the newly perceived tasks of educational institutions.

Conclusions

There is a growing awareness that a theoretical uniformity in the regulations governing educational institutions does not lead to real equality; more particularly because there are elements outside the educational sector which influence the effectiveness of measures taken within the sector.

It is very unlikely that an overall integrated social model which would include an inter-sectoral planning system for education in all its complexities could be elaborated; it is not even desirable, since, as experience shows, once elaborated, inter-sectoral systems tend to lead to excessive rigidity. On the one hand, each sector increases its own administrative capacity to deal with inter-sectoral problems from its own sectoral point of view, while on the other the "Commissariat général du Plan" - although without executive power - and various national agencies also deal with some major inter-sectoral problems. There is a growing feeling however that integration of social policies at the national level remains too abstract to lead to a satisfactory solution in the field. At the other end of the scale, too much precision in inter-sectoral planning at the national level can create excessive rigidity in the field, where the solutions proposed should be completed or even changed by other forms of action, better adapted to local conditions.

However, even if decentralisation is much discussed, it is not actually desired by most groups and lobbies within the educational sector. It is generally felt that inter-sectoral problems can be dealt with satisfactorily through the usual sectoral channels, and that better solutions may be found by dealing with each sector separately. There is a feeling that more co-ordination with other sectors at the local level might mean greater dependence on these sectors, whereas responsibility to one ministry may offer a form of protection.

THE UNDER-FIVES AND THE
CORPORATE SYSTEM OF COVENTRY

by Alberto Melo

I.   TRADITIONAL LOCAL GOVERNMENT AND CORPORATE GOVERNMENT CHANGES

Britain's system of local government, in its modern form, was
created at the end of the last century to meet new social and environmental demands arising from the industrialisation and urbanisation
of the country. Traditionally the administrative system within local
authorities has been based on self-contained professions, departments or committees, dealing separately, on the whole, with problems
arising in their individual departments, using monies from an annual
income which is divided among the departments to be used
independently.

The old structure of local government tended to confuse the
public and it was often seen as irrelevant to their problems. A
family with related social problems could not have them tackled as
a whole, and was unable to identify them with individual departments. The new system evolving in Coventry since the mid-sixties
attempts to overcome such disadvantages by overlapping traditional
departmental boundaries.

The drawbacks of non-integrated local authorities were systematically attached in several official reports on matters of local
government published during the sixties. The Maud Report stressed
"the absence of unity in the internal organisation of a local authority which is the result of the close association of a particular
service, the service committee, the department concerned and the
hierarchy of professional officers" (Maud Committee on Management in
Local Government, 1967 Vol. I, p. 57, HMSO, 1967). Similarly, the
central message of paragraph 2.11 of the Bains Report (The New Local
Authorities: Management and Structure, HMSO, 1972) is that the traditional departmental attitude of much of local government must give
way to a wider unifying corporate outlook.

The use of words like "unity" and "unify" leads to the idea of
corporate planning, a technique among others which involves the
uniting and drawing together of professional and other skills and
resources in order to attack the complex problems now facing local
government.

Coventry was chosen for this study because it was known to be developing a systematic approach to corporate planning. It is, for instance, stated in paragraph 5.77 of the Bains Report that "although many authorities are making increasing use of multi-disciplinary working groups for specific projects, few, if any, have gone as far as we now suggest. Coventry CBC /County Borough Council7 is probably as far along this particular road as anybody and we found an impressive sense of commitment and enthusiasm there which contrasted sharply with the very mixed feelings in some of the other authorities which had undertaken substantial changes in management structures."

The main features of the Coventry system are directed towards:

i) identifying the needs and problems which the city faces as a whole;

ii) formulating the main policies which the City Council wishes to pursue and the plans which need to be made to achieve them;

iii) estimating the level of resources likely to be available from central government and local sources;

iv) concentrating on what the Council seeks to achieve overall rather than on the individual services they wish to develop;

v) investigating different ways of achieving the Council's aims with a view to making the best use of the resources available;

vi) monitoring achievement and keeping matters under continuous review.

Did this new approach to management and planning provoke any drastic changes in the organisational structure of the Coventry Council? The initial intention was to preserve as much as possible the old structure, based on Departments and Committees, and to knit these together by means of the corporate, multi-disciplinary, structure, based on Programme Area Teams (PATs).

PATs are at the very heart of the system. Unlike traditional local authority departments, with their origin in the professionalisation of particular disciplines or in the powers and duties given by Parliament to local authorities, the PATs consider related activities grouped together, with a common over-arching objective set for each group. The City Council, in January 1971, agreed to a statement of its objectives for the city. There are nine prime objectives, each of which is concerned with a wide area of activity over which the Corporation has control or influence:

1. To enrich the lives of the people by the optimum personal development of each individual in the community (PAT Education);

2. To assist in achieving and maintaining the optimum standard of community health and well-being for people in Coventry (PAT Community Health and Well-Being);

3. To promote consumer services, environmental hygiene and public safety (PAT Public Protection);

4. To secure an adequate and proper distribution of satisfactory housing accommodation to meet the social and economic needs of the city (PAT Housing);

5. To ensure the existence of facilities for the movement of persons and goods (PAT Transportation);

6. To ensure appropriate provision of facilities for the whole community to enjoy their free time and in particular to encourage those pursuits which contribute to the development of the individual and family life and to voluntary participation in the life of the community (PAT Leisure);

7. To promote commercial and industrial development of the city and of the region in order to meet the optimum employment and social needs of the city, consonant nevertheless with the needs of industrial and commercial concerns which may be involved (PAT Commerce-Industry);

8. To achieve a satisfactory physical environment for the community in all its activities (PAT Environment);

9. To provide support and to deal with other unassignable functions (PAT General Support).

Each of the PATs oversees the activities leading to the achievement of one of these prime objectives. PATs are multi-departmental: representatives are drawn from the principal officers of the Departments whose activities are covered by the Team's objectives. Each is led by a Chief Officer nominated by the Chief Executive and Town Clerk.

PAT, No. 1, Education, is composed of 17 officers recruited from the following departments: Architecture and Planning (2), Associate Town Clerk's (3), Health (1), Libraries, Art Galleries and Museums (1), the City Treasurer's (2), Social Services (1), and finally Education (7), which provides the PAT Leader, who is the chief Education Officer.

Within PAT Education services are grouped into six sections, mainly based on the age of the clients: (1) pre-school, (2) primary, (3) secondary, (4) further, (5) special, (6) administrative and advisory activities. For each section an individual objective is defined. In the pre-school section, the authority defined as its objectives:

"to ensure in the light of parental wishes adequate educational provision appropriate to the needs of infants below the age of five years".

II. UNDER-FIVES IN COVENTRY BEFORE 1972

Before the publication of the 1972 White Paper (announcing a
new central policy of expansion of pre-school provision) the Coventry
Council was already aware of a strong public demand for greater educational facilities for the under-fives. The exact extent of demand
for nursery education was difficult to assess with any precision.
However, in July 1972 there was a total of 832 names on the waiting
lists at Coventry's nursery schools and units. In August 1972 the
Education (Planning) Sub-Committee prepared a document which listed
some alternatives for action on "Educational Provision for the under-
fives". It stated that "ideally, all children should have the benefit of a period of nursery education to prepare them more adequately
for the transition from home to school." However, with an average
age group of approximately 6,000 children (i.e. 30,000 under-fives)
and only about 1,050 nursery places available in the city, it was
clear to the Councillors and Officers concerned that a considerable time would have to pass before the ideal would be realised.
This ideal would not only be quantitative, that is providing nursery
places for 30,000 children, but should also refer to the nature of
the provision, as the existing institutions were not responsible to
the overall needs of parents and children.

Provision was made in Coventry for under-fives as follows:
(i) by the education service in infant schools, in nursery schools
and in nursery classes, (ii) by the social service in day nurseries
(iii) by voluntary play groups under the supervision of the Social
Services Department.

Statutorily, a local authority has power to provide nursery
education for children under five, and indeed is enjoined by law
"to have regard to the need" for providing nursery schools or units.
It was found by the Coventry Authority that the provision of nursery
education proved to be a great benefit to all children concerned.
They develop physically, socially, emotionally and intellectually,
and are readier to take advantage of full-time infant education when
of compulsory school age.

In addition to the provision of nursery schools, the City
Council is empowered to provide for the under-fives in two other
ways. The first is by the direct provision of day nurseries, which
come under the responsibility of a different central government
Department (Department of Health and Social Services) and also of
a different Council Department and Committee (Social Services).
Day nurseries serve a somewhat different function from nursery
schools, as they do not aim directly at providing any education
but fulfil an economic and social role (the release of women for
employment, or the meeting of particular social needs such as those
of one-parent families).

The second way in which the Council caters for the under-fives, outside the nursery schools and units, is by assisting pre-school play groups. These have grown up largely in response to the shortage of nursery places and are purely voluntary organisations which may operate in individual homes or, for example, in church halls, community centres, or indoor play centres.

It is estimated that in Coventry the following proportions are currently provided for directly by the City Council (i.e. in infant schools, nursery schools or classes and in day nurseries):

	Full-time attendance	Part-time attendance
4-year-olds	59%	7.5%
3-year-olds	6%	4 %

The services at present provided are of a mixed nature with a great variation in standards of care and stimulation for the children, and hours of opening for the parents. The position is summarised in the table on the following page.

After extensive consultation with a wide section of the population, the Council concluded that the type of institution required to satisfy the needs of both children and parents would be one which incorporated qualified teaching and nursing staff with opening hours suitable for working parents.

Furthermore, the local government decided that the education of the under-fives was to be a major input into those areas designated as deprived.

The potential demand for services provided by the local authority for under-fives was clearly in excess of the existing supply, and therefore the authority decided to expand nursery provision in the city of Coventry.

The "Nature and Extent of Educational Provision for Children under the Age of Compulsory School Attendance" was therefore defined as a "Key Decision Area", which means, in terms of the management approach used in Coventry, an issue selected for in-depth study. This implied the production of a report relating to the educational provision for under-fives with a description of the present situation and of the effects of population changes on future provision and resources. The authors of the report were required to cover the following areas:

    i)   the level of provision at which the Authority should aim;

    ii) the means by which the Authority should seek to realise
        this aim, i.e. release existing nursery units for their

Type	Hours open daily	Weeks open yearly	Full or part-time	Fees charged	Staff qualification	Provided by	Age range
Day Nursery	7.30-6.00	48	F.T. essentially	On a sliding scale from 50p to £3 a week	NNEB(*)	Social Services Dept.	0 - 4
Nursery School	8.45-3.45	40	F.T. or P.T.	Nil	Teaching Certificate NNEB	Education Dept.	2 - 4
Nursery Class	8.45-3.45	40	F.T. or P.T.	Nil	Teaching Certificate NNEB	Education Dept.	3 - 4
Child Minder	Dependent upon the child minder and the needs of the parent			From approx. £3-£5 per week	Registration with Social Services Dept.	Individual child minders	0 - 4
Play Group	Generally 9.30-12.00 or 1.30-3.30	Generally 40	P.T. for a number of sessions a week	Various	Nil. But a number of leaders are qualified teachers, nurses or NNEBs Registered with Social Services Dept.	Voluntary agencies, mostly individuals	3 - 4

*)   Nursery Nurses Examination Board

        designed purpose, provide additional accommodation, await changes in national policy, encourage part-time attendance, greater local authority encouragement of voluntary effort;

iii)   the level of teaching and ancillary staffing to be provided either by continuing existing policy, reducing existing staffing levels, or equalising levels of provision in nursery and reception classes.

    In their statement on Educational Provision for the Under-Fives as a Key Decision Area, the officers composing PAT Education developed some of the reasons for choosing this area. They found that since the war a good deal of research had been undertaken into factors affecting educational performance, and that as a result strong evidence had accumulated to show that the quality of the home environment was crucial to educational development. The officers thus concluded that if inadequacies in the home were to be countered through the educational system it was vital to start the process at "as early an age as possible". At the same time, they had to recognise that public pressure had been growing in recent years for the expansion of nursery opportunities.

Faced with a rather restrictive policy from central government in this field, the officers when defining this specific Key Decision Area in 1972 could rely only on local resources. The immediate issue which remained open was whether existing accommodation could or should be made available for nursing purposes. Such an issue was then, and still is, intimately bound up with future policy in the primary field and presents essentially two aspects; accommodation and staffing.

Over the next few years, the accommodation available would increase while the primary school population would remain static and eventually decline. However this expected surplus of accommodation could be used in a number of ways. Firstly, it would make it possible to lower the overall pupil-classroom ratio and thus reduce the size of primary classes. Secondly it could be used to get rid of some of the 124 classes housed in temporary accommodation. Thirdly, it could be used to increase the numbers benefiting from education by admitting more two- and three-year-olds. A combination of these policies could equally be adopted.

This problem was paralleled by the staffing situation in that the projected increase in teacher supply would equally allow some improvement in existing primary class size. However, at the same time, such improvement could also permit the diversion of these additional teachers to nursery education without giving rise to any worsening of the primary provision. Coventry was well aware that nursery education makes considerably greater demands in terms of staffing than primary education. A 40-place nursery unit, for example, would normally have a qualified teacher and three or four NNEB(*) trained assistants.

Without a clear central government policy, local authorities felt unable to deal satisfactorily with these serious and increasingly complex issues.

III. CENTRAL GOVERNMENT INITIATIVES

A turning-point in the recent evolution of central policy for nursery education was certainly the report of the Plowden

---

*) Nursery Nurses Examination Board.

Committee on Primary Schools, published in 1967 ("Children and their Primary Schools, report of the Central Advisory Council for Education", HMSO 1967). The Plowden Committee was not the first body to recommend an extension of nursery education, but its weighty and well-researched report put a stamp of respectability on, and hence gave new impetus to, the nursery education movement.

The report suggested that there should be a substantial expansion of nursery education. The research of child development experts, upon which this recommendation was based, was set by the Central Advisory Council for Education alongside sociological investigations which seemed to indicate that much of the difference in children's learning ability in school should be attributed to home background and parental influence. This led to the concept of "positive discrimination" in favour of the disadvantaged child. Areas of poor housing, deprived social and environmental conditions should be declared "Educational Priority Areas" (EPAs), which would receive an extra allocation of resources. The nursery programme would make its own contribution to the development of the disadvantaged child with a poor home background.

The two main governmental initiatives that came to affect the nursery field were (i) from 1968, the Urban Aid Programme, and (ii) in December 1972, the White Paper "Education - a Framework for Expansion".

a) Urban Aid Programme

On 22nd July, 1968, the then Home Secretary, Mr. James Callaghan announced in Parliament a proposal to initiate an urban programme of expenditure, mainly on education, housing, health and welfare, in areas of special social need. A list of such areas was drawn up jointly by the Home Office, the Ministry of Health and the Department of Education and Science. In the Joint Circular (Home Office No. 225/68 of 4th October, 1968) about the Urban Programme it was announced that expenditure would be approved under the programme to a limit of about £3 million on providing, expanding, or improving nursery schools and classes, day nurseries, and children's homes, and also on expenditure on additional staff, equipment, and running costs necessary to carry on the schools and nurseries. Furthermore, on the second reading of the Bill on Urban Aid the Home Secretary announced that the government were prepared to pay the new specific grant at a rate of 75 per cent towards approved items of expenditure.

The city of Coventry was not included on the list drawn up by the three government Departments, but in February 1969 it was announced that a second phase of the Programme, sanctioning further expenditure, would be started. In response to a joint circular

from the above three Departments, Coventry City Council formulated
plans for the provision of a day nursery and nursery school, as well
as a supervised indoor play centre. At about the same time, the
then Secretary of State for Health and Social Security,
Mr. Richard Crossman, invited Coventry to take part in a national
experiment in Community Development.

The expressed aim of the experiment was "to find ways of
meeting more effectively the needs of individuals, families and communities, whether native or immigrant, suffering from many forms of
social deprivation". The problems these people have to face in their
daily lives were defined by Mr. Crossman as being "interrelated".
Furthermore, it was recognised that they did not know how to gain
access to, nor how to use constructively, the services which exist
The memorandum from the Secretary of State for Health and Social
Security observed: "In varying degrees, each /of the social
services7 exists to meet a particular need or range of needs, the
assumption being that other needs will be met by the clients themselves or by the other services. This arrangement works satisfactorily for those people who are reasonably well aware of their needs
and who know how to make constructive use of the relevant services.
By contrast people who suffer from a multitude of interrelated problems and deprivations need support from the social services which is
not offered piecemeal in relation to this or that facet of the total
situation, but which can help them face these problems as a whole."

The proposed experiment involved the establishment, in a small
number of areas where severely deprived families are concentrated,
of a co-ordinated approach by an inter-service team devoted to the
total personal needs of individuals and families and of local communities as a whole. This inter-service team, one for each selected
area, was expected to draw on staff from the following local
services:

Education	e.g. teacher, education welfare officer
Child Care	e.g. child care officer
Welfare	e.g. welfare officer
Health	e.g. general practitioner, health visitor, home nurse, local authority medical officer, mental welfare officer, public health inspector
Employment	e.g. employment officer, disablement resettlement officer, youth employment officer
Social Security	e.g. supplementary benefit officer
Housing	e.g. housing officer
Probation	e.g. probation officer
Industrial Services	e.g. industrial welfare officer

Child Guidance   e.g. psychologist, social worker
Police   e.g. local constables, juvenile
                             liaison officers.

In addition, it should also include a representative of the university associated with the experiment and representatives of voluntary agencies working in the area.

In a striking parallel to the principles behind the system of corporate planning, the inter-service team was required "to explore possible ways of supplementing, but not displacing the work of the organised services and the existing machinery for inter-service co-ordination". The object of the experiment was not, in fact, to disrupt or supplant the existing channels for the allocation of resources, nor to set up some parallel organisation, but to enable each of the existing services, working closely together, "to see problems whole and to plan their decisions so that they reinforce, and are reinforced by, those taken by other relevant services".

The task assigned to each team was to make an assessment of the human and material needs and problems of the area, and then to propose an inter-service strategy for their satisfaction and solution by the services concerned, acting individually or in concert. Each member of the team was therefore expected to look at the area and its problems as a whole, "not from the exclusive viewpoint of his own service", and subsequently to act as an advocate of the proposed strategy within his own service, and to report back to the team any difficulties or objections from his service which called for some modification of the team's proposals.

b) A Community Development Experiment in Coventry: Hillfields

As a result of Coventry accepting its inclusion in the national experiment of Community Development, a Services Co-ordinating Group was formed. At their inaugural meeting (24th April, 1970) it was proposed that management of the Community Development Project in the city should be vested in two bodies to be responsible respectively for policy making and advisory functions. A Community Development Project Committee, representing the interests of the City Council and central government, was to be the means of control over the financial and establishments aspects of the project, and to confirm general policy at the local level. A Services Co-ordinating Group of Principal Officers were to act as a consortium for securing agreement and support for a programme of action from the relevant local, regional and central government services together with the relevant voluntary organisations.

A channel through which the neighbourhood could obtain access to the agencies controlling resources was made by means of a local steering group including residents who participated in the process of discussion and planning about the development of their community.

By March 1969, the Coventry City agreed that an area in the centre of the city, known as Hillfields, where the nursery and play centre were to be planned under the Urban Aid Programme, should also become the focus of Coventry's Community Development Project. Hillfields is a mainly residential redevelopment area with small industrial units. Its population of 5,700 approximately is racially mixed.

It was recognised by the Authority that the best way to respond satisfactorily to the needs of the neighbourhood was to provide full day care for at least 100 pre-school children and to keep this service available from approximately 7.00 a.m. to 6.00 p.m. for five days a week thoughout the year. By fulfilling these needs the Authority was bound to encounter strong administrative hindrances in terms of overlaps among separate services, that is, departments and committees, and of different central government departments to control and fund the project.

On 17th June, 1970 a meeting of officers was organised to discuss all problems regarding the management of Hillfields day nursery/nursery school (as it was then called). The Director of Education and the Medical Officer of Health were present along with officers from Education, Health, Architecture and Planning, and City Treasurer's Department. It was generally agreed that, in the interest of the community which the day nursery/nursery school was going to serve, both aspects should be integrated, and in order to signify this integration to the public it was accepted that the establishment would in future be known as Hillfields Nursery Centre.

The meeting discussed the obvious need for adjustment in the normal opening times, i.e. day nurseries are open from 7.30 a.m. to 6.30 p.m. five days per week 48 weeks per year, whilst nursery schools adhere to school times and terms. Staffing and financial problems were thoroughly discussed.

The Education Department is only empowered to provide nursery education for children aged from two to five years, and has no powers to charge for such education other than for mid-day meals. On the other hand, day nurseries charge for the services they provide. It was decided to charge all children a basic amount in order to meet the aims of the Urban Aid Programme and recognise the Hillfields Nursery as a particular project coming nearest to easing the difficulties which would inevitably be experienced by the Education and Health Departments vis-à-vis other nursery school and day nursery provision.

There still remained certain administrative problems to be overcome, not the least that of whether the Principal should be drawn from the nursery school world or from the day nursery world, that is

to say, whether to appoint a head teacher or a matron. It was
planned to hold classes appropriate to the needs of the parents in
the area, e.g. language classes for immigrant mothers, and the consequent need for qualified teaching staff was among the decisive
factors behind the decision to appoint a Head Teacher to take charge
of Hillfields Centre.

With a teacher as the Head and a matron (responsible to the
Director of Social Services) as the Deputy, it was finally agreed
by the officers that the Education Department was to be responsible
for the administration and running costs of the Hillfields Centre,
and the Medical Officer of Health would administer the medical
services.

In October 1973 there were at the Hillfields Centre 24 children
up to 2 years and 76 between 2 and 5. The two qualified teachers
take different groups from time to time, while the nursery assistants
and nurses concentrate on the under-threes. As the Centre remains
open from 7.00 a.m. to 6.00 p.m. and the two teachers work on rota
duties alongside the nurses, they have a worse deal than the school
teachers who work from 9.00 a.m. to 4.00 p.m.

The stringent need for extra places is behind the present programme of the Head Teacher, backed by the City Council, to organise
local annexes of the Nursery Centre: three or more using church
halls and other possible accommodation. The annexes will be temporary premises, until primary accommodation becomes available for
nursery education. To solve problems of staffing and running the
annexes, the Head Teacher is now training local mothers willing to
help. For them a basic course on Child Development was organised
over 12 sessions in the Parents' Room at Hillfields.

c) White Paper and DES Circular 2/73

The second central government initiative that greatly affected
local strategies for expansion of nursery education was the White
Paper of December 1972. In this document ("Education: A Framework
for Expansion", Cmnd 5174) the Secretary of State for Education and
Science announced an expansion of nursery education at a rate which
would enable provision to be made by 1981-1982 up to the limit of
the scale estimated as necessary by the Central Advisory Council in
1967 in the Plowden Report.

The government's policy was to provide by January 1982:
    i)   full-time education for 15 per cent of three- and four-
         year-olds;
    ii) part-time education for 35 per cent of three-year-olds;
    iii) part-time education for 75 per cent of four-year-olds.

Among other points to retain from the White Paper on the under-
fives are the following:

i) the government's view that most of the extra nursery provision should be in the form of nursery classes for the
under-fives forming part of primary schools, while significant expansion of nursery schools as such is discouraged;

ii) a proposal to convert some voluntary play groups into
maintained nursery classes;

iii) the abandonment of the phrase "Educational Priority Areas"
and the use instead of "Areas of Disadvantage" and "Substantial Areas of Social Deprivation, Urban and Rural";

iv) the maintenance of the freedom of local education authorities to decide their own priorities in preparing plans for
nursery education;

v) the stress laid upon parental involvement, particularly in
the disadvantaged areas;

vi) the plans for increasing the number of qualified teachers
on the staff of nursery schools, both from new entrants
to the profession, and by retraining of teachers hitherto
concerned with older age-groups;

vii) the promised increase up to 1976 in the resources to be
devoted to building for nursery education.

After the White Paper was published, The Department of
Education and Science advised local authorities about the intended
implementation of the programme in DES CIRCULAR 2/73. This was
primarily concerned with the mechanics of building programmes. It
is, nevertheless, significant that the Circular asks for building
proposals on the basis of multiple social deprivation, and refers
specifically to the criteria used for the Urban Programme, which
suggests that the primary objective is an improvement in the learning
capability and attainment of "disadvantaged" children, and leaves
the burden mainly on the shoulders of the local Education Committees
and Departments.

In Circular 2/73 the Department of Education and Science expressed their belief in the particular value of nursery education as a
means of redressing the educational and social disadvantages suffered
by children from homes which are "culturally and economically disadvantaged". In order to justify their decision to concentrate the
resources available for nursery education in areas of social deprivation eligible for the Urban Programme, the Secretary of State
referred to recent research findings that confirm how such children
can be greatly helped in two ways. The first is through educational
programmes which enrich their experience and thereby directly offset
their environmental handicap. The second is through increasing the
interest of the parents, particularly mothers, in such a way that
they understand more of their children's development, and are able
to assist them at home and co-operate with the teachers at school.

d) Coventry's Response to the White Paper

Coventry, as all the other local authorities, was then faced with the prospect of having to provide by 1982 nursery places for 90 per cent of four-year-olds and 50 per cent of three-year-olds. For planning purposes it was assumed as being reasonable to take each age group in the city as comprising 6,000 children. Thus the provision needed to meet the government's target was estimated as follows:

	full-time	part-time	total places
4-year-olds	900	4,500	5,400 (90%)
3-year-olds	900	2,100	3,000 (50%)
	1,800	6,600	8,400

When these target figures (to be achieved by 1982) were compared with the current provision in Coventry, it was noticed that:

i) just over 65 per cent of four-year-olds were already attending infant school, nursery school or class or day nursery;

ii) about 59 per cent of four-year-olds were attending full-time (compared with the recommended requirement of only 15 per cent);

iii) about 10 per cent of three-year-olds were attending day nurseries, nursery schools or classes.

It was clear from the above that the main area of additional provision had to be for three-year-olds, although some consideration had also to be given to part-time education for four-year-olds. It is not envisaged in Coventry that all children under the age of five will receive nursery education and for a number of years the targets set by the White Paper are not expected to be met. An unmet demand for nursery education is expected to remain for some time to come. In the meanwhile the Authority hopes to create a favourable attitude towards nursery education by the appointment of Educational Visitors, attached to nurseries and whose role would be to make contact with the parents of young children in the area served by the school and work with the mothers to establish an individual programme for the children prior to their admission to the nursery.

In order to achieve the several targets and objectives as defined by central government, local authorities had been told by the White Paper that "the main burden of responsibility must rest on education departments, but other departments of local authorities will need to share in it, and consultation with voluntary bodies will also be necessary in many areas".

IV. UNDER-FIVES IN COVENTRY SINCE 1972

Coventry, already practising a system of co-ordination between Departments by means of PATs was geared therefore to follow the guidelines of the White Paper with comparative speed and efficiency. Moreover, as the Authority was already committed to their own long-term planning, the necessary skills and structure were operable and could immediately incorporate the 10-year objectives laid down in the White Paper, as shown above.

The Social Services Act 1970, following on the publication of the Seebohm Report, radically reorganised the Local Authority's presentation of welfare and personal social services. The Seebohm Report embodied the concept of a co-ordinated service provided for the whole individual, in relation to his family and his community, rather than that of a series of separate Departmental problems. Consequently, the Social Services Act required each local authority to set up a Social Services Department in 1971 which took over the functions of the personal social services.

a) Co-ordination among Local Services

The extent to which the Social Services Department in Coventry tries to co-ordinate its activities with other Departments in order to give more satisfaction to the real needs of the population is well illustrated in a document issued by its Forward Planning Division on "Objectives in Provision for under-fives".

The first point in this document is for action to be taken in order to identify as early as possible children at risk or in need of services, so that all the help that the Social, Health and Education Services and other agencies offer can be applied where necessary. For example, babies should be screened for developmental disorders such as defects of hearing and vision, clumsiness, abnormal activity, and emotional disorder.

A policy of positive discrimination is also advocated in the provision of social and educational services for under-fives, remembering that deprivation takes many forms, e.g. environmental, linguistic, lack of social contact and interaction.

The importance of early action in dealing with children at risk (both socially and medically) is clearly recognised and it is seen as essential that teachers, GPs, health visitors, social workers, and all staff concerned with under-fives should recognise and be trained and encouraged to deal with the less acute developmental problems, e.g. slow start in speech, bed wetting.

Further action is asked in order to provide adequate support for families with under-fives, for example adequate services should be established to supplement those of the family in caring for children under five (e.g. for children of working mothers, single parent families, large families). These may take the form of domiciliary services or of child caring/educational services outside the home.

It is equally asked in this document that the importance of location in the provision of services for under fives be recognised in the planning process. "The provision of health, social work and other services dealing with children under five within physical proximity of each other should be encouraged wherever possible, to allow greater opportunity for liaison between staff dealing with the under-fives."

Finally the planning document asked for a thorough programme of action to be centred around the real needs of the under-fives in Coventry. "Attention must be given to discovering the exact needs of under-fives, in terms of the type of services that might be provided for them. It will be important to evaluate continuously the needs of under-fives, the types of provision and the adequacy and success of this provision in fulfilling these needs."

On 21st December 1972, the Director of Education, the Director of Social Services and the Director of Health Services in Coventry came together in a special meeting to discuss possibilities of a co-ordinated approach to future planning for provision for under-fives. The different responsibilities of the three Departments were generally agreed as follows:

Health Department:	responsibility for Health Visitors and Clinics and some work at the Paediatric Assessment Unit: main work is diagnostical and referral for medical, nursery or hospital care.
Social Services Department:	provision of day nurseries and supervision of pre-school play groups and child minders.
Education Department:	provision of nursery schools and classes, including nursery units at the special schools and the observation and assessment classes at the Child Guidance Clinic. Equally, provision for rising fives at infant school.

b) The Joint Working Party

The three directors agreed to set up a joint Working Party representing the three departments and whose main objective was to review provision and future policies and priorities regarding under-fives. The Education Department was to provide the Chairman, and the Social Services Department the Secretariat.

The broad brief for the Working Party was to make an analysis of the needs of the under-fives in the city. Their first meeting on the 29th January 1973 discussed possible areas for future consideration which included the following:

1. Developments in the Education Service following the "Framework for Expansion"
2. Links among the three Services concerned with the under-fives
3. Extension of hours in Nursery Schools and Day Centres
4. The input of skills from each of the Departments in all the establishments for under-fives
5. Links among Pre-School Playgroups, Nursery Schools and Nursery Classes
6. The role of Child Minding and its relationship to other services
7. The co-ordination of policy in relation to charges
8. The needs of handicapped children
9. Use of facilities in relation to treatable developmental disabilities in young children
10. Training needs of both professional and volunteer staff
11. The impact of an expansion in provision for under-fives on individual families and their social well-being.

The inclusion of members from departments other than the three which originated the Working Party had been discussed from the beginning. The admission of representatives from, say, Manpower Planning and Treasurer's Department was thought desirable and it was agreed to invite participation at a later stage.

The Working Party found some difficulty in presenting statistical data from both the Education and Social Services Departments on the same locational basis. The fact is that the Social Services basic unit of information is its District, whereas the Education unit is its Primary School catchment area. Members of the Forward Planning Divisions of the two departments were therefore instructed to investigate the possibility of grouping school catchment areas in such a way as to achieve a reasonable approximation to the Social Services districts, whilst remaining relevant to the Education Department's purposes. Moreover, information regarding one major area of need for all day care - namely children of single parent families - was at a given stage required by the Working Party, and the Health Department undertook to make available the results of a survey carried out by Health Visitors. These are some of the lines of co-ordination taken by the local Departments within the organisational structure of the Working Party. The Rationale behind it was the feeling that, firstly, the real needs of the population are not departmentalised, and secondly, that any submission to the Department of Education and Science regarding the expansion of nursery education should be supported by other than purely educational evidence: i.e. number of immigrant children on the roll, the results of a reading survey and the referral of children for special education should be accompanied by a full reference to social criteria. Thus the Working Party had to consider households without full amenities and the number of persons per household as well as the percentage of the population by socio-economical groups.

The document sees the present situation as very satisfactory and makes its position clear in support of a more systematic approach to the provision of services for under-fives: "In formulating strategies for the development of services the opportunity should be taken to integrate the contribution of the various services, both statutory and voluntary, into a comprehensive service". To this end, bearing in mind the different levels of need of the children, the combinations of provision are suggested in the table on p. 262.

In developing any strategy for implementation, it was found necessary by the Working Party to decide what combination of provision was best suited to the needs of under-fives in a particular area. The following example of "Positive Discrimination" is given:

Type of Area	Appropriate Provision
High level of need likely to persist	Nursery Centre or Day Nursery with Education support
Moderately high level of need	Day Nursery and/or Nursery Class Minding Centre (3-5) at Infant School
Medium level of need	Nursery Class at Infant School supplemented by "satellite" playgroups
Low level of need	Playgroups looking to Infant School for professional and equipment support etc.

The document further develops the idea that if a comprehensive service which is coherent for parents is to be implemented, effective arrangements for co-ordination are essential. This is even more essential now because of the re-organisation of local government in April 1974 when all local health functions will become the responsibility of the Area Health Board. It is therefore suggested that this co-ordination should rest with the Director of Social Services who should be responsible for:

1. Ascertaining the needs of the under-fives and maintaining a register in co-operation with the Area Health Authority

Need	Service	Provision Required	Ancillary Support from:
Day care for children with personal handicap and/or family difficulties			
(a) Care emphasis with educational support	Day Nursery	0-4 year-olds 48 weeks 10/12 hours	Teachers Social Workers Health Visitor
(b) Additional educational emphasis	Nursery Centre	Full- or part-time	Child Health Clinic Medical Officers
Day care for children of working mothers or "single" fathers	Child Minders (or extended hours at nurseries)	0-4 year-olds Hours and days by private arrangement	Supervision and Registration Social Workers Health Visitors
Early educational experience to offset disadvantages			
(a) Nursery education	Nursery Schools and Classes	2/3-4 year-olds School terms and hours	Health Visitor Social Worker
(b) Child minding and play facilities outside school hours for children with parents at work etc.	Child Minding Centres	Attached to Infant schools	
Education of Rising Fives - to ensure all children are receiving infant education by fifth birthday	Infant Schools: provision at nursery standards	4-year-olds School terms and hours	School Liaison Service
Pre-School social and play experience			
(a) City wide	Voluntary Playgroups	2½-4 year-olds School terms Part-time	Supervison and Registration Social Workers
(b) In areas of high need	Council organised play-groups	Hours and days as arranged by individual groups	Education Visitors
Residential Care			
(a) for children with severe handicaps	Hospital units	0-4 year-olds Long and short stay placements	Health, Education and Social Services
(b) for children with personal, social and/or family deprivation in care of the Local Authority	Residential Nursery	1-4 year-olds Long and short term care as individually required	Integrated field team support on regular case-conference basis
	Foster Care	0-4 year-olds Long and short term care as individually required	
Day care and educational facilities for physically and mentally handicapped children	Nursery Centres at Special Schools for particular handicaps	0-4 year-olds 48 weeks or less as arranged individually	Health, Education and Social Services Integrated field team support on regular case-conference basis Paediatric Assessment Unit.
	Day Nurseries and Playgroups as appropriate	Full- or part-time	Parents Advisory Centre

of all children born with physical or mental handicaps and
of other children at risk;

2. Notifying and advising the Homes and Properties Services
    on the housing needs of families with young children;

3. Notifying and advising the Education Service on the needs
    for nursery places for children under five;

4. Advising the Recreation, Planning, Libraries and other
    services on the need for informal recreation facilities
    for under-fives;

5. Arranging for professional advice and support from the
    Health and Education Services as appropriate to all groups
    providing services for under-fives;

6. Arranging jointly with the Director of Education training
    programmes for staff (including voluntary workers) and for
    community education programmes.

Finally, the Working Party expected their report to form the
basis of consultation with the public and all those groups specially
interested in the under-fives, e.g. the Pre-School Playgroup
Movement, Associations for Handicapped Children, Parent/Teacher Associations, Professional Associations of Teachers and Social Workers,
the Churches, Community Associations. The report was also to be
considered by the appropriate Committees of the City Council together
with the views expressed in the process of public participation.

V. PUBLIC PARTICIPATION

The complexity of the problem of identifying needs, the relative
failure of the many techniques that have been used to assess "need
scores", and primarily the idea that local government (as different
from local administration) is only justified because it stimulates
democratic awareness of politics and participation in decision-
making, were relevant factors behind the growing sensitivity of
local services towards the wishes of the recipients themselves.

Coventry has been conscious for a long time of the essential
necessity of keeping in close contact with the local population in
order to react quickly to their main wishes and needs. The Authority
expects that its corporate system, and especially the production of
the different plans required, should aid public understanding of
the complex interrelationships among the diverse needs and demands
arising in the area.

When preparing the Local Policy Plan in 1973, the City Council
tried to develop community interest by carrying out an extensive
programme to consult the public on the ways in which the city should
develop, not only in the physical sense but also in response to

changes in social attitudes. "The general public and the special interest groups (for example, residents' associations) into which they form themselves, wish increasingly to be involved in the Council's decision-making process.....
Coupled with the greater awareness and openness of discussion of local problems, groups and individuals are pressing more forcefully for a wide range of improvements to services. Perhaps the best examples of this trend are in the education service, expressed in growing demands nationally for nursery education and in the City to use school premises for wider community purposes, a call for closer relationships between home and school and pressure to enhance the quality of services expressed in demands for lower class numbers and better equipment."

In April 1973 the City Council published a "Statement relating to Publicity and Public Participation during the Production of the Structure Plan." This was prepared in the light of the statutory requirements set down in the Town and Country Planning Act 1971, but the city authorities went much further in their attempt to involve the local community.

Two questionnaires were produced during this participatory exercise. They were intended, firstly, as a means of informing the public of the major issues facing the Council; secondly, as a method of obtaining from the public a clear indication of priorities; and thirdly, as a means for the public to write down additional issues which they thought were important. A total of 15,000 questionnaires were distributed by means of the exhibition bus, public meetings and were sent out to some schools.

The first questionnaire asked the respondents to consider the basic objectives of the nine main areas of Council activities, to place them in their own order of priority, and to make further comments. The answers established that the majority of respondents considered the most important area of Council activity as being Health and Social Services, followed by Housing and then Education.

The second exercise was to place a number of issues within each of the Council's main areas of activity in their own order of preference. The priority given by respondents, as a whole, to the educational issues is set down below in terms of the percentage of respondents placing particular issues in first or second places:

"Give special attention to deprived children" 27
"Maintain primary and secondary education facilities" 23
"Provide better school buildings and facilities" 22
"Improve nursery education" 21
"Improve adult education facilities" 8

Given the fact that the issue of the under-fives had become in Coventry a Key Decision Area and also the general commitment of the Authority towards an increasing involvement of the public in the process of local decision-making, a series of public meetings was organised in August and September 1973. It is clearly impossible to summarise accurately all the points made on this issue during the series of meetings. There was a considerable amount of interest shown in nursery education but at some meetings the subject did not reach the level of discussion and interest anticipated by the organisers.

There was no universal agreement that the expansion of nursery education was automatically right: "This is communist practice to take the children away from their parents." A number of points were raised which implied that mothers of young children should remain at home and be responsible for their offspring: "Parents of young children should be made to realise that the final responsibility for the children is theirs. They have to be educated in this respect and encouraged to participate in any nursery education which their children may attend."

To counterbalance these views there was often enough acknowledge-ment of the importance of the first five years in a child's life and there was a resulting stress on the importance of developing nursery education, particularly for children from disadvantaged homes: "All children should go to school as early as possible;" "Is education being wasted completely?"; "This is the only country in the Common Market where there is not a right to have nursery education." Some members of the public clearly thought that nursery expansion on traditional education lines was not sufficient. In some areas there was a need for extended care along the lines provided by day nurseries and the need for Nursery Centres (as in Hillfields) was stressed.

There appeared to be general agreement that priority in the ex-pansion of nursery education should be geared towards the city's more deprived areas. However, much was equally said on the need to go further than merely "remedial" action, by implementing comprehensive programmes of social change that would decrease in time the numbers of deprived "cases". "Aren't we treating the symptom and not the cause?", was a recurring question in the debates provoked by these public meetings.

VI. SUMMARY AND CONCLUSIONS

In this paper some of the main features of Corporate Management at local government level were introduced. Firstly, the establish-ment of a structure that forces councillors and officers to come out of their committees and departments and work "corporately", especially through the introduction of PATs. Secondly, the use of multi-year plans which overlap with the annual budgets in the same way as PATs overlap with departments. And, thirdly, the utilisation of the plans, in their successive stages, as a publicity means to attract public attention and, consequently, to make the population aware that it is possible and worthwhile to influence decision-making at the local level.

The first point, that of a corporate structure, has to be related to the main function of British local governments as providers of social services. A lesson that local authorities learnt recently was that human needs represent a totality that cannot be categorised according to the administrative divisions of departments. This is particularly evident when local governments attempt to carry out preventive action (e.g. detecting families at risk) rather than mere remedial functions.

It should be repeated that the new structure - based on prime objectives and PATs - did not replace the traditional departments but overlapped with them to form a "cross organisation". Departments still have an important function to fulfil, mainly as a basis for the allocation of the annual budget, a ladder for professional careers, and consequently as the suppliers of professional expertise.

Another important point to stress now is the apparent apathy of the population regarding local government. as shown by the low rate of participation in local elections. Among other reasons, there is a widespread ignorance about what a local government can do autonomously as against central government's spheres of influence and control. On the other hand, local authorities see the whole survival of the decentralised democracy existing in the United Kingdom as depending upon the participation of many more people. As one of the councillors I saw in Coventry put it: "Certainly if we don't make it possible for people to participate more widely and therefore to feel responsible for what is done on their behalf, there will be resentment, people will not take pride, will not take interest in what is done. Therefore I see the increase in vandalism and violence as being symptoms of our ineffectiveness as politicians to involve people in a participative sense."

Corporate planning in Coventry was equally seen by councillors and officers alike as a means to revive public interest on local issues. By giving wide publicity to the 10-year plan in its early stages, and by showing how much of the city's future could be controlled locally, the Authority expected the public to feel it worthwhile to participate more fully and make their wishes known.

Whether they were successful or not is still a matter of controversy in Coventry. For some, the low response from the public made the publicity exercise a mere waste of time and money. For others, participation being a long-term objective this was a first and essential step in the right direction. Other steps, though, had

266

to follow, such as the expansion of participative schemes of nursery education.

The 64,000 dollar question, however, that still remains to be answered is: is public participation at the local level really possible?

First, will local authorities be willing to devolve part of their powers to grass-roots groups and invest them with more responsibilities as well as with the necessary means to carry them out?

Second, will the public respond positively towards such moves from the local authorities?

Third, and even more acute, have the local authorities in the United Kingdom any autonomous powers they can delegate at all? If they are to prove themselves powerless in face of an all-powerful central government, any exercise at local level will be but a gratuitous waste of time.

When, for example, last December, I saw the officer of Coventry Council responsible for Educational Planning, he was most pessimistic about the chances for public participation. He told me how well the public had responded to those meetings organised in September 1973, and especially when the topic for discussion was nursery education. Many were the demands and suggestions from the floor regarding the under-fives in Coventry, and the Council officers present had promised to follow up this issue and expand nursery education as a Key Priority Area in Coventry. Nevertheless, by the sheer magic of a mini-Budget in which central government decided to drastically cut back public expenditure, all new expansion in this field was then to be slowed down. Many were the doubts in the mind of my interviewee from the Education Department, when he asked sadly: "How are we now going to convince those people who turned up at our September meetings and were promised an important expansion of nursery facilities that we seriously want their participation? How are we going to make them come again for future meetings if they see that nothing came out of their demands?"

As long as local authorities have more responsibilities than power to carry them out it is difficult for the public to see more than propaganda in any Council initiatives for public participation. And as long as central government relies mainly on a financial strategy of stop-go for public expenditure how can local authorities seriously work in terms of ten-year plans?

THE POLITICAL USES OF "PLANNING" AND "DECENTRALISATION" IN THE UNITED STATES
by Frances Fox Piven

INTRODUCTION

Modern states have elaborated vast networks of public or publicly funded programmes, presumably to serve the needs of their citizens in such areas as education, health care, housing, transportation, communications, income security, and so forth. Once instituted,
these programmes do not remain fixed, but are from time to time reorganised, expanded or, less frequently, contracted. Periodic changes
of this sort seem to be a fairly regular feature of the public
services.

What is true elsewhere is true in the United States. A vast
array of public services have been developed, funded and mandated by
a tangled network of national, state and local agencies. Each of
these service systems is periodically reorganised, expanded or,
occasionally, contracted. When such reorganisation occurs in the
United States today the official explanation for the change often
emphasizes the need for "planning", or the need for "decentralisation", or the need for both. Government spokesmen announce that reorganisation is necessary in order to rationalise the service system,
to improve its technical capacity to achieve public goals. This is
the planning rationale. Alternatively, and sometimes simultaneously,
the public is told that reorganisation is necessary in order to make
the service more responsive to the needs of the people served, typically by delegating part of the responsibility for the operation of
the service to local units, or by enhancing the advisory or "participatory" role of the citizenry. This is the decentralisation
rationale.

But although the rhetoric of officialdom in the United States
draws increasingly on the catechisms of "planning" and "decentralisation", there is little reason to believe that the periodic reorganisation of the public services has resulted either in increasing
rationalisation (at least if the performance of the services is measured by the public goals asserted for them), or increasing responsiveness. The regularity of this discrepancy between official claims
and actual results suggests that what is actually done under the

banners of planning and decentralisation may be quite different from
what is claimed. Moreover, since the record of past failures never
seems to deter future efforts - each launched as if no one had ever
thought of being rational or of being responsive before - the persistence of this discrepancy suggests that what we are dealing with
is a new political symbolism that serves important purposes for the
public services, albeit purposes quite different from either planning or decentralisation. In the pages that follow I will argue
that what has been done under these twin banners in the United States
has more to do with the maintenance and expansion of the public
bureaucracies than with what might reasonably be construed to be the
requirements of either planning or decentralisation.

OBSTACLES TO INTERSECTORAL PLANNING

If one can speak of bureaucracies as having intentions, then
even with the best of intentions the structural obstacles to planning in the public services of the United States would be formidable.
The reason is simply that in a complex society, planning almost of
necessity implies an "intersectoral" approach. But the key sectors
are largely beyond the control of planners in the public services of
the United States.

The limited authority of public agencies

To plan is to attempt to control the future, and to do so not
by star-gazing or wishful thinking but by what are generally considered the methods of rational action. It follows that planning
requires the capacity to predict or control the key events and decisions that will shape those aspects of the future with which one
is concerned. And, in a complex, specialised and divided society
the lines of action which bear on the achievement of any given set
of public goals will be controlled by different "actors" or agencies,
located in different "sectors". Thus it is often said that to achieve
a planned approach to urban development requires that the diverse
decisions made by a range of agencies controlling aspects of urban
development - transportation, land use regulations, school locations,
and so forth - all somehow be dovetailed to realise a preferred pattern of future urban development. Everything does indeed affect
everything else, especially in matters of public policy.

The difficulties of achieving such "inter-sectoralism" among
public agencies are considerable. But co-ordination of the public
sector would in any case fall far short of what can reasonably be
called planning, simply because the primary decisions that shape the
future environment of the public services are not made in the public

sector, but in the private sector. It is the investment and production decisions of the private sector that generate the needs that public programmes are supposed to meet, and the problems that public programmes are supposed to solve. Sometimes these economic decisions are made in concert with specialised public agencies, but they are not ordinarily made in concert with the range of agencies serving broad public purposes that will be affected by these decisions.

Thus, to return to our example, the key decisions determining the future pattern of urban development are not made by the various public agencies that are usually said to require co-ordination, but by real estate and construction investors and by large-scale industrialists. These economic decision makers are often able to secure a degree of consistency in public and private decisions, between transportation and housing or commercial development, for example, when prior public investments create opportunities for profitable private development. But businessmen do not make their decisions in deference to the numerous public agencies that will soon have to build the local roads, schools, water and sewerage systems and other community facilities which a new development requires, while similar facilities go under-used in areas depopulated as a result of their investment decisions. When the decisions are made to build up a tract with new housing, or to invest in a new industrial complex, the investors expect the public services and facilities that are required to be provided, and their expectations are usually fulfilled.

The political subordination of public agencies

The insulation of the economic sector from public control is the primary limitation on public planning in the United States. But it is not a limitation inherent in formal structure alone; it does not result solely from the segregation of governmental from economic decisions under the American political system. In fact, many public agencies have the formal authority to regulate economic interests, or the formal authority at least to influence economic interests through the allocation of subsidies of various kinds. For example, city planning agencies, with the approval of local legislatures, have the authority to regulate the location of business and industrial enterprises, to regulate the kinds of structures these enterprises can be housed in, and even to regulate the manner in which these enterprises are conducted. In principle this zoning power is far-reaching. In practice, however, it is almost always exercised with the concurrence of the commercial and industrial interests to be regulated. The reason is simply that the planning agency is politically vulnerable to these interests. It requires their support at crucial junctures when the agency's budget and mandate are under review.

Similarly, federal agencies administer the subsidies and loans, the interest rates and tax incentives on which the housing industry has come to depend. The Defense Department administers contracts and subsidies that can influence the location and operation of major industries throughout the country. And federal highway subsidies virtually determine the shape of metropolitan areas, and also determine the prosperity of the auto, trucking, petroleum and construction industries that depend on the highways. (By comparison, local public services, such as the schools, have far less formal authority. When unemployment rises or falls in a particular locality as a result of a change in the flow of federal defence contracts, or when new federally subsidised highways ringing a city drain population and business to the suburbs, local public agencies merely try to adapt.) But the federal agencies that do have considerable authority do not use that authority to plan, or at least they do not plan in terms of public goals. Instead, they tend to follow and serve economic interests, simply because they are dependent on the interests which in principle they regulate. In other words, even when public agencies do have sufficient formal authority to make a degree of planning possible, they do not have the political independence of major economic interests that public planning in the public interest requires.

These basic limitations are rarely acknowledged, however, by those who plan for the public services in the United States. Consider, for example, the current campaign for reorganisation of local services on what is called a metropolitan or regional basis. This form of reorganisation has been a recurrent theme of city planners and civic reformers generally, for many decades. Urban development cannot be rationally guided or efficiently serviced, it is said, until municipal boundaries are made coterminous with expanding areas of settlement. It is even said that metropolitan government can overcome segregation by class and race by breaking down city-suburban lines. In the past, proposals by cities to annex adjacent areas were usually defeated by the voters, and received little support from economic interests. Now, however, new metropolitan super-agencies are in fact being created, with support from local business groups. But they are not being created to plan the pattern of urban development; that has long since been done, for better or worse. "Suburban sprawl", and the chaotic relationship of land uses and services that it implies, already exists, and metropolitan agencies will do nothing to reverse it. What these agencies can and will do is service the sprawling residential and industrial developments that now surround and engulf American cities. Whether or not one approves such a method of adapting public and private decisions, it is clearly not a planned or "inter-sectoral" approach.

The case of the schools: the unplanned 1960s

The education system in the United States is perhaps especially helpless before the exigencies created by economic decisions, and therefore without the capacity to plan in any significant sense. The events of the past decade provide ample evidence, for during that decade the urban primary and secondary schools of the United States were swept by problems generated by rapid changes in economic, social and political spheres, changes which the school systems could hardly have been expected to predict, and which they were certainly helpless to control.

The sources of many of the problems confronted by the schools lay in decisions made not by any school systems, but by large land holders in the south who were rapidly mechanising (encouraged, to be sure, by the pattern of federal agricultural subsidies) and enlarging their holdings. Mechanisation meant the displacement of millions of black families who had been sharecroppers, tenant farmers, or day labourers, and the enlargement of land holdings meant the displacement of others who had somehow managed as independent subsistence farmers. Deprived of their livelihood on the land, many of these people made their way to the cities, concentrating in the older large cities which already had settlements of blacks. Between 1940 and 1960 nearly four million blacks left the land for the cities. By the end of this period one in five of the residents of the 50 largest cities were black. In the biggest cities, the proportions were much greater.

Under the best of circumstances the migration would have posed substantial problems for the urban school systems of the United States. It was not merely the large numbers of new children that had to be absorbed by the schools, but also the special difficulties posed by the experience the children brought with them to the schools, an experience rooted in the culture of the feudal and depressed rural south, overlaid with the new experience of disorientation and unemployment in the cities. None of this was planned by the urban school systems. Neither could planning by the schools have averted it.

The problems of the schools were compounded by the political disturbances which resulted from the migration, disturbances which came to reverberate on the educational system. Massive shifts of population are almost always disruptive to a political system, for relations have not yet been formed between the political stratum and the new groups.(1) In this case, the disturbances were aggravated by race and class antagonisms. The masses of incoming lower class blacks aroused ferocious hatred among existing city residents, especially

_____

1) See Samuel P. Huntington, <u>Political Order in Changing Society</u>, Yale University Press, New Haven, 1968 pp.88-89.

272

among the white ethnic groups who lived in neighbourhoods bordering the ghettos, and who felt their homes, and especially their schools, endangered. In the face of such high-pitched feelings, efforts by the schools to deal with the demands of different groups only inflamed the situation. The ensuing turbulence signalled by waves of parents' boycotts, student walkouts and teacher strikes, was not planned by the schools, nor could planning have prevented it.

That much of the race conflict in American cities came to focus on the schools had to do not only with the fact that the schools play a central role in the intergenerational transmission of culture and class, but also with the fact that the schools are central in local patronage politics. Education is the single largest service run by localities, accounting for 40 per cent of the outlays of state and local government in 1968. The huge expenditures are also potential benefits - jobs for teachers, contracts for maintenance and construction and educational services for children - to be gained by different groups in the local community. Accordingly, the educational system became a main target of black demands, at first mainly in the form of demand for integrated schools. Later, worn down by resistance to integration, blacks began to demand a share of the jobs, contracts and status positions that the school system provides. Boards of education began hiring more black teachers, and ensconced local black leaders in the lower echelons of the school hierarchy. But these developments infringed upon the terrain of those who had traditionally been the recipients of school patronage, primarily the teachers and supervisory personnel, who were lodged within the school bureaucracy. These "producer" groups were numerous and well organised, and reacted to threats to their traditional turf with strident efforts to secure their existing privileges and benefits, and to enlarge them. The result was a scramble of escalating demands, backed up by teacher strikes in most of the big cities of the country. Over the course of the decade of the 1960s, teacher salaries in many of these cities doubled. Nationally, teacher salaries rose by 8 per cent each year between 1965 and 1969. This was not planned by the urban school system. Or at least it was not planned as a strategy to achieve educational goals.

In other words, the school systems, like most other public services, strain to adapt to decisions made elsewhere, in economic and in political spheres. They do not plan, at least they do not plan the significant dimensions of their service, because they have no control over the decisions that will ultimately shape the significant dimensions of their service.

Planned or not, there is not much reason to think that these transforming changes of the 1960s improved education; quite the contrary. For what it is worth as evidence, reading scores in the big

273

city schools with large proportions of black pupils have been falling. Nor is it even clear that the schools can do very much to reverse this, were they inclined to try. A people reared to till the land in the South were uprooted, their traditional way of earning a living suddenly taken from them, their communities scattered, and then left to languish in urban ghettos in which the rate of sub-employment now averages about 30 per cent. These experiences educate children as much as the schools do. They educate them to the fact that their work is likely to be menial, if they work at all; that above all, their future is terrifyingly uncertain. Can children so educated on the streets be educated differently in the schools?(1) It may be that even within the narrow realms of pedagogy the schools are at the mercy of decisions made within economic spheres that even in this area they can only strain to try somehow to cope with the problems created elsewhere.

THE POLITICAL USES OF "PLANNING"

Despite these limitations on the capacity to plan, the public services in the United States, including the school systems, engage in a considerable amount of activity that is often called planning, sometimes called policy research, or simply research:

> "This is the age of planning: the expert briefing, the flip chart, facts and figures from computer output, forecasts and trend analyses, the invention and use of social measurements for policy formation and feedback evaluation, programming of sequential action programmes, management information and control systems, PERT (programme evaluation and review technique), CPM (critical-path method), cost-benefit analysis models and simulation, and statistical decisions." (Guy Benveniste, The Politics of Expertise, Glendessary Press, Berkeley, 1972, p.4.)

Planning as public relations

Almost every public service has a department that collects large amounts of data on current needs, projects and analyses trends and undertakes to explore the impact of alternative programmes. Sometimes all of this is very well done: the data are reasonably accurate and competently analysed. But often they are not. Sometimes the variables studied bear directly on the activities of the service. Often what is studied is only vaguely related to the service. Incompetence and irrelevance is not, however, the main problem.

---

1) Greer reports that United States census data for 1910, 1920, 1930 reveal that occupational mobility preceded the success of different ethnic groups in the United States schools. Colin Greer, The Great School Legend: A Revisionist Interpretation of American Education, Basic Books, New York, 1972, p.85.

While this sort of activity looks like planning, and in principle provides the basis for a more rational and far-seeing approach to public decisions, in fact it often seems to have very little to do with actual decisions made by the public services. Reports are published in glossy volumes, accompanied by press conferences; academics and other dignitaries give their opinions about this latest compilation on the future of housing, or of the schools, or of the city as a whole. What all this suggests is not improved decision making, but improved public relations. The very weight of the documents seems to lend weight to the agency's efforts.

For example, two years ago the New York City Planning Commission finally issued a long-awaited Master Plan for the city. The document occupied six large volumes, each replete with photographs and graphics.(1) Now in American cities, widely aired agency decisions are almost always attacked by one group or another, for the very sound reason that such decisions almost always affect some group adversely, or at least less favourably than other groups. The Master Plan in principle contained the decisions that shaped the city's future development. In actuality the "Plan" consisted mainly of speculations of what might possibly happen in the city, depending on the decisions made by the private sector and the federal agencies. Accordingly, it was hardly attacked at all, except for some who sensibly objected to the sheer mass of the document as an indication of waste. That such activities turn out to be so uncontroversial is evidence of their small importance insofar as public decisions are concerned.(2)

A similar example of planning as public relations was recently provided by the New York City Department of Human Resources, which administers the public welfare programme. The Department, much maligned for the "welfare mess", which in New York means the fact that so many people are on welfare, inaugurated a series of large-scale studies of various dimensions of the welfare "problem" in New York City in collaboration with the Rand Institute. The studies were heralded from the first: the Mayor gave the public to understand that the prospects for attacking the welfare problem were hopeful indeed, especially now

1) "If the Master Plan is beautifully printed, with elaborate charts, tables and pictures, one may be sure that it does not represent what is going on or that - as is often the case - nothing is going on." Bertram M. Gross, Organisations and their Managing, The Free Press, New York, 1968, p.578.

2) The sections of the six-volume Master Plan that dealt with valuable Manhattan real estate were perhaps of more significance, not because they represented decisions made by the city planners, but because they were suggestive of major investment decisions being planned by private developers with the co-operation of the city planning department and other public agencies. The "National Centre" proposed in the plan is a good example, for it describes the development of 30 million square feet of new office space, a major exhibition centre, new hotels and so forth.

that the prestigious Rand "think tank" was pitching in. In due
course the studies were completed, and each was summarised in a
press release. Then a conference was called to which were invited
the academic and government élite of the social welfare field, and
the press. The Department was complimented on the seriousness of
its research efforts. As it happened, the studies were very well
done and, somewhat unusually, had direct bearing on the Department's
activities. One study showed, for example, that two-thirds of the
Department's decisions in terminating clients were unrelated to the
clients' needs. Another study showed that at least 500,000 eligible
people were not receiving aid from the Department. These findings
were not much discussed. Instead, the Commissioner used the occasion
to call for full employment policies in the United States, and the
revamping of all federal income maintenance programmes to ensure uniform benefits and lower local costs. Almost everyone in the room
could agree with the Commissioner's objectives, as would almost
everyone in the city. However, these objectives had no relationship
whatever to the studies or, indeed, to the administration of the
Commissioner's department, which had no jurisdiction over employment
policies, and certainly not over the federal income maintenance programmes. This being the case, there was no cause for acrimony what-
soever, and the conference ended with cordial good feeling for the
Human Resources Administration. Of course, nothing had changed in
the administration of public welfare in New York City as a result of
all this.

Planning as a rationale for bureaucratic expansion

If planning activities were always merely a public relations
facade for the regular operations of the public services, perhaps
they would not be of much importance one way or the other. Sometimes, however, they are a public relations facade for changes in the
public services, changes that usually involve increased centralisation of authority, increased specialisation, or new devices to improve co-ordination - all or any of which usually entail increased
funding for the public agency. These kinds of developments are consistent with the classic pattern of bureaucratic entrenchment and
expansion. The significance of most planning activity is not that it
causes bureaucratic expansion but that it justifies it.

Like bureaucracies generally, the public agencies strive to
maintain the conditions necessary for their stability and expansion.
Since they are public agencies, these conditions depend on a continued public mandate, and continued public funding. To protect
their mandate and budget, and to expand them, the bureaucracies require the support of legislative and executive leaders, and the tacit support at least of those organised forces that watch over

governmental policies and can threaten intervention in governmental decisions. Bureaucratic stability and expansion, in other words, depend on political support.

Ordinarily, the public bureaucracies try to ensure support by operating their services and distributing their benefits in ways which suit the interests of governmental leaders and of those constituent groups that are sufficiently powerful either to influence governmental leaders or to intervene directly in the operations of the public itself. And so long as political arrangements remain relatively stable, the operation and organisation of the public services is also likely to remain relatively stable, and to expand only gradually. Conversely, disturbances in the political environment are likely to be reflected in changes in the organisation and operation of the public services. These disturbances are broadly of two kinds. First, a new political leadership may win office, displacing the incumbents to whom bureaucratic officials were related, and to whom they may even have owed their existence. Second, new discontents and new demands regarding the public service may emerge among constitutent groups. The public agencies will have to adapt to these disturbances. In doing so, however, both politicians and bureaucrats will co-operate in trying to reorganise and reform the agencies in ways which create the least internal stress. At the same time, bureaucratic leaders will strive to use these occasions to enlarge their public mandate and their public funding. To this end, the public service agencies characteristically propose solutions to political problems which draw uniquely on bureaucratic resources, which emphasize reliance on the technical expertise and organisational elaboration as a solution to political problems. These proposals look very much like planning activities. In practice, however, they ordinarily do not result in planning, but in bureaucratic entrenchment and expansion.

Political succession is one kind of problem with which the bureaucracies in the United States must regularly contend. On one level the problem is relatively straightforward, for it consists simply in the need to develop regular liaison between the bureaucracy and the new political officials. It is ordinarily simply solved by the appointment of administrators who are linked to the new political officials. The problem is more serious when the new office-holders represent different constituencies than the previous incumbents, when a Republican President succeeds a Democrat, or when an Italian succeeds an Irish mayor in the ethnic politics of American cities. When that happens, one ordinarily sees a more extensive effort at reconstituting the upper hierarchies of the public service so as to make them more responsive to the interests of the new officials (and so as to make bureaucratic patronage available to the new

officials). Thus, President Nixon made a strenuous effort to replace the entire upper echelon of the federal bureaucracies after
his election in 1968. That much is to be expected, at least in
American politics.

As a matter of fact President Nixon's way of going about the
restaffing of the federal bureaucracies was somewhat unusual, and
accordingly widely criticised as blatantly "political". Indeed the
Civil Service Commission recently called for the resignation of three
high Nixon Administration officials for hiring political favourites
to fill career civil service jobs.(1) The trend in the handling of
problems of political succession seems to be not to revamp the bureaucracies or to replace large numbers of bureaucratic personnel,
but instead to create new tiers of organisational hierarchy, which
can be staffed with people loyal to the new incumbents. Thus the
election of a new Mayor or a new President or a new Governor is frequently accompanied by the announcement that a new super-cabinet or
new super-agencies are to be created. This method solves the problem
of succession while leaving the public agencies relatively intact.

For example, when Mayor Lindsay of New York took office in
1965 he did so on the basis of support from upper-middle class districts, and at least tentative support from ghetto districts. He represented, in other words, an entirely different constituency from
the working class and ethnic groups that had been the basis of traditional Democratic politics in New York. Accordingly, he had to
struggle to gain control of the New York City public agencies. One
of his first efforts was to "reorganise" the numerous agencies of the
city into nine umbrella "super-agencies". This was not done simply.
Outside experts were called in, studies commissioned, and elaborate
reorganisation proposals finally issued, each purporting to be a
technically based plan for the rational organisation of a set of city
services. The reorganisation did not much affect the operation of
the individual agencies, however. What it did do was create an opportunity for the appointment of a new level of officials loyal to the
Lindsay administration. And when Lindsay retired from office in
favour of a new mayor more closely identified with the old Democratic
party, the dismantling of the super-agencies began.

The emergence of new discontents, of new demands, constitutes
the second type of political change to which the bureaucracies must
respond. When a new demand is put forward by a large and influential
organisation that is a regular constituent of the bureaucracy, the
response to the demand is a relatively simple matter. The bureaucracy acts to meet it. Thus when major truckers or airline companies

---

1) The three were among nine officials of the Department of Housing
   and Urban Development who made inquiries "into the political affil-
   iation of hundreds of applicants and employees". New York Times,
   20th March, 1974.

or industries that are regularly related to a transportation agency make demands for a new service it is in the bureaucracies' interest to act on it, for these groups are its allies, ready to offer support in political spheres and collaboration in administrative spheres. And if the added services require expanded authorisation or funding the bureaucracy will go before political leaders well-defended by the groups it serves.

Sometimes, however, new discontents and new demands may emerge among groups with which the bureaucracy has no regular and amicable relationship. Any number of circumstances may lead to this. Economic or technological dislocations may activate groups that previously asked little of government, as in the 1930s. Or groups may rise in the economic structure, acquiring political force and pressing new demands. Or large-scale migration may alter the political balance among groups, as occurred in the big cities of the United States in the 1960s. These kinds of political disturbance ordinarily emerge first in political spheres, rather than bureaucratic spheres, simply because political leaders tend to be more quickly vulnerable to popular disturbances that can easily become electoral disturbances.

What political leaders seek under these circumstances is a way of placating those who are making the new demands without jostling other groups on whose support they rely. The public service bureaucracies are ready to help. What to the politician is a disturbance in his constituency and a threat to his majority is for the bureaucracy an opportunity to extend their public mandate, resources, and jurisdiction. The bureaucratic solution, whether to poverty, or poor health care, or unemployment, or air pollution, or crime, or racism, or dirty streets, or educational under-achievement, is to entrench and expand the bureaucracy by elaborating mechanisms for specialisation, centralisation and co-ordination, and above all by increasing budgetary allocations.

This solution is not usually put forward straightforwardly. Ordinarily, the first step initiated by political leaders is to appoint a task force or a commission of experts to study the problem. The very invoking of the expert task force is a step toward solving the politician's problem, for the task force typically succeeds in converting political problems into technical problems. Issues which are rooted in group conflict, which have been framed as "who gets what", are transmuted into issues of method and framed in terms of a technology. That the technology is obscure is largely an advantage; the terminal political issue of "who gets what" is thereby also obscured. Moreover, the authority and prestige of expertise, and the faith in science and progress which it calls forth, are added to the political equation, and made still more compelling by the complexity of the proposal. (Indeed, the ultimate public action may be a programme of research and demonstration to devise or advance the

279

necessary technology.) As a result, political leaders are able to offer their constituencies programmes which inspire confidence and assuage conflict by their very technicism.

The bureaucracies are, of course, key actors in this process. In fact, the task force or commission is typically dominated by representatives from the bureaucracies. Who else, after all, fully understands the problem? Robert Alford showed, for example, that bureaucrats, whom he calls "corporate rationalisers", predominated in each commission established to investigate the health delivery system in the last 25 years.(1) Invariably, bureaucrats see the solution to problems as requiring the expansion of the resources and mandate of their bureaucracies. The justification for such expansion, just as invariably, is in the language of planning. Thus Alford went on to show that the recommendations of the numerous health commissions consistently called for greater co-ordination of health care services through the hospital or medical centre. The major consequence, according to Alford, has been to complicate and elaborate the dominant bureaucratic structures in the health field, while expanding their functions and resources.(2).

One variant of this type of bureaucratic expansion in response to political discontents has all the appearances of "intersectoralism". It is easily recognised as the multifaceted or multidisciplinary approach. In responding to political problems, and converting them into political opportunities for bureaucratic expansion, agency experts put forward the view that what the public service requires to solve this new problem is the incorporation of new or more proficient experts as staff or consultants.

The political significance of this ploy deserves examination. Acknowledgement of expertise is a component of the political mandate initially granted to the public agency. It is implicit in political acceptance of technical definitions of problems and their solution, and it is also implicit in political reliance on complex bureaucratic structures to implement these solutions. Once the mantle of expertise is bestowed upon the bureaucracy, it is used to entrench and expand the role of expertise, and therefore the bureaucracy. Nor is it easy to thwart this tendency. To grant expertise in a given area is to grant authority. By its nature, expertise is obscure and its appropriate boundaries cannot easily be judged by the non-expert. It is therefore difficult to contain the propensities of expert

---

1) The Political Economy of Health Care: "Dynamics Without Change", Politics and Society, Winter 1972.

2) Benveniste acknowledges this: "Therefore, a principal function of the apolitical definition of the policy expert's role is the exact opposite of the definition: it provides access to social power without political election". op.cit. p.65.

bureaucrats to elaborate even further the specialised knowledge and technique presumably required in the recognition and solution of public problems.

This propensity is facilitated, moreover, by the development of coalitions of experts, both within and among organisations. Problems are interpreted not only as highly technical, but as multifaceted, and therefore requiring the application of a wide variety of expert skills. Consequently, the public bureaucracies are increasingly staffed by experts from a variety of professions. A non-expert trying to appraise the claims of the professional bureaucrats has virtually no recourse once the importance of expertise is acknowledged, but to turn to other experts. A competitive pluralism among organisations and professions thus would provide some counter to bureaucratic domination, not only by generating alternative programmes, but by encouraging diversity and disagreement among the experts whose competitive opinions would provide some basis for evaluating and controlling the bureaucracies. Coalitions of experts, by contrast, constitute monopolies on expertise and foreclose alternative appraisals. Electoral leaders, the general public, special interest groups are all confronted with a virtually impenetrable professional phalanx.(1)

Planning as a political defence

Occasionally, it should be said, the paraphernalia of technical expertise and organisational elaboration - of planning - is used simply defensively, when an agency is under assault, and may actually cloak the contraction of the agency's domain. Most usually this occurs in those public agencies that are charged to deal with outcast groups, and so suffer under a continuous political vulnerability, particularly when they expand. Recent attacks by liberal reformers on Willowbrook, a New York State institution for the mentally retarded, resulted in the agency's proclaiming that it had adopted a new and innovative plan for "community based care" which would enable it to discharge some of its clientele. What this meant was that inmates were being boarded out with farm families, who were reportedly glad to have the free labourers. Similarly, big city welfare departments, in response to widespread attacks on "welfare dependency", are now in the process of bringing "scientific management" techniques to bear on the conduct of their operations. The premise is that the enlarged welfare rolls in the United States signify that public welfare arrangements have somehow run amok, with the result that many people have come to be on welfare who do not belong there. The proposed

1) "Planners consolidate their monopolistic position by (i) acquiring widespread external professional consensus on policy issues and (ii) creating large integrated research teams whose advice cannot be easily dismissed." Benveniste, op cit., p. 126.

bureaucratic remedy is good management - organisational reforms that
will enable departments to discern and serve the truly needy, while
rejecting the cheats and malingerers whose presence is believed to
account for the swollen caseloads. What is in fact being initiated
under guise of management reform is, however, a pervasive and un-
selective drive toward restrictiveness, the ultimate result of which
will be to reduce the welfare caseload, and thus reduce popular antagonism to the welfare departments.

The case of the schools: politics, planning and educational expansion

The educational system of the United States, particularly the
urban school systems, has also been shaped by a history of bureaucratic adaptation to political exigency. The urban schools are particularly vulnerable to the stresses resulting from large migrations
to the cities, partly because it is their distinctive function to absorb somehow the children of the newcomers and shape them into law-
abiding workers and citizens. The schools have never had an easy time
of this; the evidence on the role they actually played in education
or failing to educate the children of the immigrants is mixed. Moreover the nature of that education is debatable. Several contemporary critics, Katz, Gintis and Bowles among them, have argued persua-
sively that the American schools educated - perhaps socialised is the
better word - children to a bureaucratically styled acquiescence,
varying this "education" according to the performance expected of
children of different social origins. But whatever the schools did
or did not accomplish, there can be little question that they were
very much at the centre of the disturbances accompanying large-scale
migrations to the big cities of the United States.

One such period began early in the twentieth century, when Euro-
peans were coming to the United States at the rate of a million a
year. The large influx of foreigners naturally caused tensions in
American cities, tensions which took form in political struggles as
the business and middle-class reform groups began to challenge the
big city political machines that claimed the large numbers of immigrants as followers. These reformers were dedicated to divesting the
machine of its various bases of patronage and power. They were particularly committed to removing the urban schools from local and machine control.

This was never defined, however, as a struggle over who would
control the schools, but rather as an effort to make the schools more
effective. The immigrant children were "social problems", the offspring of impoverished and undisciplined families, which the school
ought somehow to cope with. The new methods of coping were several,
and reflected the pattern for bureaucratic reform of the school system

282

that has been repeated during other periods of stress. First, the
schools, which in many places had been run on a neighbourhood or ward
basis, were reorganised under central school boards. Second, these
central boards were "taken out of politics", which meant that they
were taken out of machine politics and put squarely under the control
of the reformers. Third, the school bureaucracy was enlarged: children entered the schools at younger ages with the spread of kinder-
gartens, left at older ages with the spread of high schools, and
school budgets grew. Meanwhile, the internal bureaucracy of the
schools was elaborated: central departments were established within
the school system to specialise in one or another aspect of the educational process; specialised schools, such as vocational high
schools were established to deal with specialised needs; specialised
personnel, such as guidance counsellors, were introduced; and the
professional training requirements of regular teaching personnel were
extended.

A not dissimilar process has been apparent in the 1960s, as the
schools once again became the focus of the social and political turmoil engendered by large-scale migration to the cities, and once again
responded to that turmoil by enlarging and elaborating the educational
apparatus. Shortly after the Second World War, the school bureaucracies began to generate the proposals for specialised programmes
to meet the needs of the so-called educationally deprived which, by
that time, meant black children. And as black migration continued
and the numbers of black children in the schools increased, so did
the demands on the school system, both from black groups demanding
the benefits of equal education and from white groups demanding that
the schools somehow solve the variety of problems associated with the
"educationally deprived". As during the earlier periods, the schools
responded with special "compensatory" programmes, which also meant
vast expansion of the professional and supervisory personnel employed
by the schools, and vastly increased budgets. Between 1960 and 1970,
the costs of primary and secondary education in the United States
quadrupled, reaching 50 billion dollars by the end of the decade.

In sum, American school systems cannot plan, largely because
they have no ability to predict, much less control, the economic,
political and social changes which necessarily affect educational institutions in critical ways. The schools can only adapt to these
changes. But they do not merely adapt, for in the process of responding to external crisis, the educational system, like other public and
quasi-public services, has grown to become a complex and formidable
bureaucracy, representing in its own right large concentrations of
money, and controlled by the powerful vested interests that have
stakes in this bureaucratic agglomeration. That process has not been
planned, but it has been facilitated by activities called "planning".

THE POLITICAL USE OF DECENTRALISATION

Parallel to the growth of the public service bureaucracies, and to their increasing centralisation and specialisation, one can observe periodic surges of activity which are often defined as efforts at decentralisation (although more recently in the United States the terms "community participation" and "community control" have come into vogue). As others have observed, decentralisation means different things to different people or, more to the point, different things to the different participants in decentralisation efforts. While it is quite possible, and for some purposes useful, to develop an elaborate taxonomy of these different meanings of decentralisation,(1) for our purposes a single distinction will suffice. From the perspective of the public service agency, decentralisation usually involves either locating staff and operations closer to the client population, or delegating some decision-making authority to operating staff, or both. The values associated with this type of decentralisation are those of flexibility and responsiveness in service delivery, presumably facilitated by the proximity of the decision maker to the people affected by the service. Thus among the publicly defined aims of New York City's neighbourhood government programme initiated in 1972 were:

> To improve the delivery of municipal services by making city agencies more responsive and accountable at the neighbourhood level
>
> To reduce the distance that citizens feel exists between themselves and government.(2)

Sometimes this form of decentralisation also includes efforts at developing procedures for citizen participation in the administration of the public service, usually through the establishment of citizen advisory councils, which may be appointed or elected but whose role is ordinarily closely delimited.

From the perspective of the citizens who are affected by the service, decentralisation often has a different meaning. It often means a degree of control over the public service agency, and control over the public agency, in turn, means control over the resources that the agency dispenses. Resources include not only the services

---

1) For examples of such taxonomies, see Eric Nordlinger and Jim Hardy, "Urban Decentralisation: An Evaluation of Four Models", Public Policy, XX, 3, Summer 1972; Henry J. Schmardt, "Decentralisation: A Structural Imperative", Neighbourhood Control in the 1970s, edited by George Frederickson, Chandler, New York, 1973.

2) Quoted in Ira Katznelson, Urban Counter Revolution, 1984, Revisited, edited by Robert Paul Wolff, Knopf, 1972, p.150.

which the agency is mandated to perform, but the honours and jobs and contracts which the agency generates in the course of performing that service. Decentralisation understood as control is itself variously interpreted, of course, with more radical critics viewing decentralisation as merely the first step in a strategy to achieve the ultimate dismantling of the corporate state. But whatever the degree of control envisioned, control over the public services is quite different from, even contradictory to, the bureaucratic interpretation of decentralisation. This contradiction is rarely clarified in specific decentralisation activities, however, perhaps because the duality permits the activities to go forward, attracting support from different groups on different grounds.

Neither of these versions of the goals associated with decentralisation goes very far towards explaining the periodic emergence of decentralisation efforts. It is only at certain times that bureaucratic leaders become concerned with creating devices for bringing services "closer to the people" and it is only at certain times that citizen groups begin to demand a degree of control over the public services. Why this occurs when it occurs is an interesting question, the answer to which may help to explain decentralisation not in terms of the manifest goals of particular parties to the process, but in terms of the functions such efforts serve for the maintenance of bureaucratic agencies.

First, it is worth reiterating that efforts at decentralisation have developed in the context of increasing political centralisation of the public services in the United States. Services which were once controlled by local governments are now increasingly dependent on the state and federal government for their funding. One evidence of this is the changing pattern of government revenues and government expenditures in the United States. As recently as the 1930s municipalities collected over half of public revenues; now they collect less than 7 per cent. The expenditures of local governments have not declined proportionately, but have in fact risen sharply as a share of total government expenditures. The resulting differential is made up by state and federal grants-in-aid to localities. Each of these grants-in-aid is also an instrument of influence. In order to receive state and federal funds, localities must submit to state and federal guidelines. Thus a whole range of services that were once largely controlled by local governments, including public welfare, transportation, policing, housing, and education, are now subject to the conditions laid down by state and federal bureaucracies, and by state and federal political leaders.

Of necessity, state and federal funding means the imposition of state and federal decisions on local services, including the schools. Centralisation does not result solely from the fact of state and federal financing, however. It is also that the removal of key decisions regarding the operation of the public services from the local level changes the political environment in which public service decisions are made. It facilitates political centralisation by screening out of the decision-making process those groups that do not have the political capability to exercise influence on the state and federal level. Thus it is not that the federal experts rule, but that they rule with a narrower range of interests in mind. Groups that are better organised and better financed can operate very effectively on the state and federal level, and perhaps more effectively because the field is clear of cantankerous local influences. Accordingly, the expansion of the federal role in the management of the public services has been paralleled by the expansion of federally-oriented lobbies that participate in the administration of increasingly centralised public services. The national housing lobbies grew as federal housing programmes expanded; the massive highway lobby enlarged to match the enlargement of federal highway expenditures. And the inauguration of major federal programmes in health and education in the 1960s was accompanied by the enlargement of national health and education lobbies, composed of the professional and bureaucratic interests that depend on federal health and education funds and programme authorisation.

These changes have been proceeding for some time. Many of the federal initiatives began in the Great Depression, when localities were under enormous strain as local needs rose with mass unemployment while local revenues fell. As a matter of fact, compared with some of the other services, the political centralisation of the schools is relatively unadvanced, and accomplished largely indirectly, as a result of the influence of national professional associations. Although state education departments date from the 19th century, federal financing of education did not begin until 1965, and local school boards still have some decision-making latitude.(1)

Centralisation is not without its problems, however. Periodically, the centralised services are subject to what might be called crises of legitimacy, crises that are probably rendered more likely by the process of bureaucratic and political centralisation. Diminished local influence and diminished local access to the service, and the increasing rigidity in the distribution of bureaucratic patronage that ordinarily accompanies centralisation of themselves might

---

1) The best known critics of centralisation of the school systems are, in fact, critics of administrative centralisation within one city. See for example, David Rogers, 110 Livingston Street, New York, Random House, 1968; Marilyn Gittell, Participants and Participation, Centre for Urban Education, 1967; Peter Shrag, Village School Downtown, Beacon Press, Boston, 1967.

be expected to create strain, or at least alienation, among the citizens who are presumably the constituents of the public agencies. Strain is even more likely during periods of economic and social change, when new groups are politically activated, and new discontents emerge, often taking form in dissatisfaction with the public services. This is, of course, what happened in the big cities of the United States during the 1960s; the new groups that were activated were primarily urban blacks. The response by the government agencies was "decentralisation".

In most places the formula was relatively simple, and similar. First, access to the services was made easier by the establishment of local outposts that received housing complaints or handled welfare applications or offered medical care. In some cities the various public services joined together under mayoral leadership in establishing these local outposts, which were then called little city halls or neighbourhood governments. Second, some agency functions were often delegated to these outposts, or to local districts carved out of the public agency's jurisdiction. Third, new roles were created within the bureaucracies for local citizen representatives, sometimes as staff in the local outposts, sometimes by establishing committees of citizen advisors. Fourth, lower level bureaucrats were exposed to "community relations" training programmes which presumably equipped them to understand and respond to the citizenry.[1] The urban school systems employed this formula as well. In cities where agitation by blacks against the school system was intense, various measures were taken to delegate some of the administrative responsibility for the schools to local districts established for the purpose; citizen committees were established, and more blacks were hired as teachers or as "teacher aides".

These devices no doubt produced some gains in improved accessibility to the public agencies. They even resulted in the spinning off of some agency resources to local areas in the form of new jobs and facilities. These gains have, however, been relatively small, and do not really counteract the main tendencies toward centralisation. The purpose of such changes is not to decentralise control of the agencies, but to give people the sense that the public services are responsive and accessible by creating the illusion of democratic participation in the administration of the public services. The fact that much of this participation has to do with minor aspects of administration also helps to divert popular discontent from the public

---

1) Lipsky calls these "street level bureaucrats". See "Street Level Bureaucracy and the Analysis of Urban Reform", Neighbourhood Control in the 1970s, edited by George Frederickson.

service itself to the local outpost. Alan Altshuler put it baldly in his well-known book on community control.(1)

"Perhaps its (decentralisation's) most important positive potential, from the standpoint of city-wide elected officials, would
be to divert much of the force of community dissatisfactions
from them to neighbourhood leaders. There would still be pressure on the city-wide leaders to find resources for the decentralised functions, but they would be far less vulnerable than
currently to blame for day-to-day operations. The community
leaders who came to the fore, moreover, ... would probably be
more moderate than today's most visible ghetto spokesmen ...
Responsibility for the operation of complex services would be
likely to sober the successful candidates in the neighbourhood
elections still further, and in any event to absorb much of the
ghetto's political energy ... City officials who supported limited devolution of authority to the neighbourhood level would be
likely to reap a harvest of good will in the black community ..."

The main achievement, in short, of this type of decentralisation
is to shield the public services from the pressures of popular dissatisfaction which, if left unchecked, might conceivably force larger
and more fundamental responses to popular demands - a process one
might indeed reasonably call decentralisation.

CONCLUSION

If this perspective on planning and decentralisation activities
in education in the United States has validity, then the possibility
exists that similar processes underlie such activities in other countries. At the very least, examination of the political uses of planning and decentralisation would yield knowledge of a dimension of
such activities which is usually ignored. Several areas of inquiry
might be included in such an examination:

1. In the preceding pages, I argued that activities called planning,
or research, or policy research, were often of little consequence in
guiding public agency decisions. These activities could in fact be
better understood as public relations than as planning. The most
straightforward way to investigate this possibility is close empirical observation of:

    a)   the problems identified for research and planning, and their
        relevance or lack of relevance to the decisions with the
        agency's control; and

---

1) Community Control: The Black Demand for Participation in Large
American Cities, Pegasus, New York, pp.112-113.

b)   the actual use made by the agency of the research or plans
     that are produced. It hardly needs to be added that when
     activities are consistently used for public relations pur-
     poses and not for agency decision making, the process is
     probably not accidental.

2.   I also argued that planning activities often cloaked agency
efforts to entrench and expand their domain. This use of planning
is less readily verified by simple observation, simply because agency
expansion may look very much like planning or intersectoralism.
Nevertheless, it would be useful to attempt such an appraisal by:

a)   analysing the political context which prompts new planning
     efforts, and examining the match between the political de-
     mands made upon the agency and the agency's own presumed
     new planning goals;

b)   identifying the role of bureaucratic representatives in fos-
     tering one or another planning alternative as a solution to
     a political problem; and

c)   evaluating the benefits which accrue to the agency as a re-
     sult of the new planning activities, such as an expanded
     public mandate and increased personnel and budget. These
     benefits may be achieved directly by the agency, or may be
     the result of the new liaisons with other agencies called
     for by the "plan". Once again it is reasonable to presume
     that when political demands are transmuted into proposals
     that result in agency expansion the result is at least not
     entirely accidental.

3.   Finally, activities which are called decentralisation can be
evaluated not merely by observing the shifts in intra-agency chains-
of-command, or the formal procedures for "citizen participation" or
feedback, but by evaluating the actual political leverage on the
agency, particularly leverage in matters regarding the allocation of
tangible resources, including the hiring and firing of personnel,
which accrues to citizen groups, especially those citizen groups
which have not previously been regarded as significant constituents
of the agency. While such a "test" of decentralisation may seem
crude, in the turgid realms of bureaucratic policy the simplest
test of power may be the most reliable.

REFERENCE FRAMEWORK FOR THE REPORTS

Prepared by the Secretariat

EDUCATIONAL PLANNING IN AN INTER-SECTORAL CONTEXT

The OECD has made the commitment to assist its Member governments to reach new social objectives set for economic growth in the
1970s, based on higher expectations for human welfare. Thus, a
recent report by the Secretary-General(1) quotes the 1970 discussion
of the OECD Council on quantitative and qualitative objectives:

"... Ministers stressed that 'growth is not an end in itself,
but rather an instrument for creating better conditions of life'
and that 'increased attention must be given to the qualitative
aspect of growth, and to the formulation of policies with
respect to the broad economic and social choices involved in
the allocation of growing resources'. Ministers emphasized
that 'an important task of OECD will be to assist Governments
in these aims'."

The work which has been developing during recent years in
various parts of the Organisation on this basis places each major
sector, like education, within the context of comprehensive social
and public policy which must deal with such real issues as the
irreversible destruction of the natural environment, transportation
gluts, pollution, the social consequences of technology, massive
urban malaise, steadily increasing inequities, violence, and the
alienation of whole population sectors - problems requiring an un-
precedented co-ordination of public policies and programmes.

As a basis for developing a system of indicators to monitor
social progress in such areas, Member countries have agreed to a
list of 24 "Social Concerns Common to Most Member Countries" cover-
ing "the fields of health, individual development through learning,
employment and the quality of working life, time and leisure, command
over goods and services, physical environment, personal safety and
the administration of justice, and man's place in society". As noted
in the report by the Secretary-General, "the detailed identification,
clarification and classification of these concerns represent a
significant step both technically and politically". /C̲(73)104, p.6̲7

In this same report it has also been recognised that such comprehensive public policy involves "decisions which are of a complex,

1) Doc. C(73)104 OECD Council: Preparations for Meeting of Council
   at Ministerial Level, 6th-8th June; Agenda Item 2; Activities of
   the Organisation, Including: Work on Qualitative Aspects of
   Economic Growth (Report by the Secretary-General).

horizontal and interacting nature" /paragraph 5, C(73)104⁷/, which go
beyond the mere arithmetic summation of the traditional government
sectors. For example, the competing objectives within society for
the allocation of resources cannot usefully be treated as if this
were a competition between such sectors as health, education and
public transportation - as if individual objectives were particular
to individual sectors. In other words, for a sector like education,
the objectives are larger than the sector: the measures taken in
education to serve "its" objectives must be supported by further
measures in other fields like health, urban policy and employment.
Policy for any one sector as now defined in government must be related to policies of other sectors if they are to become practical
and effective.

In the field of education there are significant country developments in this direction. For example, in France each successive
five-year plan has witnessed a notable increase in the number of
inter-sector committees involved in proposals about education.
Policy discussions and proposals for developing recurrent education
in countries like Sweden and the United States have explicitly
recognised general societal contexts. In the recent review of
Japanese educational policy it was authoritatively announced - and
this was again confirmed this year - that it was the official policy
of the Government to make a decisive shift in its overall national
investment policy, from investment yielding direct financial returns
to investment in the social infra-structure, so as to ensure that
economic growth would increasingly be directed toward raising the
quality of life of the Japanese people. The role of education at
the heart of this infra-structure was spelled out in some detail in
the OECD report on the review of Japanese educational policy.(1)

Internal changes in the field of education further emphasize
its inter-sectoral character. The core of education, the part subject to governmental public policy, must make radically new relationships with the whole field of educational activity as it expands
and diversifies throughout the society. Current institutional
arrangements cannot long withstand the widening gap between the
growing legitimate demand for education and the available resources,
and education is being forced to change its social parameters.

The study of education in an inter-sectoral context also
suggests that what happens to the individual as a target of policy
could provide a practical position from which to view the combined
effects of various public policies and programmes. Focus on the
individual - on the status and conditions of people - could become
an organising principle for combined policy.

---

1) Reviews of National Policies for Education: Japan, OECD, 1971.
   pp. 155-6.

The above considerations suggest that it is now opportune to examine selected country experience in planning and developing education in its specific interrelationships with other sectors, and within general government policy.

THE NEED FOR INTEGRATION IN GOVERNMENT POLICY PLANNING

The difficulties in the way of developing education in an intersectoral context cannot be over-stated, and must be approached through an effort to understand that the planning problem faced by governmental sectors - along with their size and complexity - has rapidly increased, each new sector in general representing a new problem area coming within the province of government and giving rise to an extended set of governmental objectives.

However, the accelerating pace of modern social and economic development throws up fundamentally new problem areas and new goals far more rapidly than government seems to be able to create new agencies or even to reorient the directions of old ones. Adding to this historical slowness in the building of government structures and organisations is the complicating fact that as modern government has spread out to embrace the whole social and economic fabric the effectiveness of each sectoral service becomes increasingly dependent upon its interrelationships to other sectors.

Thus, experience reveals the shared character of goals. The major goals of any sector are always larger than the sector itself, and the so-called operational goals conceived within the sector are seldom without important "inputs" from other sectors. Furthermore, it has become obvious that this comprehensive reach of government goals implies a long-term perspective in planning while, at the same time, government programmes are seen to directly affect the fate of individual citizens who begin to demand more demonstrable participation in the setting up and direction of such programmes.

These major developments strongly suggest that government structures and procedures will have to provide at least for:

a) 'horizontality' in policy making, programme formulation and execution, responding to problems in a manner making for co-ordinated use of the whole range of relevant government services;

b) autonomy and localised authority so that inter-sectoral co-ordination can occur at practical operating levels;

c) 'action research' or experiments reorganising administrative structures to allow top level political policy to be made on a basis of political and social goals which cut horizontally across government service sectors and their dominant disciplines;

d) 'staff' services which enhance such horizontally oriented policy efforts and action, and which facilitate critical questioning, variations, innovations, and experimentation at field operational levels. Such staff services would include studies of long term implications of existing and proposed programmes, and technical assistance to planning activities at all levels of the government and in its various sectors.

It is such policies for a macro-framework that could be expected to facilitate efforts to close the persistent gap between macro-level policies and those operations which have practical applicability on a local and inter-personal level.

CURRENT GOVERNMENT STRUCTURES

The usual structures and procedures of modern governments are far indeed from meeting such needs, and the Organisation is beginning to study the policy-making process itself and related procedures and structures with a view to stimulating innovation $\underline{/}\overline{C}(73)104$, paragraph 18$\underline{7}$. Very generally described, each sector of modern government now consists of its own organisational pyramid within which the lines of relationships are meant to be primarily vertical, answering to the policy expressed, typically, by a cabinet minister. Each sector then naturally develops its own bureaucracy and a vested interest in the performance of its service within the established structure. Such services create a particular professional rationale, often drawing viewpoints and theoretical positions from a predominating academic discipline. Staff services tend to become specific to the sector concerned and analytical work is 'contained' within the dominant disciplines.

There is no doubt that this form of government organisation has contributed to substantial advancement in governmental services, often bringing to bear in a pointed way the application of major academic disciplines to various social sectors. A great deal of experience has been accumulated in these governmental services and their social, psychological and institutional dynamics are too fundamental to be suddenly revolutionised. Nevertheless, the planning and operation of government sectors as if they represented largely unique functions in society have tended to make such services increasingly less responsive to the policies and commitments of government's top political authorities and, at the same time, less sensitive to the actual results of such services for the masses of the constituency.

POLITICAL NATURE OF INTER-SECTORAL PLANNING

Thus, it is not surprising that there is a demand for change in the way government develops and executes policy, and there are various statements of intent, experiments and on-going developments among Member governments. Examples of such general approaches would include current efforts by the governments of Japan, Scandinavian countries, France and the Netherlands. In other instances governments have been rearranging the ministerial sectors or creating "super-ministries" (e.g. the Department of Health, Education and Welfare in the United States), but the regrouping of sectors does not necessarily guarantee policy integration. The Federal Government of Canada and the provincial Government of Ontario have installed in different forms ministers for planning in the cabinet, without executive functions, to co-ordinate overall policy. And many governments are developing forms of programme budgeting and systems analysis and have strengthened staff, planning or expert advisory functions with the aim of increasing co-ordination and consistency in total policy.

Effective study of this broad problem, however, begins with the recognition that these administrative methodologies are the tools of actual politics used in the particular situations of different countries and times. The working out of prevailing policy is a political process which is usually so fluid as to be revealed only by means of description and analysis of the position and development of formal and informal relationships among relevant competing groups. The "model" of policy making includes the use of the existing segmented structure in bargaining for political advantage, and programme integration among sectors will be seen in terms of political costs and benefits for groups contending for power.

It should be emphasized that the perspective of this paper is not the need for or the possibility of developing some over-arching system of analysis in the service of expert controls which would replace such political processes. Bargaining for resources between the sectoral programmes is moderated by such factors as the levels of political articulation (in parliament, parties, media, etc.), agreement among the leadership, the "qualities" of the leadership and of the operational staff. The planning question is: how can a planning process contribute toward these moderating forces so that they can converge on policies which better meet the realities of social needs? Such a planning process in effect would aim not at enabling planners and experts to 'manage' the integration of sectoral programmes but rather at establishing conditions in which the people involved, from top policy makers to those in the 'field', would be enabled to integrate the growing array of such programmes.

It will be useful at this point to outline some of the main features
postulated for such a planning process.

SECTORAL PLANNING FOR THE INTEGRATION OF
GOVERNMENT PROGRAMMES

A framework of analytical work and supporting organisational
features which would be characteristic of integrated inter-sectoral
planning can be briefly outlined as a guide to any effort to look
at existing government situations. This framework does not represent
a utopian perspective, despite its obvious distance from current
conditions and practice in governments. Today all governments do
in fact have inter-sectoral policy in the sense that policies,
though stated for sectors, actually have an inter-sectoral impact,
which goes largely unrecognised and unplanned. Thus today inter-
sectoral policy is in fact made in the absence of inter-sectoral
planning to the mounting cost of gaps and redundancies. The stage
is thus set for profound changes in government structures and procedures. The next step is to recognise the main features of inter-
sectoral planning as they would affect any single sector, and on this
basis it will be possible to propose a more definitive inquiry into
educational sector planning.

1.   Characteristic Analytical and Technical Tasks

A)   Clarification of Inter-Dependencies

The most distinctive feature of sector planning oriented toward
integration would be its effort explicitly to recognise and to clarify
inter-dependencies. Fundamental to this kind of inquiry would be
the delineation of goal inter-dependencies in that:

- goals, considered individually, are most often served by
  instruments, measures or means distributed organisationally
  among a wide range of the operating units from many sectors;
- specific operational instruments, measures or means emanating
  from any given sector, usually influence more than one, and
  often a wide range of objectives;
- process-oriented goals, so important in social programmes
  such as education, require particular recognition in the study
  of inter-dependencies. Such goals represent instances when
  the 'output' of a programme is the very process involved in
  it, as well as (or instead of) some end 'product'.

This exploration of the nature and consequence of inter-
dependencies will be shown to underlie all subsequent aspects of
planning for any single sector.

297

B) Sectoral Planning in the Context of Inter-Dependencies

i) The Sectoral Plan

The sector would be conceptualised and defined in terms of a given set of instruments, measures or means, and the sectoral plan would be concerned with their use. Thus it should be emphasized that no objectives or goals would be identified as the exclusive province of the sector under consideration, since virtually no objective can be shown to be served only by the measures, means or instruments of any one sector. In other words, the sector defined by the means at its disposal would never be delineated according to any goals or objectives exclusively served by (or "assigned" to) the sector.

The nature and the dynamics of the relationship of the contributions of other sectors to any goal or set of goals served by the sector should be examined in such terms as:

a) how these other contributions affect the functioning of the sector's various instruments, measures or means;

b) the extent to which other sectoral inputs can be substituted for these means.

Thus the sectoral plan would explore its borderlines and inter-relationships with activities in other fields. In each 'round' or 'cycle' in the development of such sector plans this exploration could be extended and deepened.

ii) Indicators

Indicators of progress toward goals would be expressed in terms of their inter-dependence with other indicators and goals. A sector could not be planned or regulated by indicators limited to the performance of measures within the one sector. Process-oriented goals would require the development of indicators which are "descriptors" of the state of the process, and would rest on efforts to understand better the nature of the processes involved.

iii) Long-term Perspectives

The analysis of long-term futures would constitute an increasingly essential 'service' to the sectoral planning process. Such analysis would be designed to illuminate the consequences of current premises and decisions; in particular, it would not aim at 'fixing' what the future will or should be.

iv) The Autonomy of Sectors

The extent to which integration of the sector is based on its 'dependence', on its need to 'fit' into the larger trends of society and of all other sectors, will determine the rigidity of such planning. The exploration of inter-dependencies should notably involve a recognition of the impact of the sector's programmes on trends beyond the sector. The extent to which a sector plan can envisage maximising its societal impact, and hence maximising the 'freedom' of the sector, is a matter for on-going political bargaining. Planning should be designed to inform this process, but surely in the case of major social sectors like education the direction should be towards increasing their impact on trends rather than submission to them.

v) Open-ended Outcomes

The complexity raised by inter-sectoral planning calls for an increasing tolerance of indeterminate outcomes. This kind of development would be facilitated by studies to better determine the boundaries and the conditions for such open-ended operations.

vi) Data Problems

Data for sectoral programmes would characteristically have only limited value for planning in an inter-sectoral context. The lack of concepts upon which to base the collection of such data and the lack of organisational motivation for developing concepts and data are two main targets of inter-sectoral planning policy.

vii) Delineation of Sectoral Groups

Planning analysis would attempt to identify the groups related to the goals served by the sector, organising this inquiry to promote wide and effective participation.

C) Participatory Planning

The need for horizontal lines of communication and action at all levels, and for pragmatic acceptance of concepts which bridge across sectors, imposing new views on inputs and outcomes, requires the kind of widespread initiative which calls for participatory rather than prescriptive planning. The technical problems of planning committed to the promotion of participation are an integral part of the problems of inter-sectoralising the planning process. The trends, problems and requirements for participatory planning in education arising from country experience are dealt with at length elsewhere.(1) However, the main lines of development involve creating an infra-structure and a programme structure for participatory planning in education.

i) The Infra-Structure

Consists of at least four main elements:

---

1) See, Participatory Planning in Education, OECD, 1974.

a) a <u>network of communication</u>, particularly providing the basis for horizontal linkages throughout the system;

b) a <u>framework of information</u>, stressing data whose substance and form would facilitate popular planning activity;

c) special <u>planning support for deviation, experiment and innovation</u>, as an essential technical service to activities which might otherwise remain isolated;

d) a <u>planning agency for participation</u> whose major terms of reference would include not planning for the organisation but the development of planning throughout the organisation, expertise in the functioning of participation and the contribution of critical information designed for widespread understanding of problems.

ii) <u>The Programme Structure</u>

Includes at least the following major elements:

a) a continuing <u>socio-technical study</u> of the organisation, including the "mapping" of the various groups to inform them of the facts of their interrelationships and their roles in the educational organisation and processes;

b) major contributions to the <u>establishment, maintenance and evaluation of the participation process</u> as a whole, particularly encouraging other educational sectors to engage in evaluation studies;

c) <u>supply of data and analysis</u> on substantive educational problems in a manner to encourage further independent study and contribute to the larger flow of information relevant for planning;

d) <u>development of planning techniques and provision of training</u> in practical skills needed by people engaged in the planning process.

2. <u>Supporting Organisational Features</u>

To perform the above technical and analytical tasks, particularly those stressing inter-dependencies in a manner such as to make them operationally meaningful, there would be need for specific organisational developments. For example, in the definition of goals there will be political, popular and "scientific" notions about goals, all of which have validity in their own right. The task of defining goals and relating them to specific programme measures can only be fulfilled in the process of close relationship to activities in the field, their observation, description and evaluation. The organisation in support of this kind of planning will have to include an appropriate communications system and structure of relationships in order both to conduct and to make use of such inquiries.

It is not possible here to give details as to specific organisational forms required for inter-sectoral planning except to indicate tendencies which would facilitate and be compatible with such planning. For example, rewards and recognition would have to be offered to groups horizontally across sectors for reaching a common goal. Exclusively sectoral rewards for the efficient management of the means within each given sector would perhaps be maintained but with the recognition that such means are never the exclusive contribution toward any goal. The horizontal lines of relationships and local autonomy would tend to gain force counter to the vertical lines of authority in the traditional sector pyramid. In this more complex world of inter-dependency the end results would be more problematic, and organisation forms would tend to protect deviation and flexibility and give less value to consistency - a mainstay of older-style planning. Planning analyses would be more designed to encourage supporting studies in the field than to give definitive programme specifications. Planning bodies would be less firmly attached to the top of the sector hierarchies.

STUDY OF INTER-SECTORAL PLANNING FOR EDUCATION:
SUGGESTED ANALYTICAL OUTLINE

Education is a sector in which it has been abundantly illustrated that effective policy and action are dependent on the development of inter-sectoral relationships, and it is proposed to initiate an investigation on how this kind of development seems to be taking place in a number of Member countries. The perspective outlined above for inter-sectoral planning can in fact be readily applied to education. For example, there are some objectives to which education is commonly assumed to make the major contribution but which are not attainable without major contributions from other sectors. Such an objective is the intellectual and emotional development of deprived children, which cannot be generally accomplished if other social problems, such as the unemployment (or excessively low income) of parents, social decay of neighbourhoods, etc., remain unsolved. Conversely, there are other objectives which are usually considered the prime concern of other government programmes but to which education is understood to make an important contribution. An example is the goal of furthering the equalisation of income, to which education in its function of human capital formation is a heavy contributor.

Considering these two examples together, it can be seen that in the first case the education of deprived children requires an important "input" of income equalisation, while in the second case, the measure of human capital actually formed will depend upon how much intellectual and emotional development has actually taken place in the process of schooling. The planning process for education, or for any other sector, cannot be expected to produce answers to such problems immediately. The governmental problem is how to set up structures and procedures which facilitate the recognition and exploration of such problems and the broadest participation in appropriate planning and action.

The following outline suggested the main lines along which further study in the field might proceed, and to which the papers in this book responded.

1. Overview of Issues

This opening section would attempt to identify major theoretical issues arising from inter-dependence between education and other sectors. It would survey and account for a wide range of problems, whose resolution would be relevant to possible choices among alternative approaches to inter-sectoral planning, leading to the development of operational hypotheses, which could be further explored and developed by the empirical analysis of country examples.

2. Sectoral 'Ecologies' or 'Policy Systems'

A primary task of the analysis would be the clarification of inter-dependencies among the goals, programme content and operational measures of related governmental sectors which interact with education. This would involve the investigation of the 'shared' objectives and values among sectors and the implications of these relationships. Individual sectors would need to be viewed as a total 'ecology' or as a total 'policy system' characterised by congruencies and incongruencies in relationships to other sectors.

Sectoral policy systems, related to and including education, can be analysed from the viewpoint of (a) delivery systems, (b) social systems, (c) political systems and (d) conceptions of service. While interrelated each of these may be considered in turn.

a) Delivery systems

Each sector constitutes an institutionalised delivery system to client populations which overlaps with other sectors. Variations in value emphasis and practice between education and other sectors which have implications for discontinuities of service can be seen in a comparison of such delivery systems. In the case of education, the differences in the knowledge bases, hypotheses and assumptions which are available for delivering different types and levels of education also affect the nature of its relationships to other sectors.

b) Social systems

Social systems are established in each sector including systems internal to its institutions and extending to its client populations. These social systems are usefully described in terms of group statuses, prerogatives, traditions and self-concepts. The social system includes both the formal structure of the organisation of the sector and its network of informal group relationships which together constitute the social structure of the sector. Descriptive analyses of inter-dependencies among sectors can only be realistic if they include the interrelationships of such social systems.

c) Political systems

Political systems are constituted in terms of the power relationships established among the various articulated groups within the sectors. These groups are not at all identical to the groups identified in the social system, to which they are nevertheless related. A practical analysis of inter-sectoral relationships must include the functioning of the political systems of each sector as they can be made operational for inter-sectoral planning and action.

d) Conceptions of the service

Conceptions of the service - in this case education - which are held by various social and political groups involved in the service affect possible inter-relationships with other sectors. Such conceptions involve the values, purposes and biases of these groups and affect their various perceptions of the educational process. Thus, for example, a conception of education as a preparation for skilled participation in the economy will have different implications with respect to other sectors compared with a conception of education as a vehicle for collective political and cultural expression.

3. The Political Economy of Inter-sectoral Planning

By "political economy" of inter-sectoral planning involving education is meant the attempts to deal with the political resolution of the dilemma of costs and the paradox of efficiency in education. A descriptive analysis of the cost/efficiency problem leads to a search for organisational and political means for horizontal co-ordination and integration without centralisation.

Costs and efficiency

Education is one of those social services - usually rendered by government - whose unit costs rise faster than the costs of most other activities in society. To this trend is added the increasing absolute demand for such services. These trends lead to budgetary pressures and the search for efficiency by means of rationalisation, co-ordination and integration. However, when over-arching or integrated programmes are introduced they have always revealed that the formerly fragmented programmes left unmet needs which cannot be sidestepped: the result is therefore higher resource demands and rising costs.

Horizontal co-ordination without centralisation

Experience suggests the hypothesis that while the problems of effective service to client populations demand horizontal co-ordination, and possibly a move towards integration of traditional services, this development cannot be made operational by means of all-embracing technocratic control structures. However, traditional representative administrative systems cannot cope with the strain placed upon them by the need to provide the expanding complex of services demanded. Thus, focusing on education in this complex of services, inter-sectoralisation involves exploration of new organisational directions such as:

a) 'loosening' administration to allow for initiatives to develop within and outside vertical organisational hierarchies;
b) institutionalisation of arbitration among groups involved in new programme relationships;
c) establishment of new rights for client and lower echelon intervention in the planning and policy of programmes;
d) development of more significant roles for informal systems, joined to formal systems, in the design, implementation and regulation of programmes.

4.   Inter-sectoral Planning

It is hypothesised that the role of planning theory, planners and planning agencies must be seen in terms of their contribution to this larger organisational, institutional and political framework involved in inter-sectoralisation. In terms of content, a recognition of the 'ecological' problem and a resolution of economic and political problems among related social services, suggests an entirely new emphasis in planning programmes and their methodology. Secondly, the organisation of planning activity would reflect its underlying purpose to promote widespread initiative for a very great variety of horizontal relationships 'in the field' among the various government sectors. On this basis, it is possible briefly to suggest major elements of the organisational structure and the programme structure required for inter-sectoral planning.

Organisational structure

The establishment of a <u>network of communications</u> is the first element of such an organisational structure, providing the basis for horizontal linkages within and between sectors.

The planning structure would also provide particular support for experiment, innovation and deviation as an essential technical service to such activities, which might otherwise decline in isolation.

More generally, planning services would be directed less towards the top of the hierarchy of service organisations and more towards the development of planning competence throughout the organisation, including the development of planning techniques and the provision of training towards this end.

In the case of education particular attention has earlier been given to the way in which its technical mission - the pedagogical mission - is closely related to the style, manner and content of planning of education, since planning itself has a pedagogical function within any system as a whole.(1)

Programme structure

The programme structure could be expected to emphasize <u>long-term futures analysis</u>, <u>socio-technical analysis</u> and <u>evaluative analysis</u>. While interrelated, these three kinds of study should be seen as essential inputs with unique functions in developing the knowledge base for inter-sectoral development.

<u>Long-term futures analysis</u> is beginning to be recognised as a practical and powerful policy tool for developing interrelationships among sectors. It is in the extension of the time dimension that the consequences of interrelated programmes can be assessed. Such information about alternative futures would aim at developing a greater capacity in people - particularly the clients of the service - to decide what the future should be.

<u>Socio-technical analysis</u> aims at mapping the various groups involved in related sectors in such a way as to inform them on how their group roles fit into the technical operation of their sectors and its institutions. Such an analysis aims at providing a factual basis upon which 'bargaining' among groups in a situation of change can take place.

<u>Evaluative analysis</u> should be encouraged as a process taking place throughout horizontally provided services. The technical planning service to such evaluative activities should prominently

---

1) See, <u>Participatory Planning in Education</u>, op. cit.

include the development of <u>indicators of progress</u> towards inter-dependent goals shared by related sectors.

5. <u>Towards Policy: Operational Forms of Inter-sectoral Planning and Action</u>

The search for operational forms of educational planning in the context of inter-sectoral planning and action is illustrated in a number of different approaches in Member countries which are related to various aims and assumptions. Examples from this experience include:

a) the formal or informal co-operation between agencies which remain separate;

b) the creation of a centralised 'umbrella' agency leading to bureaucratic unification;

c) similar bureaucratic unification at a regional or even more local level;

d) development of a unified organisation which is sufficiently innovative to break down the old services and to create new delivery systems;

e) co-option of services from various agencies and their incorporation into a single agency;

f) consumer sovereignty strategies which allow the demands of the clients to serve as the agent of co-ordination.

Therefore, the policy questions which are posed include: what are the essential aims and assumptions served by these or other such approaches to inter-sectoral planning in education? What are minimum necessary conditions needed for effective inter-sectoral planning of various types involving education? What policy measures would be implied from answers to these questions?

THE PARTICIPANTS IN THE STUDY

David Cohen	Professor, Harvard University
Yehezhel Dror	Professor, University of Jerusalem
Kjell Eide	Director, Research and Planning, Ministry of Education, Oslo, Norway
Amitai Etzioni	Professor, Columbia University
Herbert Gans	Professor, Columbia University
Maurice Kogan	Professor, Brunel University Uxbridge, United Kingdom
Olav Magnussen	Professor, Rogaland District College Stavanger, Norway
Thierry Malan	Chargé de Mission à l'Inspection Générale Ministère de l'Education, France
Alberto Melo	Professor, Open University, United Kingdom
Maurice Peston	Professor, St. Mary's College University of London
Frances Fox Piven	Professor, Boston University
William Westley	Professor, McGill University, Montreal
The Secretariat:	Beresford Hayward, Head of Country Programmes for Educational Policy Planning

OECD SALES AGENTS
DÉPOSITAIRES DES PUBLICATIONS DE L'OCDE

ARGENTINA – ARGENTINE
Carlos Hirsch S.R.L., Florida 165,
BUENOS-AIRES, ☎ 33-1787-2391 Y 30-7122

AUSTRALIA – AUSTRALIE
International B.C.N. Library Suppliers Pty Ltd.,
161 Sturt St., South MELBOURNE, Vic. 3205. ☎ 699-6388
658 Pittwater Road, BROOKVALE NSW 2100. ☎ 938 2267

AUSTRIA – AUTRICHE
Gerold and Co., Graben 31, WIEN 1. ☎ 52.22.35

BELGIUM – BELGIQUE
Librairie des Sciences,
Coudenberg 76-78, B 1000 BRUXELLES 1. ☎ 512-05-60

BRAZIL – BRÉSIL
Mestre Jou S.A., Rua Guaipá 518,
Caixa Postal 24090, 05089 SAO PAULO 10. ☎ 261-1920
Rua Senador Dantas 19 s/205-6, RIO DE JANEIRO GB.
☎ 232-07. 32

CANADA
Renouf Publishing Company Limited,
2182 St. Catherine Street West,
MONTREAL, Quebec H3H 1M7 ☎(514) 937-3519

DENMARK – DANEMARK
Munksgaards Boghandel,
Nørregade 6, 1165 KØBENHAVN K. ☎ (01) 12 69 70

FINLAND – FINLANDE
Akateeminen Kirjakauppa
Keskuskatu 1, 00100 HELSINKI 10. ☎ 625.901

FRANCE
Bureau des Publications de l'OCDE,
2 rue André-Pascal, 75775 PARIS CEDEX 16.
☎ 524.81.67
Principal correspondant :
13602 AIX-EN-PROVENCE : Librairie de l'Université.
☎ 26.18.08

GERMANY – ALLEMAGNE
Verlag Weltarchiv G.m.b.H.
D 2000 HAMBURG 36, Neuer Jungfernstieg 21.
☎ 040-35-62-500

GREECE – GRÈCE
Librairie Kauffmann, 28 rue du Stade,
ATHÈNES 132. ☎ 322.21.60

HONG-KONG
Government Information Services,
Sales and Publications Office, Beaconsfield House, 1st floor,
Queen's Road, Central. ☎ H-233191

ICELAND – ISLANDE
Snaebjörn Jónsson and Co., h.f.,
Hafnarstraeti 4 and 9, P.O.B. 1131, REYKJAVIC.
☎ 13133/14281/11936

INDIA – INDE
Oxford Book and Stationery Co.:
NEW DELHI, Scindia House. ☎ 45896
CALCUTTA, 17 Park Street. ☎ 240832

IRELAND - IRLANDE
Eason and Son, 40 Lower O'Connell Street,
P.O.B. 42, DUBLIN 1. ☎ 74 39 35

ISRAËL
Emanuel Brown: 35 Allenby Road, TEL AVIV. ☎ 51049/54082
also at:
9. Shlomzion Hamalka Street, JERUSALEM. ☎ 234807
48 Nahlath Benjamin Street, TEL AVIV. ☎ 53276

ITALY – ITALIE
Libreria Commissionaria Sansoni:
Via Lamarmora 45, 50121 FIRENZE. ☎ 579751
Via Bartolini 29, 20155 MILANO. ☎ 365083
Sous-dépositaires :
Editrice e Libreria Herder,
Piazza Montecitorio 120, 00 186 ROMA. ☎ 674628
Libreria Hoepli, Via Hoepli 5, 20121 MILANO. ☎ 365446
Libreria Lattes, Via Garibaldi 3, 10122 TORINO. ☎ 519274
La diffusione delle edizioni OCDE è inoltre assicurata dalle migliori
librerie nelle città più importanti.

JAPAN – JAPON
OECD Publications Centre,
Akasaka Park Building, 2-3-4 Akasaka, Minato-ku,
TOKYO 107. ☎ 586-2016

KOREA – CORÉE
Pan Korea Book Corporation,
P.O.Box n°101 Kwangwhamun, SÉOUL. ☎ 72-7369

LEBANON – LIBAN
Documenta Scientifica/Redico,
Edison Building, Bliss Street, P.O.Box 5641, BEIRUT.
☎ 354429–344425

THE NETHERLANDS – PAYS-BAS
W.P. Van Stockum,
Buitenhof 36, DEN HAAG. ☎ 070-65.68.08

NEW ZEALAND - NOUVELLE-ZÉLANDE
The Publications Manager,
Government Printing Office,
WELLINGTON: Mulgrave Street (Private Bag),
World Trade Centre, Cubacade, Cuba Street,
Rutherford House, Lambton Quay, ☎ 737-320
AUCKLAND: Rutland Street (P.O.Box 5344), ☎ 32.919
CHRISTCHURCH: 130 Oxford Tce (Private Bag), ☎ 50.331
HAMILTON: Barton Street (P.O.Box 857), ☎ 80.103
DUNEDIN: T & G Building, Princes Street (P.O.Box 1104),
☎ 78.294

NORWAY – NORVÈGE
Johan Grundt Tanums Bokhandel,
Karl Johansgate 41/43, OSLO 1. ☎ 02-332980

PAKISTAN
Mirza Book Agency, 65 Shahrah Quaid-E-Azam, LAHORE 3.
☎ 66839

PHILIPPINES
R.M. Garcia Publishing House, 903 Quezon Blvd. Ext.,
QUEZON CITY, P.O.Box 1860 – MANILA. ☎ 99.98.47

PORTUGAL
Livraria Portugal, Rua do Carmo 70-74, LISBOA 2. ☎ 360582/3

SPAIN – ESPAGNE
Mundi-Prensa Libros, S.A.
Castelló 37, Apartado 1223, MADRID-1. ☎ 275.46.55
Libreria Bastinos, Pelayo, 52, BARCELONA 1. ☎ 222.06.00

SWEDEN – SUÈDE
AB CE FRITZES KUNGL HOVBOKHANDEL,
Box 16 356, S 103 27 STH, Regeringsgatan 12,
DS STOCKHOLM. ☎ 08/23 89 00

SWITZERLAND – SUISSE
Librairie Payot, 6 rue Grenus, 1211 GENÈVE 11. ☎ 022-31.89.50

TAIWAN – FORMOSE
National Book Company,
84-5 Sing Sung Rd., Sec. 3, TAIPEI 107. ☎ 321.0698

TURKEY – TURQUIE
Librairie Hachette,
469 Istiklal Caddesi, Beyoglu, ISTANBUL. ☎ 44.94.70
et 14 E Ziya Gökalp Caddesi, ANKARA. ☎ 12.10.80

UNITED KINGDOM – ROYAUME-UNI
H.M. Stationery Office, P.O.B. 569,
LONDON SEI 9 NH. ☎ 01-928-6977, Ext.410
or
49 High Holborn, LONDON WC1V 6 HB (personal callers)
Branches at: EDINBURGH, BIRMINGHAM, BRISTOL,
MANCHESTER, CARDIFF, BELFAST.

UNITED STATES OF AMERICA
OECD Publications Center, Suite 1207, 1750 Pennsylvania Ave.,
N.W. WASHINGTON, D.C.20006. ☎ (202)298-8755

VENEZUELA
Libreria del Este, Avda. F. Miranda 52, Edificio Galipán,
CARACAS 106. ☎ 32 23 01/33 26 04/33 24 73

YUGOSLAVIA – YOUGOSLAVIE
Jugoslovenska Knjiga, Terazije 27, P.O.B. 36, BEOGRAD.
☎ 621-992

Les commandes provenant de pays où l'OCDE n'a pas encore désigné de dépositaire peuvent être adressées à :
OCDE, Bureau des Publications, 2 rue André-Pascal, 75775 PARIS CEDEX 16.
Orders and inquiries from countries where sales agents have not yet been appointed may be sent to:
OECD, Publications Office, 2 rue André-Pascal, 75775 PARIS CEDEX 16.

OECD PUBLICATIONS, 2, rue André-Pascal, 75775 Paris Cedex 16 - No. 38 461 1977
PRINTED IN FRANCE

1023   2090